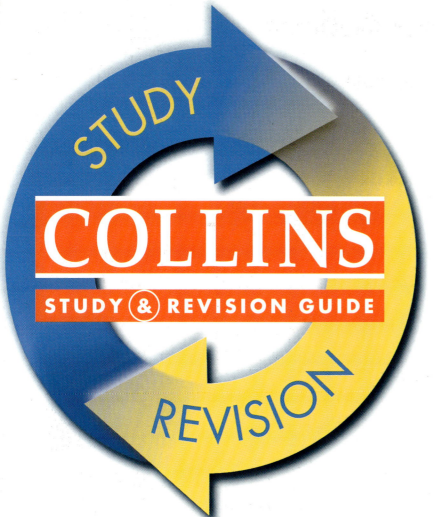

STUDY

COLLINS

STUDY & REVISION GUIDE

REVISION

D&T
RESISTANT MATERIALS
GCSE Key Stage 4

▶ Colin Chapman

▶ Series Editor: Jayne de Courcy

Collins Educational
An Imprint of HarperCollinsPublishers

Contents

How to boost your grade

A Study Guide <u>and</u> a Revision Guide – in one book

You may be starting – or part of the way through – your GCSE Design and Technology course. You may be thinking about your coursework, part way through it or getting close to mock or final exams. Wherever you are in your course, this book will help you. It will improve your understanding of Design and Technology. It will help you to boost your coursework grade. It will show you the best way to answer exam questions. These three pages will show you how to get the most out of this book so that you can boost your grade!

An up-to-date book to match your course

This book has been written specifically to match the new GCSE Design and Technology syllabuses and covers the syllabus content that is common to all of the Examination Boards. Your teacher will tell you which syllabus you are following and which topics you need to cover. Use the contents list and the index to find quickly and easily the topics that you want to study or revise.

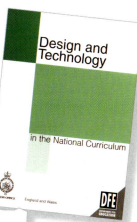

Short, manageable sections to study

The major sections of this book are divided into short chapters that you should be able to cover in around 45 minutes. The headings tell you clearly what you are going to read about. Short chapters mean that you can concentrate on understanding a small area before moving on. This also makes it quick and easy to find what you want when you are revising or doing homework.

Revision hints

- It is a good idea to divide your revision into small, manageable chunks: the sections in this book are ideal.

- Don't always start from the same place. Sometimes start towards the end of chapters to make sure you cover all the sections – not just the easiest stuff!

Check yourself

QUESTIONS

Q1 Explain what is meant by the term 'standard components'. Give two ways in which the use of standard components could help a manufacturer save money.

Q2 Compare the use of nails and screws in respect of their holding strength in soft wood.

Q3 What particular aspect of modern furniture manufacture has made 'knock-down' fittings popular and cost effective?

Check yourself **sections let you check your progress quickly and easily. They tell you where you might have gone wrong and how to boost your grade.**

At the end of each short section, there is a *Check yourself* panel which consists of several short questions that will let you see if you have read and understood the section properly.

We have purposely placed the answers straight after the questions so that you can **either**:

- Cover up the answers so that you can test yourself properly. When you have written down your answers, check whether you are right.

or:

- Read through a question, then read through the answer and tutorial. Here you're not using the *Check yourself* as a test; you're using it as an interactive way of revising.

Tutorial help – upgrade your exam result

The examiner has written a *Tutorial* for every question. If you did not get the answer right, the *Tutorial* will tell you where you may have gone wrong and will guide you back to where you can find more help. Many of the *Tutorials* point out where candidates often make mistakes in the exam. They also show how you can improve an answer to boost your grade, e.g. from a D to a C or a B to an A.

Every answer is accompanied by helpful advice in a *Tutorial*.

ANSWERS

A1
1 Wear an overall or apron
2 Wear eye protection
3 Check the condition of tools and report damage
4 Get help when carrying large or heavy objects

A2 Working from a datum is particularly important when marking out the position of a number of features such as holes. By taking each measurement from the datum the risk of cumulative error is reduced.

TUTORIALS

T1 This is a correct answer which would have gained four out of four marks. However, the first two points both relate to clothing and the question does ask for 'different aspects'; if a further point within the answer had also been about clothing then it is possible that a mark could have been lost.

T2 This is the correct answer; remember that cumulative error will only occur in marking out when progressing in steps away from a datum.

Planning your revision time

Use the *Check yourself* questions to plan your revision time. Close to exams, use them as tests. They'll tell you which topics you're weakest at. You'll need to spend more time reading through these sections again. It's tempting to spend lots of time on topics that you feel confident with already, but you should concentrate on what you **don't know**.

Revision hint

Be active when you revise! Write summaries of sections and make short notes on the questions.

Practising real exam questions

At the end of each section you will find some past-paper questions to practise on. One of these has sample student's answers with examiner's comments underneath. The others are for you to try. The answers are at the back of the book so that you can treat the question just as you would in the exam.

You can practise with real exam questions and then check the answers to see how you've done.

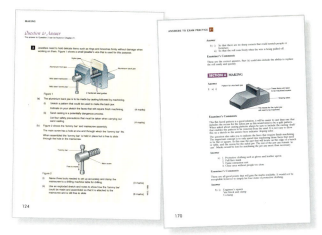

Examiner's comments – upgrade your exam result

The sample student's answers and the answers at the back of the book have mark schemes and detailed examiner's comments on them. These show you:

- **how to tackle the questions**
- **common mistakes to avoid**
- **how marks are awarded**
- **how to improve your answer to boost your grade**

Final revision – using the Examination checklist

There is a checklist at the end of each chapter. This summarises all of the key ideas in the topic. Use this to tick off the areas that you know about and to spot the ones where you may need to do some more work.

EXAMINATION CHECKLIST FOR THIS SECTION

After studying designing you should be able to:

- recognise design needs and opportunities taking into account the considerations of other people and recognising conflicting needs and demands;
- gather, organise and present research data;
- develop a design specification;
- generate a range of ideas whilst recognising constraints;
- develop, model and test ideas using a variety of graphical means including CAD systems;
- communicate design proposals appropriate to the needs of an audience;
- evaluate design proposals and develop working drawings and plans for scheduling manufacture.

Feeling confident

Using this book will help you to enjoy your course because you'll understand what is going on. You'll feel confident and ready to take your exams. And remember –

for every topic and every question, there are Answers, Tutorials and Examiner's comments, so you're never left without help!

v

Resistant Materials Technology

GCSE Syllabuses

All the Exam Board syllabuses have to meet the requirements of National Curriculum Design and Technology. This means that they are all quite similar. This book has been written to support all the GCSE Resistant Materials Technology syllabuses and provides help and guidance for both the written examination and coursework.

What is assessed?

In GCSE Design and Technology, you have to develop your knowledge and understanding of materials and components, design techniques, systems and control, and manufacturing industry. All these areas are covered in this book.

You then have to apply this knowledge through the skills of designing and making.

Designing is about knowledge and understanding combined with the design and communication skills needed to design products for a specific purpose.

Making is about the knowledge and understanding of tools, materials, techniques and processes in order to make products for a specific purpose.

In GCSE Design and Technology, you are assessed on your ability to design and your ability to make and this applies to both your coursework and your written exam. The marks are allocated like this:

> *Designing – 40% of the total marks*
>
> *Making – 60% of the total marks*

Coursework and written exam

Your final GCSE grade is make up of the marks that you have gained for your coursework and your exam. Your coursework makes up 60% of your final GCSE grade and your exam 40%.

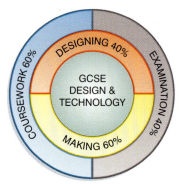

The key to getting a good grade in Design and Technology is to plan your coursework well, to finish it on time and to achieve a high standard. Section I of this book gives you lots of guidance on how coursework is assessed and how to gain high marks.

Foundation and Higher tier papers

Your coursework is not tiered but in the written exam you will be entered for either the Foundation or the Higher tier. The Foundation tier allows you to obtain grades from G to C. The Higher tier allows you to obtain grades from D to A*.

Higher tier							
A*	A	B	C	D	E	F	G
			Foundation tier				

There is no difference in the syllabus content for both tiers. Your teacher will have marked your coursework before your exam entry is finalised. This means your school will have a good idea about which is the most appropriate exam tier to enter you for.

The aim of coursework within Design and Technology is to provide you with the opportunity to demonstrate the application of your skills, your knowledge and your understanding of the subject. This section of the revision guide will provide you with guidance that will help you to get a better mark within the coursework element of your GCSE course. Subsequent sections of this book contain those aspects of knowledge and understanding that you should be demonstrating through your coursework.

Make sure that you are familiar with the process of designing that is set out in the introduction to Section 3 'Designing'. This process provides the framework for the organisation of your coursework and for its assessment.

The assessment of coursework is made within your own school and by your own teacher. The teacher's marks are then moderated by a representative of the examination board. Moderation is a process that ensures the marking has been properly carried out and the marks awarded are to the same standard across a range of schools. This makes sure that it is a fair and equal process wherever you may live or go to school.

It is very important that you are familiar with the assessment process that will be applied to your coursework. Your teacher will have this as part of the examination syllabus and will make a copy of it available for you at the start of your GCSE coursework. Your coursework will be measured against these criteria so you need to understand them.

The following are samples of coursework assessment that have been taken from a range of examination boards. You will quickly see that there is very little difference between the boards. The other thing to notice is how closely they follow the design process model that appears in Section 3 of this book and is the basis of all of your work.

The assessment process is broken down here into four stages:

- Design brief, specification, research and investigation;
- Generation and development of design solutions;
- Making;
- Evaulation.

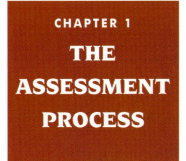

CHAPTER 1
THE ASSESSMENT PROCESS

DESIGN BRIEF, SPECIFICATION, RESEARCH & INVESTIGATION

Figure 1.1 shows part of an assessment grid covering two areas of assessment: 'Formulation of the design brief and specification' and 'Research – investigation'. To make an assessment your coursework is compared with the descriptions in the boxes and the marks allocated are taken from the range shown above the box, depending upon how well they fit.

Assessment Note 1

If you have needed a lot of help to write a design brief and you have written only a limited specification then you can only be awarded between 0 and 3 marks out of a total of 15 for this section. If, on the other hand, your work fits with the description in the box on the right-hand side then you can be awarded between 13 and 15 marks.

Assessment Note 2

To move from the 11–15 mark box in 'Research – investigation' to the

16–20 mark box you need to have identified the source of information, and organised your research. This emphasises the importance of being methodical and organised. It is often quite easy to move up into a higher mark range if you study the mark scheme and understand what is required.

ASSESSMENT GRID

This assessment grid describes, for each assessment heading, a continuum of performance based upon an expectation of what candidates can achieve at the end of Key Stage 4. The descriptors placed along the assessment lines assist teachers in making a judgement which reflects the candidate's performance and enables a best fit to be made between the work and the mark awarded.

FORMULATION OF THE DESIGN BRIEF AND SPECIFICATION				
0　1　2　3	4　5　6	7　8　9	10　11　12	13　14　15
Requires considerable help to formulate a design brief. A very limited specification with key features missing.	Can react to suggestions and begin to formulate a design brief. Is able to prepare a limited specification/ list of design criteria which identify some features.	Can prepare a design brief but may need occasional advice. Is able to formulate a coherent specification but with some aspects missing that are relevant to the design.	Can identify a primary need/approach and prepare a suitable design brief. Is able to formulate a list of design criteria/specification which takes into account appearance, function, safety and reliability.	Can independently identify an original problem and produce a brief which clearly outlines the design objective, supported by a concise list of design criteria and a specification.

RESEARCH – INVESTIGATION				
0　1　2　3　4　5	6　7　8　9　10	11　12　13　14　15	16　17　18　19　20	21　22　23　24　25
Can collect only basic information from a severely limited range of sources. Only limited use is made of existing knowledge of familiar products when planning and making.	Can gather basic information from an available range of sources by starting to recognise that users have preferences, and to take some of them into account when designing. Draws upon existing knowledge of familiar products, materials and processes when planning and making.	Can collect a useful range of information and data that are relevant to their designing activities. There is some organisation and collation of research material in order to support the designing and making process.	Can identify appropriate sources of information for designing and making which: • justify needs/ opportunities • help generate ideas • provide information to assist • planning and making Shows some evidence of sorting/organisation and analysis of research information.	Can identify how the needs and preferences of users are reflected in existing products and markets and relate these to their own work in order to • justify needs/ opportunities • inform their design decisions • support planning and making Shows discrimination in the collection, selection, organisation and analysis of research information.

Figure 1.1 *AQA, SEG 2000 syllabus – design brief, specification and research.*

CHECKLIST

To gain marks within the top bands of 'Design brief, specification, research and investigation' for all examination boards you must have in your portfolio:

- the identification of an original problem;
- a brief that outlines your design intention;
- a specification that includes a list of design criteria;
- a study of existing products that are similar to your design and reference to how these meet the needs of the users of those products;
- reference to how existing products have influenced, justified and supported your own design decisions;
- organised and sorted research that is relevant to your project;
- an analysis of the research that has been carried out.

If the assessment grid in Fig. 1.1 is not the one that you are using then study yours and compile a similar checklist.

GENERATION AND DEVELOPMENT OF DESIGN SOLUTIONS

The assessment grid examples here are from another examination board; they are set out differently but what they say and the way that marks are allocated are very similar.

DESIGN & TECHNOLOGY COURSEWORK ASSESSMENT

Generation of Design Solutions

Level of Response	Mark range
One or more solutions proposed. **Little or no** evaluation. The work presented displays a **low standard** of communication techniques.	0–3
Several solutions proposed. A **cursory** evaluation. **Unsupported** choice of design proposal. Communication will be of a **reasonable standard** using a **limited** number of techniques.	4–6
A **range** of **appropriate** solutions proposed. Design proposal chosen, **supported** by **clear evaluation**. Communication will be of a **good standard**, well presented using a **range** of **appropriate** techniques.	7–10
A **wide range** of **appropriate** solutions proposed. Design proposal chosen as a result of **detailed evaluation** and **consideration** of the **need** and **fitness for purpose**. Communication will be of a **high quality**, well presented and using a **wide range** of **appropriate** techniques.	11–14
TOTAL	14

Product development

Level of Response	Mark range
Some materials and production methods identified. Has **attempted** to model part of final solution. **Limited details** given for final solution. The work presented displays a **low standard** of communication techniques.	0–3
As a result of **investigations some decisions** made about **materials, production methods** and **manufactured items**. Has used **modelling** to **check** that the product meets the design brief. **Some important** details given about the final solutions and how more than one of the product could be made. Communication will be of a **reasonable standard** using a limited number of techniques.	4–6
Some testing and trialling resulting in **decisions** about **materials, production methods** and **manufactured items**. Used **modelling and testing** to **ensure** that the product meets the design brief. **Most details** given about final solution and its relevant system of manufacture. Communication will be of a **good standard**, well presented, using a **range** of **appropriate** techniques.	7–10
Appropriate testing and trialling resulting in **reasoned decisions** about **materials, production methods** and **manufactured items**. Has used **modelling** and **test** procedures to **identify** any **necessary modifications** and to **ensure** the product meets the design brief. **Full details** about the final solution and the effective control over the system needed to produce the product in quantity. Communication will be of a **high quality**, well presented and using a **wide range** of **appropriate** techniques.	11–14
TOTAL	14

Figure 1.2 *OCR syllabus – generation of design solution and product development.*

3

Assessment Note 3

Look carefully at the stages in the marks for 'Generation of design solutions' and notice the progression. For example, the strand that refers to 'solutions proposed' is graded from 'one solution' to 'several solutions' to 'appropriate solutions' and finally to 'wide range of appropriate solutions'. To gain high marks you must have design solutions that are:

- wide ranging – not all variations on the same idea;
- appropriate – relevant to your design specification.

Assessment Note 4

Within the assessment of 'Product development' there are four clear strands:

1 Materials and manufacturing
2 Modelling and testing
3 Details of the final solution
4 Quality of communication

You will see that this is typical of all the assessment grids. You must make sure to achieve an equally high standard in all of these strands. You will not be able to gain marks from the top range 11–14 if, for example, your standard of communication is so poor that it is within the mark range 4–6.

CHECKLIST

To gain marks within the top bands of 'Generation and development of design solutions' for all examination boards you must have in your portfolio:

- a wide range of appropriate design solutions;
- an evaluation of your design solutions that refers to the need for the product and its intended purpose;
- results of testing and trialling of materials and manufacturing processes;
- models (not necessarily 3-dimensional) that you have used to test and modify your design;
- a good standard of communication that demonstrates that you are able to use a wide range of communication techniques such as sketches, presentation drawings, word processing, computer-aided drawing, etc.

If the assessment grid in Fig. 1.2 is not the one that you are using then study yours and compile a similar checklist.

MAKING

The assessment grid example here in Fig. 1.3 is from an examination board that uses a grade system rather than a mark system. You will see that the description of a student's ability to 'make' is structured in line with GCSE grades G to A.

Assessment Note 5

It is important to remember that 'making' contributes 60% of the marks of your GCSE award. This is a very important aspect of your design and technology. You must plan your making with care, carry out your work to the highest possible standard, and stick to time targets that are set. We will

Assessment Criteria
Candidates will have

Grade	Making
G	1 used equipment safely under close supervision; 2 produced an undemanding or incomplete outcome.
F	1 demonstrated negligible forward planning; 2 used equipment correctly and safely; 3 produced a largely complete but undemanding outcome; 4 demonstrated accuracy and finish in some parts of the product.
E	1 demonstrated some forward planning; 2 corrected working errors where necessary; 3 used equipment and processes correctly and safely; 4 produced a recognisable outcome; 5 demonstrated accuracy and finish in the product.
D	1 planned sequence of making activities; 2 appropriately corrected working errors; 3 used appropriate equipment and processes correctly and safely; 4 produced a largely complete and effective outcome; 5 demonstrated a reasonable level of accuracy and finish in the product.

Assessment Criteria
Candidates will have

Grade	Making
C	1 planned the correct sequence of making activities; 2 recognised the need for and justified any changes or adaptations; 3 used appropriate equipment and processes correctly and safely; 4 produced a complete, effective and well-assembled outcome; 5 demonstrated a level of accuracy and finish in the product which satisfies most of the demands of the design solution.
B	1 planned the correct sequence of making activities; 2 recorded and justified the need for any changes or adaptations; 3 used appropriate equipment and processes skilfully, correctly and safely; 4 made a complete, effective and skilfully-produced outcome; 5 demonstrated a level of accuracy and finish in the product which satisfies the demands of the design solution.
A	1 produced a correct sequence of activities which shows where, why and how practical production decisions were made; 2 recorded and justified the need for any changes or adaptations; 3 used appropriate equipment and processes consistently correctly, skilfully and safely; 4 made a complete product of high quality; 5 demonstrated an ability to satisfy accurately and completely all the demands of the design solution.

Figure 1.3 *AQA, NEAB syllabus – making.*

return to planning and managing your time later in this section. Remember also that 'making' is assessed through the knowledge and understanding that you have about 'making processes' that are tested in your examination.

Assessment Note 6

If you follow the 'outcome' strand within the assessment grid you can easily see that it is not possible to gain above a grade D if your product outcome is incomplete. Refer to the section on 'choosing a project' in Chapter 2.

Assessment Note 7

Compare carefully the difference between a grade D and grade A. There are a number of key words that make all the difference:

- **correct** sequence of activities;
- **recorded** and **justified** changes;
- **consistently** correctly;
- **complete** product;
- demonstrated an **ability**.

CHECKLIST

To gain marks within the top bands of 'Making' for all examination boards you must:

- plan by producing a correct sequence of activities which shows where, why and how practical production decisions were made;

- record and justify the need for any changes or adaptations;
- use appropriate equipment and processes consistently correctly, skilfully and safely;
- make a complete product of high quality;
- demonstrate an ability to satisfy accurately and completely all of the demands of the design solution.

If the assessment grid in Fig. 1.3 is not the one that you are using then study yours and compile a similar checklist.

EVALUATION

This final assessment grid example is from yet another examination board. The four assessment grids in this chapter together cover all of the major examination boards.

EVALUATION	
Pupils should show evidence of continuous reviewing, testing and evaluation against the criteria of the original need or opportunity, and of resultant decisions taken	
Mark	**DESIGN AND MAKE TASK**
Low 0–3	• Evaluate alternatives within a selected scheme with chosen solution not justified. • Compare end-product with initial idea. • Propose tests to end-product. • Relate in simple terms, what end-product does to how it does it.
Med 4–7	• Evaluate alternative approaches and justify a chosen solution. • Show evidence of research and modelling, including a systematic approach. • Compare end-product with design specification but make little comment on discrepancies or their significance. • Test end-product and compare results with identified need. Make a reasonable evaluation of work during the manufacturing process.
High 8–10	• Provide a detailed argument for and against a range of alternatives. • Support chosen solution by further research, synthesis and modelling. • Adopt a systematic and analytical approach throughout. • Critically assess chosen solution in its entirety, including evidence of market evaluation where appropriate. • Compare end-product with design specification accounting for discrepancies and assessing their significance. • Make suggestions for further developments. • Test end-product in relation to the original brief, design specification. • Make a detailed evaluation of work over production lifetime with explicit recognition of strengths and weaknesses.

Figure 1.4 *EDEXCEL, London syllabus – evaluation.*

Assessment Note 8

Evaluation of your work must be ongoing. You need to carry out evaluation of your ideas, evaluation of your making and evaluation of your final product outcome. Make sure that this is recorded as a strand throughout your design portfolio.

Assessment Note 9

Your coursework evaluation should be objective rather than subjective. Refer to Section 3 Chapter 11. Evaluate your product outcome against your design specification because this should reflect the intention of the 'design and make' activity. You may need to revisit your specification; do not change the original but rather take the opportunity to justify changes and draw up a revised list of criteria for your evaluation.

CHECKLIST

To gain marks within the top bands of 'Evaluation' for all examination boards you must have in your portfolio:

- a systematic and analytical approach to your evaluation;
- evaluation of alternative design solutions and support for the chosen solution through research and modelling;
- comparisons between the product outcome and the design specification;
- a record of tests that have been carried out with suggestions for further development and improvements;
- an evaluation of your work during the manufacture of the product outcome.

Note

Note all of the above points will come at the end of your coursework; your evaluation should be ongoing.

If the assessment grid in Fig.1.4 is not the one that you are using then study yours and compile a similar checklist.

COURSEWORK ASSESSMENT KEY POINTS

- Coursework assessment is a positive exercise, your teacher will be looking to give you marks where possible and marks can only be rewarded for work that is there.
- You can help your teacher to award you marks by first assessing your work yourself and filling the missing gaps.
- Use the assessment grid to guide your work, don't spend lots of time on things that gain you no credit.
- Organise your portfolio so that it fits with the assessment grid.
- Presentation is important. Well presented work is more effective in communicating quality than untidy work.
- Your work is judged by how good it is, not how big it is.

CHAPTER 2

GETTING ORGANISED

Coursework is as much a test of your ability to get yourself organised and pursue a task through to the end as it is a test of your design and technology ability. More students lose marks by having to rush or not getting finished than by any other failing that they may have. Look back at the assessment of 'Making' in Chapter 1. You can't get above a grade D with an unfinished project.

CHOOSING A PROJECT

Be clear about what a GCSE course is designed to do; a GCSE in Design and Technology is a qualification to be gained that will enhance your prospects of higher education or provide support for a chosen career. Do not be tempted to confuse it with an opportunity to make something that you need at home, as part of your hobby or would just like to have a go at making. You need to tackle a piece of coursework that interests you and motivates you to do well but think carefully, it is most important that your choice enables you to demonstrate your ability and also to succeed.

Here are some points to consider. Choose a project that:

- is just beyond your current ability so that during your course you are stretched and learn more;
- interests you – if you lose interest then you will not be motivated to finish your work to a high standard;
- has a number of design solutions so that you are able to look at a range of options and carry out wide-ranging research;
- enables you to demonstrate your ability to work with more than one material and use more than one aspect of ICT (information and communication technology), where it is relevant;
- is relatively small; large projects often create large problems, and there is also more area to clean up and make presentable;
- you can finish before the deadline so that you can carry out a proper evaluation and return to any weak areas of your work.

Figure 2.1 shows a range of products based upon lighting in the home. This is a good example of the opportunities that exist within an area such as lighting. There any number of materials and design solutions that could be used and the products are all manageable in size and can be finished to a high standard. The main materials used in these examples are acrylic, in sheet and rod form, and aluminium.

Other topics such as clocks and children's toys offer similar opportunities for sensible and realistic project choices.

Figure 2.1

MANAGING YOUR TIME

The examination boards do not tell schools when students should start their projects, but they do state the date by which the project should be marked and ready for moderation. Your teacher will tell you when your coursework starts and may give you a theme, topic or design brief to work with. You will also be told the date by which your work should be complete and ready for marking. It is up to you to plan your time with care between start and finish. It is a good idea to construct a project management graph like that shown in Fig. 2.2.

Follow these steps:

1   Fill in the horizontal axis time line with dates from the start to the final deadline. Be sure to add the holidays. It will be up to you whether holidays are time off or time for intensive activity: a bit of each is advisable.

2   Mark the vertical axis with the stages of your project. It is a good idea to divide the manufacturing up into realistic manufacturing stages. This will help you to monitor the progress of your manufacturing.

3   Using the graph is easy, the important aspect is to keep yourself in the area marked 'good progress'. Once you slip into the 'danger zone' your graph must become steeper to reach the target date. It is hard to climb back up, so keep on the good side of the target line.

The graph has the progress of two projects plotted on it. Look how far apart the two projects have become. Example 2 now has a very steep climb to make the finish deadline, there will be little time available for making improvements.

Another way of managing time is to use a Gant chart. These are used a lot in industry to plan activities that may take place at the same time (concurrently). With a Gant chart you are able to plot activities with start and finish times that overlap each other. The example shown in Fig. 2.3 is taken from a GCSE project folder. It shows only the stages for the manufacture of the product but it could easily have been extended to include the whole project.

Figure 2.2 *Project management graph.*

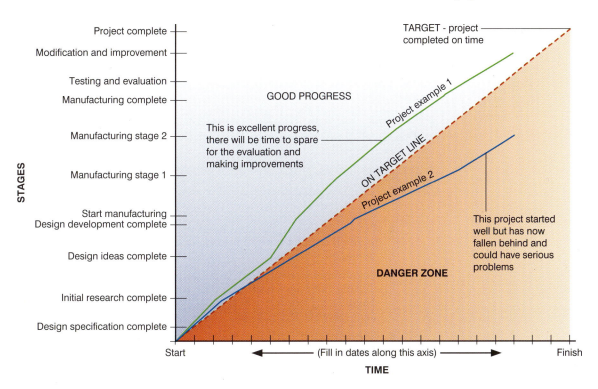

Gant chart for the production of my product

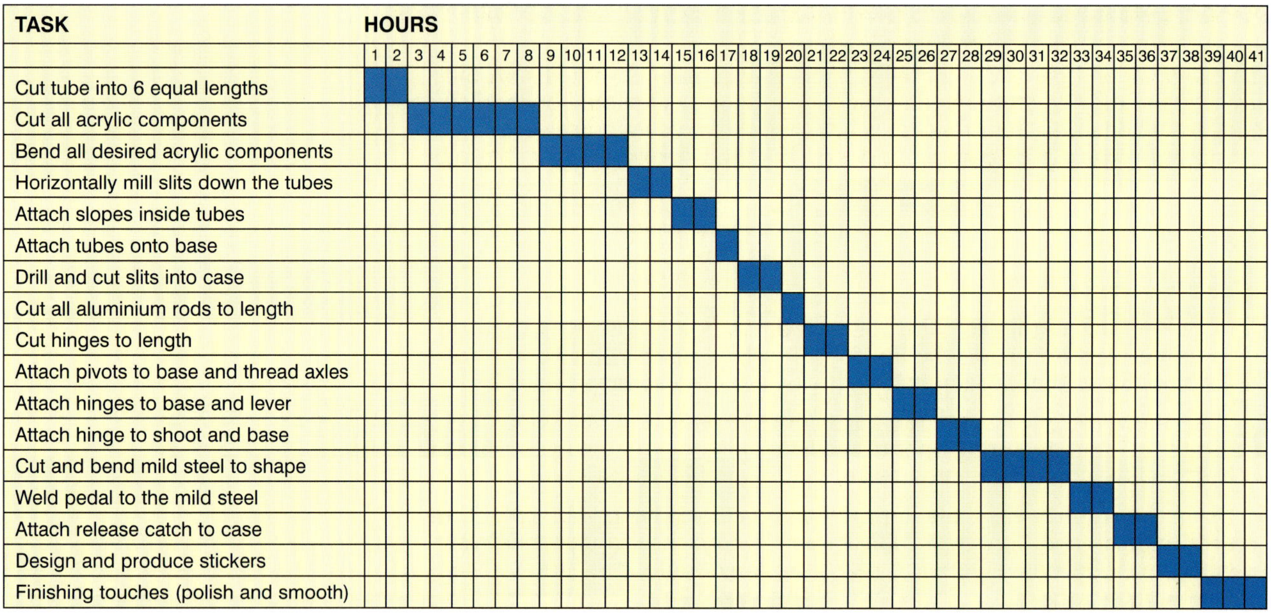

TASK	HOURS
	1 2 3 4 5 6 7 8 9 10 11 12 13 14 15 16 17 18 19 20 21 22 23 24 25 26 27 28 29 30 31 32 33 34 35 36 37 38 39 40 41
Cut tube into 6 equal lengths	1–2
Cut all acrylic components	3–8
Bend all desired acrylic components	9–12
Horizontally mill slits down the tubes	13–14
Attach slopes inside tubes	15
Attach tubes onto base	16–17
Drill and cut slits into case	18
Cut all aluminium rods to length	19–20
Cut hinges to length	21
Attach pivots to base and thread axles	22–23
Attach hinges to base and lever	25
Attach hinge to shoot and base	27
Cut and bend mild steel to shape	29–31
Weld pedal to the mild steel	33
Attach release catch to case	35
Design and produce stickers	37–38
Finishing touches (polish and smooth)	39–41

Figure 2.3 *Gant chart.*

RESOURCING YOUR PROJECT WORK

Any amount of careful planning of your time will come to very little if you are faced with major delays. Think ahead if you are using materials or components that need to be ordered and delivered. Place any orders early even if you are assured that the company has next day delivery, and avoid the Christmas period when postage can be delayed.

ORGANISING YOUR PORTFOLIO

Candidates for examinations often let themselves down in very simple ways. You must remember that your work is to be assessed by both your teacher and by an examination board moderator. If it is hard for them to locate work that should gain you credit then there is always the chance that it will be missed and the marks not given. It is not possible to see what is in your head or know what you have done other than by the work that is presented for assessment.

PORTFOLIO CHECKLIST

- Presentation is important. Keep your work clean and tidy and allow yourself enough time to rework sheets that have become scruffy or damaged.

- Plain paper benefits from a border, but don't spend so long on making the pages look nice that you neglect the content of the page. Fancy borders will present your work nicely but they will not gain marks in themselves.

- Organise your portfolio in line with the examination board's mark scheme. This will provide a structure for you that will help you to make sure that you haven't missed things out, and it will help the person marking your work.

- Number the pages in pencil to begin with. You may need to add pages when you come to review your progress; pages numbered 5a and 5b, etc. suggest a lack of planning. When you are certain that you have finished then you can make the page numbers permanent.

- Do not be tempted to include lots of manufacturer's information leaflets, etc. just to make it look more. You should sort through your research and include only what is relevant with suitable notes and comments.

- Marks are awarded for the use of ICT such as for word processing, CAD drawings and spreadsheets. Make sure these are used where it is appropriate to do so. Be sure to also include other forms of communication. Marks are often awarded for demonstrating a range of techniques.

- Your name and the name of your school should appear on the front of your work and you should clearly state the examination for which you are entered.

- Store your work flat and when it is complete, clip or bind the sheets together with a cover and a stiff back, or alternatively use a folder. Your teacher will have many portfolios to store and look after. It is easy for single sheets that slip out to become damaged or even lost.

MONITORING PROGRESS AND SELF ASSESSMENT

Monitor your progress and check your work regularly. This will enable you to ensure a high standard is reached. If you leave it too long then it is often difficult to get back on track again. Self assessment is a means of quality control. With any form of quality control you need to be aware of the standard that you are trying to achieve. The mark scheme sets out what is required but this is often too complex for everyday use.

COURSEWORK MONITORING AND SELF-ASSESSMENT SHEET

The sheet provided in Fig. 2.4 will help you monitor your progress and assess your own work. The assessment objectives may need adjusting to suit your examination syllabus, but any changes will be minor.

Progress monitoring

Fill in the date required for completion of the work described and then in the 'completed' column add the date when the work is completed. The next column is important. If the work is complete, where is it located? Insert in this area the appropriate page number in your portfolio or the location of your practical work.

GCSE Design and Technology Coursework monitoring and self assessment	date required	date completed	location/page no.	Self assessment				Action		
Assessment Objectives				poor	satisfactory	good	excellent	none	re-work	revised deadline
Research, analysis and design specification Range of initial ideas										
Intended use of product examined ⟶										
Research and analysis ⟶										
Design specification ⟶										
Initial ideas ⟶										
Design development Modelling, testing and selection										
Design development ⟶										
Modelling and testing ⟶										
Materials and manufacturing ⟶										
Working drawing ⟶										
Planning Manufacture of the product										
Plan for manufacture ⟶										
Knowledge of materials ⟶										
Knowledge of tools and equipment ⟶										
Manufacturing processes and safe working practice ⟶										
Quality product outcome ⟶										
Final testing and evaluation										
Testing ⟶										
Evaluation ⟶										
Conclusions and proposals ⟶										
Information and Communication Technology Presentation										
Use of ICT ⟶										
Presentation of portfolio ⟶										

Figure 2.4

Self assessment

Tick the column that you think applies to your work. Self assessment is an important part of your own personal development. When making judgements about your own work you must ask yourself some questions that you must answer honestly.

- Could I do better if I worked harder?
- Could the outcome be improved by a little more attention to detail?
- Have I allowed enough time to test, evaluate and make any necessary modifications?
- Is this really the best I can do or am I under-achieving?

If you feel that you could do better then use the 'action' column.

Action

When you have completed your work to the best of your ability then you can tick 'none' to indicate that no further action is necessary. If you decide that your standard of work could be improved then tick 're-work' and set yourself a revised deadline date to complete the work to a higher standard.

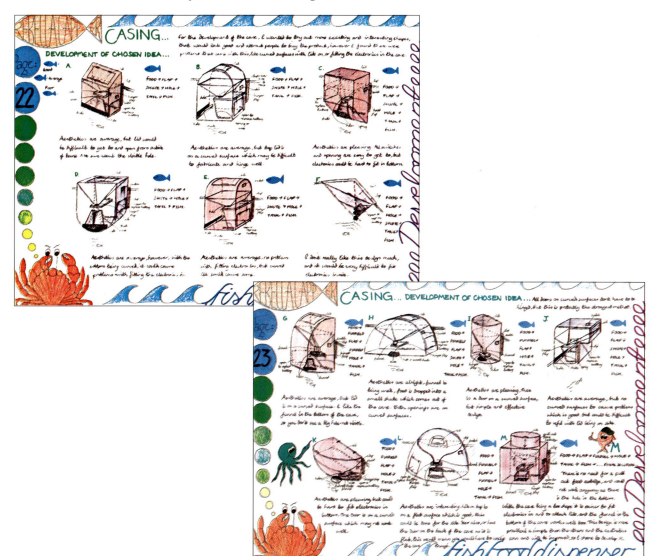

CHAPTER 3

PRESENTATION

In Section 3 'Designing', you will find some useful advice and some exercises designed to develop your basic graphic techniques. This chapter will show you how to further develop those basic graphic techniques and use them to good effect within your coursework portfolio.

LIGHT, SHADE AND COLOUR

Using light and shade will give form to object drawing that is intended to appear three-dimensional. Shapes such as circles and squares are two-dimensional – they are flat. Objects such as spheres and cubes are three-dimensional because they have form as well as shape. Simple shading using a pencil will give an object form and by indicating where light is falling on the object it will also give it realism.

Figure 3.1 *Form with light and shade.*

Figure 3.2 *Using colour.*

If you consider the sphere in Fig. 3.1 without the shading there would be no form and it would not be possible to determine whether you were looking at a sphere or a circle.

Colour brings drawings another step closer to realism but you must think carefully how and when you use colour in your design portfolio. Too much colour or the wrong choice of colour will spoil your drawings. Figure 3.2 shows how colour can be used in different ways to highlight and communicate design solutions.

Learn about colour from what you see around you. Look at posters and advertising and ask yourself why things are as they are. Sometimes colour is used to harmonise and allow things to blend with each other and with their surroundings such as in the window display example in Fig. 3.3.

The alternative is for colours to contrast. This has the effect of making words, symbols and objects stand out from their surroundings. Colours that contrast are used in road signs and warning signs in order to draw your attention to the message. Within your design work it is often important to make ideas stand out from their surroundings so contrasting colours and other techniques can be used to good effect. Highlighting is an effect created by using colour or shade to contrast with the form of the object or the whiteness of the paper.

Figure 3.4 is a good example of both highlighting and the use of colour to draw attention to aspects of the design ideas that need further development. There are a wide range of graphic media that can be used to highlight ideas in this way:

Figure 3.3 *The effect of colours that harmonise.*

- crayons;
- pastels;

- water colour paints
- spirit markers;
- text 'highlighter' pens;
- spatter effects using a tooth brush or spray.

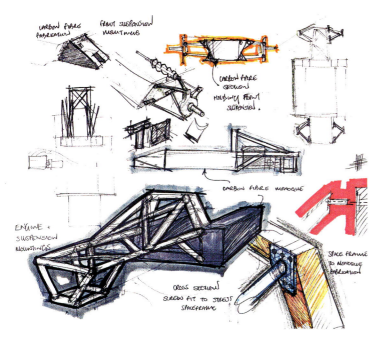

Figure 3.4 *The effect of highlighting ideas.*

Use colour, shading and highlighting in order to achieve the effect that you want. Don't 'colour in' your drawings for the sake of it or the effect will be lost.

Figure 3.5 shows the effect of using a technique called 'weighted line'. This is another form of highlighting, one that involves drawing a darker or thicker line around an object to make it stand out from its background.

The drawing in Fig. 3.6 of a bicycle crank mechanism is an ink drawing carried out using a technical pen with a highlight achieved by using water colour paint. Fine fibre-tip pens and ballpoint pens can also be used to good effect when drawing and presenting design ideas. It is important to experiment and use a medium that suits you.

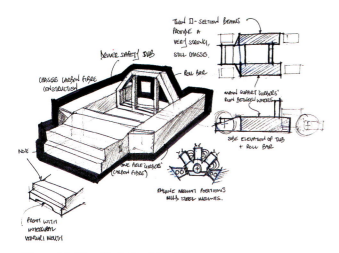

Figure 3.5 *The effect of weighted line.*

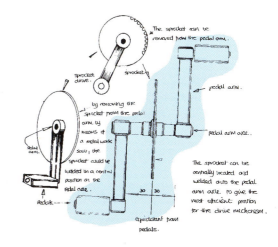

Figure 3.6 *Ink drawing with water colour highlight.*

15

DESIGN PORTFOLIO EXTRACTS

CANDLEHOLDER BY HANNAH LOY

Figure 3.7 *Candle holder.*

Figure 3.9 *Hannah's research is presented here in an imaginative manner. Many pupils include extracts from catalogues and magazines but do not always make any use of them or use them to inform their design thinking.*

Figure 3.8 *This is another interesting candle holder. This has been cast in aluminium and mounted on a wooden base. The 'hand' was first made in plasticine from which a rubber mould has taken; this is also in the photograph. Plaster of Paris was cast in the rubber mould and then the plaster 'hand' was used as the pattern for the aluminium casting process.*

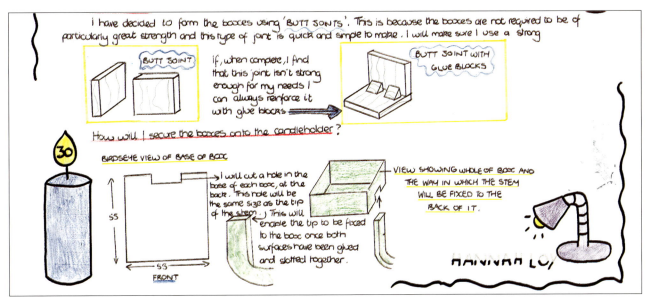

Figure 3.10 Hannah has used a 'chatty' approach to her work and has kept a real sense of continuity within her folder by using the candle page numbers. Remember – do not to spend too much time on this aspect of your work.

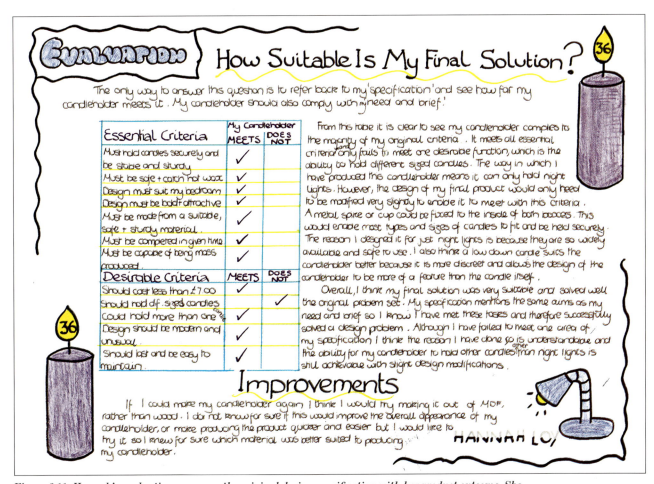

Figure 3.11 Hannah's evaluation compares the original design specification with her product outcome. She also talks about modifications and suggests further work that she could carry out. One way that Hannah could have improved upon her work would be by doing tests to determine the stability of the candle holder. She has stated that stability is an essential part of the product's design.

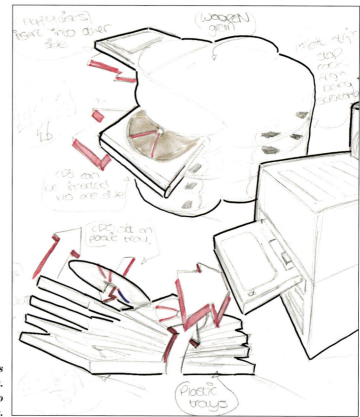

CD STORAGE RACK BY XERXES SETHNA

Figure 3.12 *CD rack.*

Figure 3.13 *This selection from Xerxes' range of ideas is lively and uses an interesting variety of graphic media. He has used crayon and fine fibre tip drawings, and also pencil with spirit markers and weighted lines.*

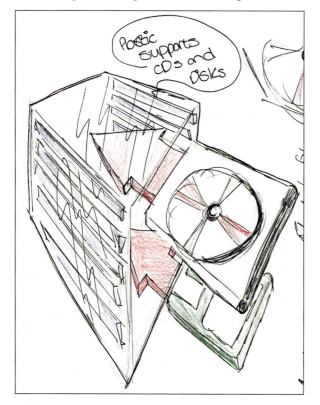

Evaluation

MARKS OUT OF 10?	WOULD YOU BUY IT?	HOW MUCH WOULD YOU PAY?	£0 - £10	£11 - £20	£21 - £30	£30+	ANY COMMENTS?
10	YES	→				✓	"It's pretty damn perfect but there isn't enough capacity"
10	YES	→			✓		"Shiny and well finished"
10	YES	→			✓		"Looks really professional"
9	YES	→			✓		"A bit sharp on the corners, otherwise very professional"
10	YES	→				✓	"Very professional"
10	YES	→		✓			"Looks good"
10	YES	→		✓			"Pretty good but a bit small"
10	YES	→		✓			"Very, very good"
8	NO	→	✓				"Attractive but over-engineered"
8	YES	→		✓			"Bit sharp on corners"

Figure 3.14 *Xerxes' design portfolio uses a large amount of ICT to good effect and a professional appearance. The evaluation – just a part is included here – is very thorough and is enhanced by the inclusion of interesting photographs.*

Analysing Results

The results show that my CD Rack scored 95/100 marks. 9 out of 10 people would buy the CD Rack if they saw it in a shop.

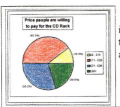

As the graph on the left shows, 40% of people interviewed would pay between £11 and £20 for the CD Rack and 30% would pay between £21 and £30 for the CD Rack.

Evaluation

Criticisms

The major criticism levelled at the CD Rack was that it was a safety hazard because of it's sharp corners. I had already identified this problem.

The second criticism was that it was not capacious enough to suit the needs of the user. In industry, a small module CD Rack would not be manufactured to be over capacious in the hope that users would buy multiple CD Racks to store their CD collection in. A future idea could be the possibility of some sort of linkage to join one CD Rack module to another - with one standing on top of the other.

Feedback

Generally, however, my CD Rack was praised for its quality finish which impressed the target group with its level of professionalism. The CD Rack is indeed very attractive, quite bold and "macho." The surface finish is aesthetically pleasing and futuristic with the myriad light reflections that play across the Aluminium, and the colour changes that occur in different lights.

Above: Only 88 components. Easy to assemble (honest)

The finished prototype.

Above: Just one of the many ways that CDs can be displayed in the Rack

FISH FOOD DISPENSER
BY REBECCA CAPPER

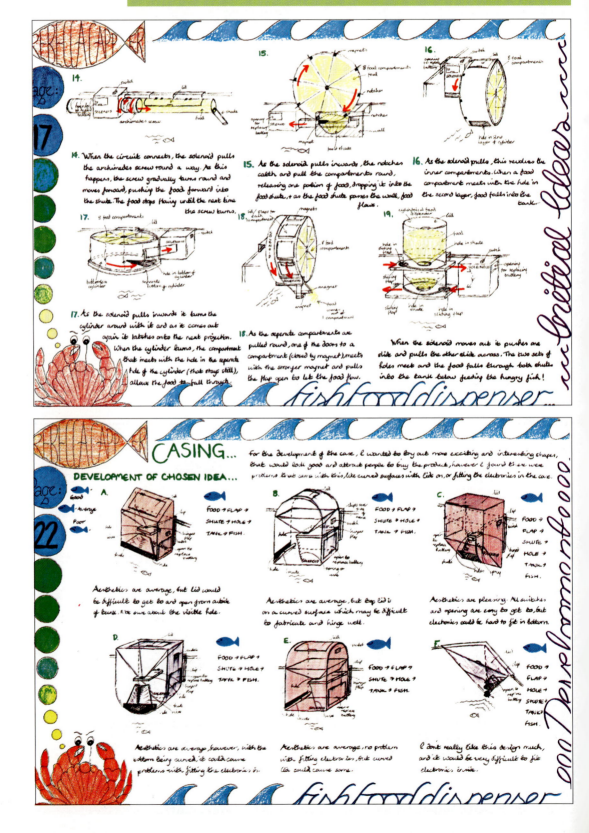

14. When the circuit connects, the solenoid pulls the archimedes screw round a way. As this happens, the screw gradually turns round and moves forward, pushing the food forward into the shute. The food stops flowing until the next time the screw turns.

15. As the solenoid pulls inwards, the notches catch and pull the compartments round, releasing one portion of food, dropping it into the food shute, + as the food shute passes the wall, food flows.

16. As the solenoid pulls, this revolves the inner compartments. When a food compartment meets with the hole in the second layer, food falls into the tank.

17. As the solenoid pulls inwards it turns the cylinder around with it and as it comes out again it latches onto the next projection. When the cylinder turns, the compartment that meets with the hole in the separate hole of the cylinder (that stays still), allows the food to fall through.

18. As the seperate compartments are pulled round, one of the doors to a compartment (closed by magnet), meets with the stronger magnet and pulls the flap open to let the food flow.

When the solenoid moves out it pushes one slide and pulls the other slide across. The two sets of holes meet and the food falls through both shutes into the tank below feeding the hungry fish!

CASING...

For the development of the case, I wanted to try out more exciting and interesting shapes, that would look good and attract people to buy the product, however I found there were problems that came with this, like curved surfaces with lids on, or fitting the electronics in the case.

DEVELOPMENT OF CHOSEN IDEA...

Good
Average
Poor

A. FOOD → FLAP → SHUTE → HOLE → TANK → FISH.

Aesthetics are average, but lid would be difficult to get to and open from outside of tank. Not sure about the visible hole.

B. FOOD → FLAP → SHUTE → HOLE → TANK → FISH.

Aesthetics are average, but top lid is on a curved surface which may be difficult to fabricate and hinge well.

C. FOOD → FLAP → SHUTE → HOLE → TANK → FISH.

Aesthetics are pleasing. All switches and opening are easy to get to, but electronics could be hard to fit in bottom.

D. FOOD → FLAP → SHUTE → HOLE → TANK → FISH.

Aesthetics are average, however, with the bottom being curved, it could cause problems with fitting the electronics in.

E. FOOD → FLAP → SHUTE → HOLE → TANK → FISH.

Aesthetics are average, no problem with fitting electronics, but curved lid could cause some.

F. FOOD → FLAP → HOLE → SHUTE → TANK → FISH.

I don't really like this design much, and it would be very difficult to fit electronics inside.

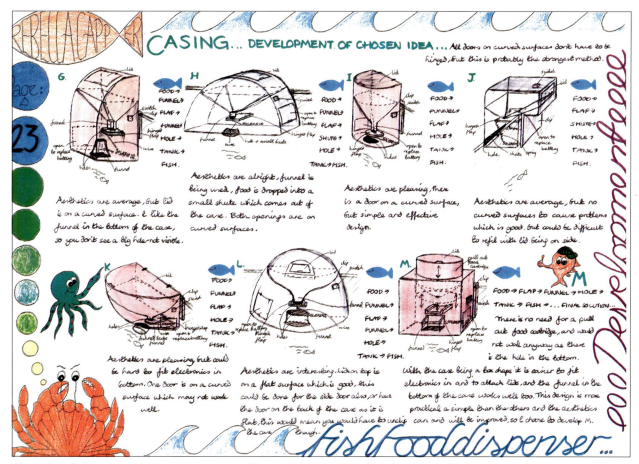

Figure 3.15 *Rebecca's portfolio contains a very wide range of ideas all of which have a sensible commentary and evaluation. Her design development is equally well structured and thorough. She has used fine fibre-tipped pen and a simple colour wash using water colours. This is a good example of how to explore and develop design ideas. The border of her design sheets have been photocopied with the title and colour added later.*

MECHANICAL TOY BY JASON GUNN

Figure 3.16 *Chameleon toy.*

Figure 3.17 *Jason's initial ideas sheet explores a wide range of ideas associated with the brief to design and make an amusing mechanical toy. There is no consideration at this point as to how the particular movement could be achieved – this means that the flow of ideas is not limited.*

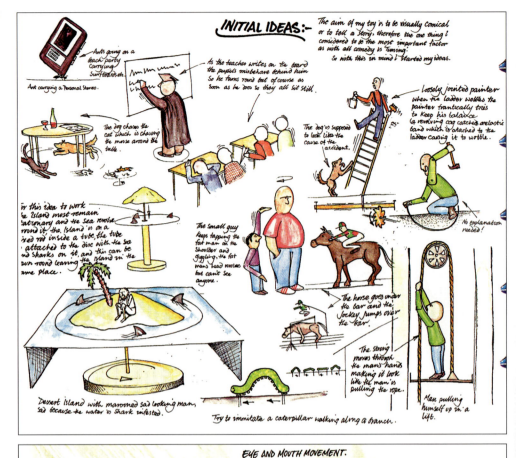

Figure 3.18 *When the decision has been taken to develop a fly catching chameleon then Jason has worked on paper and with card to model the way that the desired effect could be achieved. He looks at cams and cranks and then investigates how these could be incorporated within a base for the toy that will also serve as a housing for the mechanism.*

MOUTH MECHANISM II

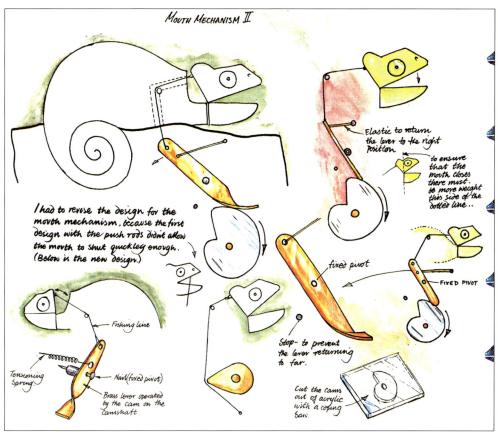

I had to revise the design for the mouth mechanism, because the first design with the push rods didn't allow the mouth to shut quickly enough. (Below is the new design.)

Elastic to return the lever to the right position

to ensure that the mouth closes there must be more weight this side of the dotted line..

fixed pivot

FIXED PIVOT

Stop- to prevent the lever returning to far.

Cut the cams out of acrylic with a coping saw.

Fishing line

Tensioning Spring

Nail (fixed pivot)

Brass lever operated by the cam on the camshaft.

MECHANISM LAYOUT AND CONSTRUCTION

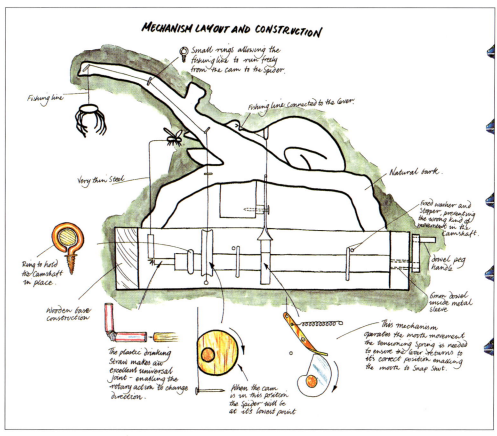

Small rings allowing the fishing line to run freely from the cam to the Spider.

Fishing line

Fishing line connected to the lever.

Natural bark.

Very thin Steel

Fixed washer and Stopper preventing the wrong kind of movement in the camshaft.

Ring to hold the camshaft in place.

dowel peg handle

6mm dowel inside metal sleeve

Wooden base construction

The plastic drinking Straw makes an excellent universal joint - enabling the rotary action to change direction.

When the cam is in this position the Spider will be at its lowest point

This mechanism operates the mouth movement the tensioning spring is needed to ensure the lever returns to its correct position enabling the mouth to Snap Shut.

23

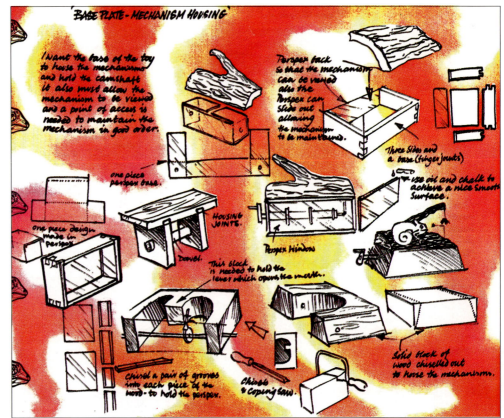

Figure 3.19 *As an extra development for this project Jason has looked at ways in which his toy design might be packaged for sale. The ideas include using card, metal, plastic and wood.*

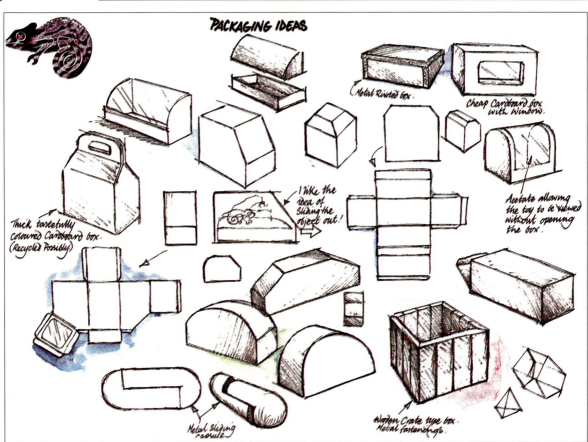

PORTFOLIO CHECKLIST

The key to a well-presented design portfolio is you having a pride in your own work. You need to be able to recognise weaknesses and have a willingness to re-work aspects that you are not 100% happy with.

You need to:

- look for opportunities to make each page interesting. An A3 sheet of paper covered in writing is a daunting task for any examiner.

- make intelligent use of all graphic media and be critical of your own work. Don't overdo it with strong colours and felt-tip pens. Less can often be more.

- always look at display and presentation ideas in advertising and magazines and consider whether you could adopt them to improve your presentation.

- check for spelling mistakes. It is very easy when working on large headings and title pages to leave letters out of words.

- review your work on a regular basis. Over a period of time you may find that changes in style have crept in.

- spend enough time to make your portfolio look good but never forget that it is the content that carries the marks, not the presentation. Presentation is, as the word implies, a means of presenting your work.

CHAPTER 4

SELECTION AND CHOICE

Being able to choose the correct material for any particular task is essential for a manufacturing activity. It is therefore important that you have a sound knowledge of materials in order to achieve success within design and technology. Selection is not always easy and there is often a compromise to be made. Choice must, however, be based upon an understanding of a material's properties and its application.

When you are making comparisons between materials you should be able to demonstrate awareness of the use of a materials database in order to assist you in sorting, comparing and making decisions.

You need to consider the following points when selecting a material for a particular application:

- The functional requirements, also called functionality;
- The manufacturing demands;
- Availability and supply;
- Economics.

THE FUNCTIONAL REQUIREMENTS

This refers to the function of the finished product and what demands will be made of any material that is to be used. It is about matching the task to the material.

Examples of functional requirements are: resistance to wear, hardness, toughness, appearance, surface texture, electrical conductivity, etc. You can see that the functional requirements of the material depend upon the product's requirements so it is important to be clear about what those are. For example, it may be important that a container for chemicals is light in weight and resistant to corrosion. Its electrical conductivity will be of no importance because conductivity is not a functional requirement of a container.

THE MANUFACTURING DEMANDS

It is always necessary when choosing a material for you to consider how the product might be made and the scale of production, that is, how many will be made. Some materials are easier to work and join than others. Many have the ability to change shape under certain conditions, often by using heat processes to melt or soften them. These are materials that can be cast, deformed, reformed and moulded. Other materials can be easily joined using fabrication techniques such as welding or by using adhesives. Some materials are suitable for a number of manufacturing processes and it is then usually the scale of production that determines the choice. For example, many plastic materials that can be successfully joined using adhesive can also be moulded through injection moulding or casting processes. These latter processes, however, can have expensive tooling costs and are therefore only appropriate when considering large scale production.

AVAILABILITY AND SUPPLY

Most materials for workshop use are available only in standard forms and sizes. These are known as **standard forms** and **standard preferred sizes**. To go outside of these standards is very expensive and only appropriate for very large scale production. The form (cross-section) of the material is described in relation to the type of material. For example, metals are available in wire, round, square, strip, sheet, bar, tube, angle and channel forms; wood is available rough sawn or with planed edges in a wide range of sizes; plastics are supplied in forms similar to metal and also as granules and liquid resins.

ECONOMICS

Cost is always an important part of choice. Some materials, such as precious metals, are much more expensive than others. This does not mean that you cannot consider them under some circumstances; silver, for example, could be an appropriate choice for a small item of jewellery, but it would not be an appropriate metal for a CD rack. The method of manufacture, dependent upon the material, is also an economic choice. Materials that take longer to work or that demand costly joining processes will result in a more expensive product outcome. You can see that within a high volume manufacturing industry this becomes a major consideration.

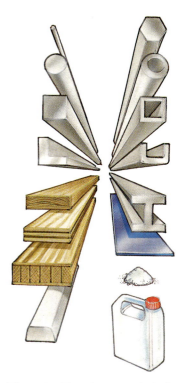

Figure 4.1 *Form (cross-section) of common materials.*

PROPERTIES OF MATERIALS

It is important that you have an understanding of the properties of materials and are able to use the correct terminology associated with those properties. It is not appropriate to use the term 'hard', when you actually mean 'tough'. Glass is hard because it resists abrasive wear such as scratching, but it certainly is not tough. Toughness is the ability to resist fracture when subjected to a sudden shock.

There are two principle categories of material properties:

● **Physical properties** These are the properties associated with the actual chemical or atomic make-up and structure of the material.
● **Mechanical properties** These are the properties associated with how a material reacts when subjected to external forces. These properties are often of greater concern to the designer and technologist.

PHYSICAL PROPERTIES

Density is mass per unit volume, this means how much matter (mass) is contained within a certain space (volume).

Fusibility is the ability of a material to change into a liquid when heated to a particular temperature, the **melting point**. This is important for processes such as casting, welding and moulding. Metals and thermoplastic plastics can be melted if raised to an appropriate temperature. Thermosetting plastics and organic materials such as wood cannot.

Electrical conductivity is the ability of a material to conduct electrical current. Metals – in particular, copper, brass, silver and gold – are good **conductors** of electricity. Non-metals – in particular, ceramics, glass and

Figure 4.2 *Ceramic insulators on an electricity pylon.*

Figure 4.3 *Saucepans have metal bodies for thermal conductivity and plastic handles for thermal insulation.*

FORCE per unit is called STRESS

Displacement (distortion by extension or compression) per unit length is called STRAIN

$$Stress = \frac{Load}{Area}$$

$$Strain = \frac{Extension}{Overall\ length}$$

Figure 4.4 *Force, stress and strain.*

plastics such as PVC and nylon – offer a high resistance to the flow of electricity. These materials are known as **insulators**.

Thermal conductivity is the ability of a material to conduct heat. Metals are good conductors of heat and non-metals are good insulators. As a general guide, materials which have good electrical conductivity also have good thermal conductivity. Air is a particularly good thermal insulator so those materials that trap pockets of air, such as woollen clothing, are also good insulators.

MECHANICAL PROPERTIES

Mechanical properties are the properties associated with how a material reacts when subjected to external forces. It is important that you understand the effect of force upon materials. Force will cause material to become stressed. **Stress** relates to how much load is applied to a given area. **Strain** is another result of the application of force. This is defined as the amount of distortion (extension or compression) that takes place per unit of length.

Strength is the ability of a material to withstand force without breaking or permanently bending. Figure 4.5 shows how different types of strength resist different types of force.

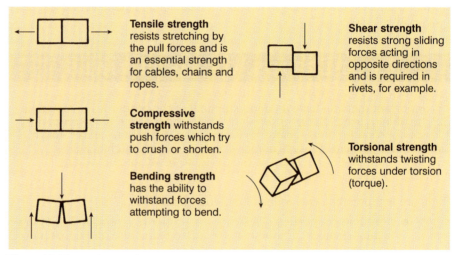

Tensile strength resists stretching by the pull forces and is an essential strength for cables, chains and ropes.

Compressive strength withstands push forces which try to crush or shorten.

Bending strength has the ability to withstand forces attempting to bend.

Shear strength resists strong sliding forces acting in opposite directions and is required in rivets, for example.

Torsional strength withstands twisting forces under torsion (torque).

Figure 4.5 *Types of strength.*

Elasticity is the ability of a material to bend and flex when subjected to a force and then to return to its previous form when the force is removed. Structures such as bridges and tall buildings must have a degree of elasticity.

Plasticity is the ability of a material to be changed permanently in shape (deformed) by the application of an external force without breaking or fracture. Most materials become more plastic when heated. The extent to which a material's shape can become changed by hammering, rolling or pressing is called **malleability**. Another associated term is **ductility**; this is the ability to undergo cold plastic deformation by bending or stretching. All ductile materials are malleable, but all malleable materials are not necessarily ductile.

Hardness is the ability to resist abrasive wear, indentation and deformation. This is the important property of cutting tools such as turning tools, drills, files and saws.

Order	Malleability	Ductility
1	Silver	Silver
2	Copper	Iron
3	Aluminium	Nickel
4	Tin	Copper
5	Lead	Aluminium
6	Zinc	Zinc
7	Iron	Tin
8	Nickel	Lead

Figure 4.6 *Comparative table of common metals: 1, most to 8, least.*

Toughness is the ability to withstand sudden stress in the form of shocks or blows without fracturing. It is also the ability to resist cracking when subjected to bending forces. Repeated bending will cause the toughness of some materials to break down such that they will eventually fracture.

Brittleness is the opposite of toughness. A brittle material will not withstand shocks or bending without fracture.

Durability is the ability to withstand wear, tear and deterioration with time. Durability refers to both the mechanical properties and the appearance of the material. The term used to describe weathering and chemical attack of the surface, particularly of metals, is **corrosion**. Plastic materials are generally less prone to corrosive effects and are therefore durable.

Stability is the ability to resist changes in shape and size over time. Wood is particularly unstable and tends to warp and twist with changes in humidity. Metals and some plastics tend to gradually deform when subjected to stress over long periods; this process is known as **creep**.

Check yourself

QUESTIONS

Q1 How is the selection of materials related to design considerations?

Q2 What is meant by the 'mechanical properties' of a material and how do these differ from the 'physical properties'?

Q3 Explain what is meant by durability and give three different examples where durability is important.

Q4 Explain the difference between elasticity and plasticity.

REMEMBER! Cover the answers if you want to.

ANSWERS

A1 Material choice is determined by the function of the product. The properties of the material should be matched to the requirements of the product being designed.

TUTORIALS

T1 *The key reference here is to the 'function' of the product and to the match or appropriateness of the material's properties to fitting the requirements of that function. As an example consider the appropriateness of aluminium, a light, relatively strong, corrosion resistant material, for use within aircraft.*

ANSWERS

A2 Mechanical properties are those properties associated with how a material reacts when subjected to force. Physical properties are properties associated with the make-up of the material and not related to any external influence.

A3 Durability is the ability of a material to withstand wear and tear over a period of time. Durability is important in: garden furniture, bearing surfaces within machinery, cooking utensils.

A4 The difference is that plasticity relates to a permanent change of shape when force is applied, whereas elastic materials return to their previous shape when the force is removed.

TUTORIALS

T2 *It is important when a question asks about differences or similarities to ensure that you answer by looking for the common thread that is the root of the difference, in this case the existence or the absence of external forces.*

T3 *The question requires a straightforward response that defines the subject, durability. Wear and tear is only part of the answer, there must also be reference made to time. Any material can withstand wear for a short period.*

In the second part where examples are asked for, you should always try to have very different examples and not similar ones. A garden gate, a deck chair and a swing for example are very similar in that they could all be made of wood whose durability is increased by some form of preservative.

T4 *The key aspect of the difference between elasticity and plasticity is 'permanence'. It is important to pick up on the key word.*

KEY WORDS

These are the key words. Tick them if you think you know what they mean. Otherwise check on them.

function	stress	ductility
availability	strain	hardness
standard form	tensile strength	toughness
standard preferred size	compressive strength	brittleness
physical properties	bending	durability
mechanical properties	shear	corrosion
electrical conductivity	torsion	stability
thermal conductivity	elasticity	creep
electrical insulation	plasticity	
thermal insulation	malleability	

CHAPTER 5

WOOD

Wood is an extremely useful natural resource and one that has been used by mankind throughout history for machines, transportation, houses and furniture. The management of wood as a renewable resource is an important ecological issue. Forests are one of the few of the world's natural resources that, through careful management, can be renewed in a relatively short period of time.

Different types of trees provide different types of wood with unique characteristics including: colour, grain pattern, texture, strength, weight, stability, durability and ease of working. They divide into two major classifications:

- **Hardwoods**, from broadleaf trees;
- **Softwoods**, from coniferous trees.

HARDWOODS

It is important to realise that 'hardwood' is a botanical division and does not necessarily indicate that the wood has the property of being 'hard' as distinct from 'soft' in terms of its ability to be worked or cut.

Broadleaf trees, from which hardwoods come, grow in warm temperate climates in Europe, Japan, New Zealand, Chile and the tropical regions of Central and South America, Africa and Asia. Most shed their leaves annually; these are deciduous (leaf losing) but there are a few exceptions such as holly and laurel. Tropical hardwoods also keep their leaves and so grow larger and more quickly.

You need to be aware of the ecological issues associated with the 'harvesting' of hardwood trees particularly from areas of Central and South America and Asia. Forests that are not sustained by replanting are lost to the world for all time. This is a serious issue for the atmosphere, soil erosion, rivers, drainage and potentially therefore the future well-being of the planet.

Figure 5.1 *English oak is an example of a deciduous hardwood tree.*

SOFTWOODS

Most softwood trees are evergreen and also coniferous (cone bearing) with thin needle-like leaves. They grow in colder temperate climates notably in Scandinavia, Canada, Northern Europe and at high altitudes elsewhere. Growth is much quicker than for hardwoods with most trees reaching maturity within thirty years. This means that softwoods are cheaper for commercial use than hardwoods and easier to sustain.

Figure 5.2 *Scots pine is an example of a coniferous softwood tree.*

SELECTING WOOD FOR MANUFACTURE

Trees are converted through a process of logging, sawing and seasoning to make them into usable timber. When a tree is first cut down it contains a large amount of sap and moisture. Once cut down and cut into slabs and planks it is also hydroscopic; this means that it absorbs moisture from damp atmosphere and gives up moisture to dry atmosphere. This results in an unstable material that swells, shrinks, warps, bends, twists and splits. Seasoning is a process for treating new timber in order to bring about some stability by drying out the sap and excess moisture. Seasoning is carried out by either stacking the timber and allowing natural air seasoning or by using drying kilns.

Name	Origin/colour	Properties and working characteristics	Uses
Beech	Europe White to pinkish brown	Close-grained, hard, tough and strong, works and finishes well but prone to warping	Functional furniture (e.g. chairs, toys, tools, veneer, turned work, steam bending)
Elm	Europe Light reddish brown	Tough, durable, cross-grained which makes it difficult to work, does not split easily, has a tendency to warp, good in water	Garden furniture (when treated), turnery and furniture
Oak European English japanese	Europe Light brown	Very strong, heavy, durable, hard and tough, finishes well, open-grained, it contains tannic acid which corrodes iron/steel fittings leaving dark blue staining in the wood, expensive	High-class furniture, fittings, boat-building, garden furniture, posts, veneer
	Japan Yellow brown	Slightly milder, easier to work but less durable	Interior woodwork and furniture
Ash	Europe Pale cream colour and light brown	Open-grained, tough and flexible, good elastic qualities, works and finishes well	Tool handles, sports equipment, traditional coach building, ladders, laminating
Mahogany African (e.g. Sapele, utile)	Central-South America, West Indies, West Africa Pink reddish brown	Easy to work, fairly strong, medium weight, durable, available in long, wide boards, some difficult interlocking grain, prone to warping	Indoor furniture and shop fittings, panelling, veneers
Teak	Burma, India Golden brown	Hard, very strong and extremely durable, natural oils make it highly resistant to moisture, acids and alkalis, works easily but blunts tools quickly, darkens with exposure to light, very expensive	Quality furniture, outdoor furniture, boat building, laboratory equipment, turnery, veneers
Walnut African	Europe, USA, West Africa Yellow, brown, bronze, dark lines	Attractive, works well, durable, often cross-grained which makes planing and finishing difficult, available in large sizes	Furniture, gun stocks, furniture veneers

Figure 5.3 *Common hardwoods*

Name	Origin/colour	Properties and working characteristics	Uses
Scots pine (red deal)	N Europe, Russia Cream, pale brown	Straight grained, but knotty, fairly strong, easy to work, cheap and readily available	Mainly constructional work, paints well, needs outdoor protection
Western Red Cedar	Canada, USA Dark, reddish brown	Light in weight, knot free, soft, straight silky grain, natural oils make it durable against weather, insects and rot, easy to work, but weak and expensive	Outdoor uses, timber cladding of external buildings, also wall panelling
Parana Pine	South America Pale yellow with red/brown streaks	Hard, straight-grained, almost knot free, fairly strong and durable, smooth finish, tends to warp, expensive	Best quality interior joinery, i.e. staircases, built-in furniture
Spruce (whitewood)	N Europe, America Creamy-white	Fairly strong, small hard knots, resistant to splitting, some resin pockets, not durable	General indoor work, whitewood furniture (i.e. kitchens)

Figure 5.4 *Common softwoods*

Selection of wood for a particular application can be based upon all or some of the following criteria:

- **Weight** This varies greatly but hardwoods tend to be heavier than softwoods. The notable exception being balsa which is a very light (and soft) hard wood.

- **Colour** Softwoods are generally lighter than hardwoods and most woods fade with exposure to light (a few such as teak get darker).

- **Grain** Some are straight and others irregular, hardwoods are generally more decorative and therefore preferred for furniture. Grain is often the key to identification. **Texture** is a feature of grain.

- **Durability and resistance to decay** These are important considerations for outdoor use. Hardwoods tend to be the more durable and rot resistant. Cedar, a soft wood, is a notable exception being able to stand up against weather, insect attack and rot. This makes it popular for garden furniture.

- **Cost** Softwoods are considerably cheaper than hardwoods, mainly because of the time it takes for hardwoods to grow and mature.

- **Ease of working** Hardwoods are generally more difficult to work than softwoods and cause tools to become blunt quicker. Other factors such as knots and stability also create problems when working with wood. Always remember that wood is a natural material so it is difficult to have hard and fast rules.

AVAILABILITY AND FORMS OF SUPPLY

After conversion wood is available either rough or planed and in a number of preferred sizes.

Rough sawn is also called nominal sized because it tends to be the size specified. When it is planed in two opposite faces it is called **PBS** (planed both sides) and when planed all round it is known as **PAR**. It is important to be aware that when wood is planed all round (PAR) it will be approximately 3 mm smaller then the size stated due to the planing.

Figure 5.5 shows the standard preferred sizes in timber.

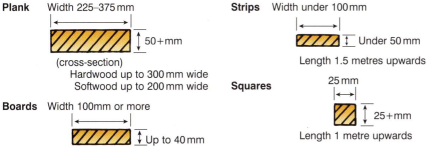

Plank Width 225–375 mm
50+ mm
(cross-section)
Hardwood up to 300 mm wide
Softwood up to 200 mm wide

Boards Width 100 mm or more
Up to 40 mm

Plank and board length varies from 1.8 metres upwards
PBS common thickness 9, 12, 16, 19, 22, 25
Sold by the square metre
Area (square metre) =
$$\text{board length (m)} \times \frac{\text{width (mm)}}{1000}$$

Strips Width under 100 mm
Under 50 mm
Length 1.5 metres upwards

Squares 25 mm
25+ mm
Length 1 metre upwards

Both strips and lengths are sold by length, i.e. per linear metre

Figure 5.5 *Standard preferred sizes in timber.*

33

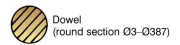
Dowel
(round section Ø3–Ø387)

Half-round

Quadrant

Architrave sections

Figure 5.6 *Examples of standard mouldings.*

Small sections of wood, usually available in 2 metre lengths, are called mouldings. Figure 5.6 shows some examples of the many forms of moulding available.

MANUFACTURED BOARD

Manufactured boards are wood-based materials manufactured by bonding together wood strips, **veneers** (thin layers), pulp or particles. They represent a very important manufacturing material particularly within the furniture industry.

Manufactured boards have a number of advantages over wide wooden board or planks:

- There is a limit to the number of wide boards that can be cut from a tree and this makes it expensive.
- Manufactured board is available in sizes up to 1525 mm wide, hardwood is typically 300 mm and softwood 200 mm maximum.
- Manufactured board is stable and of uniform thickness and consistent quality.

TYPES OF MANUFACTURED BOARD

Medium density fibre board (MDF)

This is made by compressing and gluing together tiny wood particles to form a dense board that is available in a wide range of shapes and cross-sections including mouldings and moulded panels. It is very stable and easily laminated with a thin plastic coating or hardwood veneer. MDF is used extensively for kitchen and workplace furniture.

Plywood

This is formed in large presses from **veneers** (thin layers) of wood and bonded together with adhesive. This process is called **laminating**. The veneer is laid with the grain in alternate directions to achieve maximum strength. There is always an odd number of veneers (3, 5, or 7); this ensures flat faces and stability. Plywood is used for doors and applications where it is necessary to have very thin sheet material, for example as drawer bottoms.

Blockboard

This is made by gluing together, side by side, strips of softwood and then applying a thin veneer to the top and bottom surfaces. Blockboard is very strong and it is used for furniture and heavy construction.

Chipboard

This is made by compressing and gluing together tiny pieces of wood. Chipboard is not easy to work with and not very strong. It is, however, cheap and is usually used with a hardwood or plastic veneered face in cheap furniture.

Hardboard

This is made by gluing and compressing pulped wood. Hardboard is thin and has one smooth surface and one textured. It is not very strong but provides a cheap substitute for plywood where strength is not of concern.

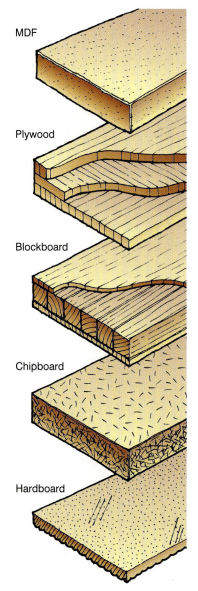

MDF

Plywood

Blockboard

Chipboard

Hardboard

Figure 5.7 *Manufactured boards.*

FINISHES FOR WOOD

The purpose of finishing wood and wood-faced manufactured board is to:

- prevent wood absorbing moisture and therefore becoming unstable;
- protect against decay and insect attack;
- enhance the appearance of the end product.

The first stage of any finishing process is preparation. Surfaces should be made smooth using a smoothing plane and/or glass paper. Remember to always work in the same direction as the grain to avoid scratching the surface.

TYPES OF FINISH

Stain

Stain is used to colour and enhance the grain. Stains can be matched to wood colours and types, for example light oak stain, or they can be used to add colour whilst allowing the grain to show. Stains are not usually protective of the wood.

Oil

This can be used to maintain a natural appearance and give some protection to the surface. Recent developments in oil-based finishes can provide protection and enhancement for external woodwork.

Polish

Beeswax polish is often used in interior 'natural' pine furniture. Traditional French polish has been replaced in most instances by modern synthetic finishes.

Synthetic resins/plastic varnishes

Modern developments in plastic-based finishes such as polyurethane varnish enable surfaces to be given attractive and tough finishes. They are available as clear or in a wide range of colours. Surfaces can be matt, satin or high gloss finished using a brush or spray. It is best to use several thin coats with a rub down using steel wire wool between coats.

Paint

Paint provides colour and protection. Knotting should be applied to knots which may leak resin and spoil the finished paint work. Then surfaces should be primed and undercoated. Several types of paint can be used:

- **Emulsion paints** are water-based and are not waterproof or durable.
- **Oil-based paints** are more expensive but are waterproof and tougher. Polyurethane paint is particularly hard wearing.

Check yourself

QUESTIONS

Q1 Compare the two main categories of wood.

Q2 In what way is the moisture content of wood likely to cause a problem?

Q3 What advantages do manufactured boards have over solid wood?

Q4 A manufacturer of wooden pull-along children's toys has a number of things to consider:

i) What are the important selection criteria to consider appropriate to this product?

ii) Explain which type of solid wood could be suitable.

iii) Give a suitable finish for the product.

REMEMBER! Cover the answers if you want to.

ANSWERS

A1 The two main categories are hardwood and softwood. Hardwoods are slower growing and more expensive than softwoods. Softwoods are generally easier to work and are used for construction work. Hardwoods are used more for high quality furniture and situations where durability is important.

A2 Moisture in wood causes it to become unstable and then to warp and twist. If this is the case then it will be difficult to work and will cause the end product to fail.

A3 Manufactured boards are wider than solid wood, more stable and of uniform thickness and consistent quality.

TUTORIALS

T1 *You need to just determine the key points that enable you to carry out the comparison. It is always important for you to show that you understand the application of materials.*

T2 *A simple statement that refers to stability is the key here. This answer shows a little more understanding of the result of the instability. It is not necessary to mention seasoning or the causes of moisture content; this is not asked for.*

T3 *The four points in the answer are the most important. You could also add that many manufactured boards are cheaper than solid timber but this is not the case with best quality plywood.*

ANSWERS

A4

i) The important selection criteria will be cost, as the toys may be made in large quantity and ease of working as they may be of intricate shapes and it would be an advantage to be tough.

ii) The best type of solid wood would be a softwood such as pine or beech which is a hardwood but works well and is tough.

iii) Either type of wood suggested can be stained and varnished or painted. It is important that the finish is a non-toxic safe material.

TUTORIALS

T4

There is often more than one acceptable response to a question of this type. The important thing is to give sound reasons for your answer that demonstrate your level of understanding. A good tip to note here: whenever a question refers to a product that involves children your response should indicate a safety consideration.

KEY WORDS

These are the key words. Tick them if you think you know what they mean. Otherwise check on them.

hardwood	pine	blockboard
softwood	PBS	chipboard
ecology	PAR	hardboard
seasoning	manufactured boards	stain
grain (in wood)	veneers	polish
beech	MDF	synthetic resins
oak	plywood	plastic varnishes
mahogany	laminating	paint

CHAPTER 6

METALS

The basic elements of all metals are found naturally occurring within the earth. After they are extracted in the form of ore they are refined and processed in a variety of ways to produce usable materials. Metals are commonly available for manufacturing use in a wide range of forms and sizes (see Fig. 6.1). The range of sizes has to be vast because, unlike wood, metal cannot easily be converted from one size to another.

Figure 6.1 *Commonly available metal forms.*

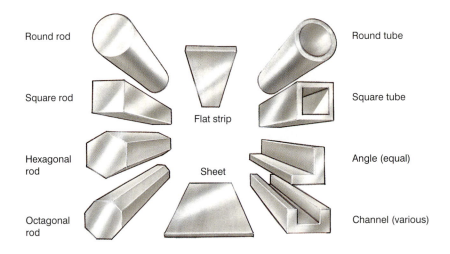

Round rod

Square rod

Hexagonal rod

Octagonal rod

Flat strip

Sheet

Round tube

Square tube

Angle (equal)

Channel (various)

TYPES OF METAL

There are two significant groups of metals:

- **ferrous metals** contain iron;
- **non-ferrous metals** do not contain iron.

FERROUS METALS

Iron is the basis of all ferrous metals but itself is of little practical use as a material. Iron ore is processed into a range of useful materials by heating and alloying processes all of which include the addition and careful control of carbon content.

Alloying refers to the process of bringing together two or more metals, often with other elements, to create a new metal that has improved properties and characteristics. Examples of ferrous (iron-bearing) alloys include **stainless steel** (steel and chromium) and **high speed steel** (steel and tungsten).

The table in Figure 6.2 shows how the addition of other metals and elements can enhance the properties of the material. You particularly need to know how materials are used and what the properties are that suit them for an application. For example, by looking at the table you should be able to determine that high-speed steel is used for cutting tools because it is very hard.

Name and melting point	Composition	Properties and working characteristics	Uses
Cast iron 1200°C	Iron + 3.5% carbon, wide range of alloys, white, grey and malleable forms	Hard skin, brittle soft core, strong under compression, self lubrication, cannot be bent or forged	Heavy crushing machinery Car brake drums or discs Vices or machine parts
Steel Mild steel 1600°C	Alloys of iron and carbon 0.15–0.35% carbon	Tough, ductile and malleable, high tensile strength, easily joined, welded, poor resistance to corrosion, cannot be hardened and tempered, general purpose material	Nails, screws, nuts and bolts Girders Car bodies
Medium carbon steel	0.4–0.7% carbon	Strong and hard, but less ductile, tough or malleable	Garden tools (trowel, fork) Springs Rails
High-carbon steel (silversteel) 1800°C	0.8–1.5%	Very hard, but less ductile, tough or malleable, difficult to cut, easily joined by carbon heat treatment, strength decreases above 0.9%	Hand tools (hammers chisels, screwdrivers, punches)
Alloy steels Stainless steel	Alloys 18% chromium 8% nickel 8% magnesium	Hard and tough, resists wear, corrosion-resistant, different forms affect malleability (types 18/8), difficult to cut or file	Sinks Cutlery Dishes, teapots
High-speed steel	Medium carbon steel + tungsten + chromium + vanadium	Very hard, resistant to frictional heat even at red heat, it can only be ground	Lathe cutting tools Drills Milling cutters
High tensile steel	Low carbon steel + nickel	Corrosion-resistant, low rate of expansion, exceptional strength and toughness	Gears/engine valves Turbines blades
Manganese steel	1.5% manganese	Extreme toughness	Chains Hooks and couplings

Figure 6.2 *Ferrous metals*

NON-FERROUS METALS

Examples of non-ferrous metals are **aluminium** (the Earth's most plentiful metal), **copper**, **tin**, **lead**, **gold** and **silver**. **Brass** and **bronze** are also non-ferrous but as you will see from the table in Figure 6.3 they are actually copper alloys. Brass is typically 65% copper and 35% zinc.

Name and melting point	Composition	Properties and working characteristics	Uses
Aluminium 660°C	Pure metal	High strength/weight ratio, light, soft and ductile (FCC), work hardens in cold state, annealing necessary, difficult to join, non-toxic, good conductor of heat and electricity, corrosion-resistant, polishes well	Kitchen cooking utensils (pans) Packaging, cans, foils Window frames
Casting alloy (LM 4) (LM 6)	3% copper 5% silicon 12% silicon	Casts well, sand and die casting, good machineability, tougher and harder, increased fluidity	Engine components, cylinder heads
Duralumin	4% copper 1% manganese + magnesium	Almost the strength of mild steel but only 30% of the weight, hardens with age, machines well after annealing	Aircraft structure
Copper (Cu) 1083°C	Pure metal	Malleable, ductile (FCC), tough, suitable for hot and cold working, good conductor for heat and electricity, corrosion-resistant, easily joined, solders and brazes well, polishes well, rather expensive	Hot water storage cylinders Central heating pipes/tubing Wire electrical Copper clad board (circuits)
Copper alloys Gilding metal	15% zinc	Stronger, golden colour, enamels. easily-joined	Architectural metalwork Jewellery
Brass 900–1000°C	35% zinc	Corrosion-resistant, increased hardness, casts well, work hardens, easily joined, good conductor of heat and electricity, polishes well	Casting (e.g. valves) Boat fittings Ornaments
Bronze 900–1000°C	10% tin	Strong and tough, good wearing qualities, corrosion-resistant	Statues Coins Bearings
Tin (Sn) 232°C	Pure metal	Soft and weak, ductile and malleable, excellent resistance to corrosion even when damp, low melting point	Bearing metals Solder
Tin-plate	Steel plate tin coated	Bends with mild steel core, non-toxic	Tin cans
Lead (Pb) 327°C	Pure metal	Very heavy, soft, malleable and ductile but weak, corrosion-resistant, even by acid, low melting point, casts well, electrical properties	Roof coverings – flashings Plumbing Insulation against radiation
Zinc (Zn) 419°C	Pure metal	Very weak, poor strength/weight ratio, extremely resistant to atmospheric corrosion, low melting point, ductile (CPH) but difficult to work, expensive	Galvanised steel, dustbins Corrugated iron sheet roof Die casting alloys and rust proof paints

Figure 6.3 *Non-ferrous metals and their alloys*

HEAT TREATMENT OF METALS

The process of heating and cooling metal can be used to change its properties and characteristics.

It is important to also be aware that **cold working** such as hammering and bending can bring about changes by introducing stress to the surface of the material. This is also known as **work hardening**. Heat treatment can be used to restore that metal's original properties.

HEAT TREATMENT PROCESSES

Annealing

This is the process by which heat is introduced to relieve internal stresses.

Ferrous metals are heated until **bright cherry red** (725 °C), allowed to **soak** at this temperature and then allowed to cool slowly.

Aluminium is heated to 350–400 °C and then allowed to cool. A temperature indicator soap is rubbed on to the surface and turns black when the temperature is reached.

Copper is heated to **dull red** and either quenched in water or allowed to cool.

Brass is heated to **dull red** and allowed to cool.

Copper and brass need pickling in dilute sulphuric acid after being treated to remove surface scaling.

Normalising steel

This process is only used for **steel** in order to refine the structure of the material after work hardening. This involves heating the steel to its '**upper critical limit**', which is between 700 and 900 °C depending upon the carbon content of the steel, soaking at that temperature for a short while, and then allowing it to cool in air.

This process results in a tougher metal than would otherwise be achieved by the process of annealing.

Hardening steel

The physical properties of steel vary according to the carbon content. Hardening of steel is achieved by heating to above the **upper critical point** and then, after soaking at this temperature, cooling rapidly by quenching. Quenching is normally carried out in water although more rapid cooling can be achieved using brine (salt water). Slower cooling can be achieved using oil. With high carbon steels, oil is used for quenching so as to reduce the risk of cracking the steel.

The degree of hardness depends upon the amount of carbon present. Mild steel, with a carbon content below 0.4% cannot be hardened in this way. High carbon steels however become so hard that they are too brittle for many applications and so they have to undergo **tempering** to make them tougher.

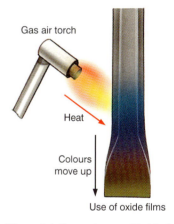

Gas air torch

Heat

Colours move up

Use of oxide films

Figure 6.4 *Tempering a cold chisel in a workshop.*

Colour	Hardest	Approx temp (°C)	Uses
Pale straw	Hardest	230	Lathe tools, scrapers, scribers
Straw		240	Drills, milling cutters
Dark straw		250	Taps and dies, punches, reamers
Brown		260	Plane irons, shears, lathe centres
Brown-purple		270	Scissors, press tools, knives
Purple		280	Cold chisels, axes, saws
Dark purple		290	Screwdrivers, chuck keys
Blue	Toughest	300	Springs, spanners, needles

Figure 6.5 *Tempering steel*

41

Case hardening

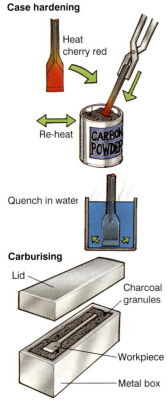

Heat cherry red

Re-heat

CARBON POWDER

Quench in water

Carburising

Lid

Charcoal granules

Workpiece

Metal box

Figure 6.6 Case hardening and carburising.

Tempering

This process involves raising the temperature of the hardened steel to 230–300°C depending upon its intended use. Within manufacturing industry this takes place in a temperature controlled oven. In a workshop tempering involves cleaning the hardened steel to brightness with emery cloth so that oxide colours will be visible as an indicator of the temperature. As the bright steel is heated using a gas air torch, coloured oxides develop and move along the steel as the heat is conducted. When the desired colour reaches the working part of the tool then the tool is immediately quenched in cold water.

Case hardening mild steel

We have seen that mild steel, because of its low carbon content cannot, be hardened by the above process. Case hardening involves introducing a surface layer of carbon to the steel so that this outer surface can then be hardened. This can be carried out either by heating the steel to a cherry red heat and dipping it in carbon – this process is repeated several times to build up a thickness – or by packing the steel in charcoal and cooking it in an oven at 900°C for several hours. Packing in charcoal is called **carburising** or pack carburising.

The steel can then be hardened as before. Case hardening does have an advantage in that the softer core of the steel remains tough whilst the outer surface is hard.

METAL FINISHING

The purpose of finishing metals is to:

- provide protection against tarnishing (oxidation) and corrosion;
- enhance the appearance of the end product.

Whatever surface finish or protection is applied to metals it is important that first the surface is 'finished' and is free from dirt, grease and oxide films. Care should be taken with handling as this is the major contributor to surface deterioration.

Hand finishing usually involves a succession of abrasive treatments: filing, drawfiling, emery cloth and polishing. These processes are dealt with in Chapter 13. Machine-finished components and products should not require these processes as it is possible on a centre lathe or milling machine to achieve a high standard of finish.

METAL FINISHING PROCESSES

Oil blacking

This traditional and simple process is normally applied to forged steel products. It involves heating the steel to a dull red heat and then quenching it in a high flash point oil. The oil burns black onto the surface providing a thin protective skin that can then be lacquered to provide additional protection.

Painting

To ensure that paint stays on metal surfaces the metal must be thoroughly cleaned and degreased using a spirit such as white spirit or paraffin, and then a primer should be applied. Metal primers such as red-oxide and zinc chromate provide adhesion to the metal surface and form a suitable surface for an oil-based undercoat followed by a top coat. It is important not to contaminate the primed surface with grease through handling.

Plastic coating

This process can be applied to most metals and is used for coating wire metal baskets, racks and handles for tools such as scissors and pliers. The product should be cleaned, degreased and heated in an oven to approximately 180°C. The coating process is called **fluidisation** and takes place in a fluidisation tank. The tank contains plastic powder with air passing through it which makes it behave as a liquid. The work is plunged in, left for a few moments whilst the plastic melts and fuses against the hot surface, and is then removed.

Returning the product to the oven then ensures a smooth high gloss plastic surface.

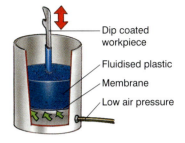

Figure 6.7 *Plastic dip coating.*

Lacquering

Lacquer involves spraying or brushing a thin layer of cellulose or varnish onto the surface to provide a clear protective barrier against tarnish and oxidisation. This is particularly suitable for items such as jewellery manufactured from attractive non-ferrous metals such as copper as it allows the colour of the metal to show through.

Enamelling

This decorative process uses powdered glass which is melted to flow over the metal to give a hard colourful and protective finish.

Vitreous (stove) enamelling is used on steel for equipment such as cookers and provides a finish which is heat, chemical, wear and corrosion resistant. Enamelled jewellery is made using a base metal such as copper or gilding metal. Small enamelling kilns are used for this purpose.

Figure 6.8 *Enamelled jewellery.*

Electroplating

Electroplating is used to give metals such as copper and brass a decorative protective finish. The product to be coated is immersed in a metallic salt solution called an **electrolyte**. A current is passed between the metal to be used for the coating and the product causing deposits of the coating to be formed on the product. Electroplating is used for chrome plating taps and silver plating jewellery.

Anodising

Anodising is a process that is used on aluminium to thicken the oxide layer of the surface. It is an electro process similar to electroplating except that no other metal is introduced. Colouring dyes are added to the process to provide a colourful 'metallic' surface finish.

Figure 6.9 *Electroplated chrome taps.*

KEY WORDS

These are the key words. Tick them if you think you know what they mean. Otherwise check on them.

ferrous metal	**aluminium**	**work hardening**	**oxidation**
non-ferrous metal	**copper**	**hardening**	**plastic coating**
alloying	**tin**	**annealing**	**lacquering**
steel	**lead**	**bronze**	**enamelling**
stainless steel	**zinc (galvanising)**	**normalising**	**electroplating**
high speed steel	**brass**	**tempering**	**anodising**
high tensile steel	**cold working**	**case hardening**	

Check yourself

QUESTIONS

Q1 Explain the term 'alloy' and give examples of two ferrous and two non-ferrous alloys.

Q2 Give one example of how the following metals might be used and state which of the material's characteristics makes it particularly appropriate for the application that you have given.

i) Cast iron
ii) Aluminium
iii) Copper
iv) Brass

Q3 Explain how the process of normalising differs from the process of annealing.

Q4 List the stages necessary to prepare a mild steel lever for plastic dip coating.

REMEMBER! Cover the answers if you want to.

ANSWERS

A1 An alloy is a metal made up of two or more other metals.

Stainless steel and high tensile steel are ferrous alloys.

Duralumin and brass are non-ferrous alloys.

A2
i) Cast iron – workshop vices – strong and has the ability to be cast easily.
ii) Aluminium – cooking utensils – good conductor of heat.
iii) Copper – water pipes – malleability.
iv) Brass – water taps – corrosion resistant.

A3 Normalising is a process that is only applicable to steel. Normalising results in a tougher steel than annealing. Within the process of normalising the temperature is controlled according to the upper critical limit of the particular steel where annealing raises the temperature to cherry red heat.

A4 The surface should be finished by filing, draw filing and then using emery cloth to remove all scratches. It should then be cleaned and all grease removed using a spirit such as white spirit.

TUTORIALS

T1 *There are not many common alloys so it is good to be aware of a few. The term aluminium alloy is used a great deal. Sports car wheels are often called 'alloy wheels'. They are in fact duralumin, an aluminium alloy that is light and strong.*

T2 *There is a range of answers to this question, but when a question of this nature arises go straight to the point and do not offer information that is not asked for. In the example of cast iron there are two properties given. No extra marks will be available for the second and you could get one of them wrong.*

T3 *Without the last sentence this answer would not have had a clear enough focus upon the question. The question asks for the difference in the process. Reference could have been made to either carbon content or upper critical limit.*

T4 *This answer is correct although it does not really matter if the actual area to be coated is free from scratches. The important point is to be free from grease.*

The word plastic is used to describe the wide range of materials that have at some point been in a plastic state, that is, the condition between liquid and solid. All of the GCSE syllabuses require only knowledge and understanding associated with synthetic (man-made) plastics but it is useful to be aware, when looking at product design and product development, that natural plastics derived from plants, animals and insects have been used in the past.

Synthetic plastics came into being during the early part of the 20th century with materials such as **bakelite**. The huge plastics industry that we know today was started up to meet the demands of the Second World War. An early synthetic rubber called **styrene** led to **polystyrene**. Vinyl provided another range of plastics including **PVC**. **Acrylic** was developed for aircraft canopies and then further refined to produce **polythene**. At a similar period **nylon** was produced which when spun into a fibre became a new fabric for clothing and furnishings. Crude oil, coal and natural gas provide the source material for the manufacture of synthetic plastics.

In general plastics do not have the strengths of many other manufacturing materials such as metal but because they can be light it is possible to achieve a good strength to weight ratio. A valuable property of plastics is their ability to resist corrosion. Whilst this is very good for providing resistance to weather and chemical attack, a near indestructible material becomes a serious environmental issue. The more that plastics replace materials such as glass for packaging and storage, the greater becomes the problem, although recent developments have resulted in a range of bio-degradable plastics. Most thermoplastics could be reused but it is not always energy and cost efficient to do so.

It is worth noting that the issues that surround environmentally responsible technology do appear in general terms within examination syllabuses and you can therefore expect them to appear within examinations. It is important that you keep up to date with developments in these areas.

Figure 7.1 *An early telephone made from bakelite.*

TYPES OF PLASTICS

There are two types of plastics:
- thermoplastics;
- thermosetting plastics.

Figure 7.2 *A modern telephone made from ABS.*

THERMOPLASTICS

Thermoplastic plastics are made from long chain molecules that are entangled but not bonded together. This means that all thermoplastics can be melted and returned to a workable plastic state, hence the term thermoplastic: 'thermo' meaning heat, and 'plastic' referring to the condition between liquid and solid.

Figure 7.3 *Examples of common plastic containers.*

THERMOSETTING PLASTICS

Thermosetting plastics (thermosets) are also made from long chain molecules but when the plastic is first formed the chains become bonded together. This means that thermosetting plastics cannot be re-melted. Thermosetting plastics are rigid and non-flexible even at high temperatures.

The tables in Fig. 7.4 cover the range of common plastics, You should be familiar with the common names, the ones in bold. It is not necessary at GCSE to know the chemical name of materials such as acrylic and ABS.

Thermoplastics

Material	Properties and working characteristics	Uses
Polythene (polyethylene) (LDPE)	Low density: tough, common plastic, good chemical resistance, flexible, soft, attracts dust, electrical insulator, wide range of colours	Detergent, squeezy bottles, toys, packaging film, carrier bags, TV cable
(HDPE)	High density: stiffer, harder, high softening point, can be sterilised, waxy feel	Milk crates, bottles, pipes, houseware, buckets, bowls
Polypropylene (PP)	Light, hard, impact resistant even at low temperatures, good chemical resistance, can be sterilised, easily joined, welded, good resistance to work-fatigue, bending, hinges, good mechanically	Medical equipment, syringes, containers with integral hinges, string, rope, nets, crates, chair shells, kitchenware, film
Polystyrene (PS)	a) Conventional: light, hard, stiff, colourless, transparent, brittle, low impact strength, safe with food, good water resistance	Model kits, packaging, disposable plates, cups, utensils, TV cabinets, containers
	b) Toughened: increases impact, strength, pigmented	Toys, refrigerator linings
	c) Expanded/foam: buoyant, lightweight, crumbles, good sound/heat insulator	Sound and heat insulation, packaging
uPVC (Polyvinyl chloride) Plasticised (PVC)	Good chemical, weather resistance, stiff, hard, tough, lightweight, wide colour ranges, needs to be stabilised for outdoor use Soft, flexible, good electrical insulator	Pipes, guttering, bottles, shoe soles, roofing sheets, records, window frames Underseal, hosepipes, wall coverings
Acrylic (Polymethyl methacrylate)	Stiff, hard, clear, very durable, IOX impact resistance of glass, but scratches easily, excellent light transmission, fibre optic qualities, safe with food, good electrical insulator, colours well, easily machined, polishes well	Light units, illuminated signs, record player lids, aircraft canopies, windows, rear car lights/reflectors, furniture, sanitary ware
Nylon (Polyamide)	Creamy colour, hard, tough, resilient to wear, low coefficient of friction, bearing surfaces, self-lubricating, resistant to extremes of temperature, good chemical resistance, machines well, difficult to join except mechanically	Bearings, gear wheels, casings for power tools, curtain rail fittings, combs, clothing, stockings, hinges, filaments for brushes
Cellulose acetate	Tough, hard and stiff (can be made flexible), resilient, light in weight, transparent, non-flammable, easily machined, absorbs some moisture	Pen cases, photographic film, cutlery handles, knobs, lids, spectacle frames, containers
ABS (Acrylonitrile butadienestyrene)	High impact strength and toughness, scratch resistant, light and durable, good appearance, high surface finish, resistant to chemicals	Kitchen ware, cases for consumer durables (e.g. cameras), toys, safety helmets, car components, telephones, food processors/mixers

Thermosetting plastics

Material	Properties and working characteristics	Uses
Urea-formaldehyde (UF)	Stiff, hard, strong, brittle, heat resistant, good electrical insulator, wide range of light colours, adhesive (Aerolite)	(White) electrical fittings, domestic appliance parts (e.g. knobs), adhesives (wood), coating paper, textile
Melamine-formaldehyde (MF)	Stiff, hard, strong, scratch resistant, low water absorption, odourless, stain resistant, resists some chemicals, wide range of colours	Tableware, decorative laminates for work surfaces, electrical insulation, buttons
Polyester resin (PR)	Stiff, hard, brittle (resilient when laminated GRP), good heat and chemical resistance, electrical insulator, resists ultra-violet light, good outdoors, contracts on curing, takes colour well	Casting, encapsulation, embedding, panels (with GRP), boats, car bodies, chair shells, containers
Epoxy resin (epoxide) (ER)	High strength when re-inforced, good chemical and wear resistance, resists heat to 250°C, electrical insulator, adhesive for bonding unlike materials, low shrinkage	Surface coatings, castings, encapsulation of electronic components, adhesives, laminating paper, PCB, tanks, pressure vessels

Figure 7.4

FINISHING PLASTICS

With excellent resistance to corrosion and decay it is not necessary to apply any finish to plastics. Plastics are regarded as **self-finishing** materials. When working with plastics, particularly in sheet form it is important to make the most of the material's finish by protecting the surface when working and polishing edges and worked-on areas.

Questions often arise within examinations related to the stages of manufacture of items using sheet materials such as acrylic. You should remember that once sheet material has been formed using heat bending, the edges are more difficult to finish. It is often necessary therefore to carry out edge finishing before the product takes on its final form.

Figure 7.5 *Edge finishing using a buffing machine.*

KEY WORDS

These are the key words. Tick them if you think you know what they mean. Otherwise check on them.

plastic	thermosetting plastic	ABS	PVC	
thermoplastic	acrylic	polythene	nylon	self-finishing

Check yourself

QUESTIONS

Q1 Compare the two main categories of plastic.

Q2 Give one example of how each of the following plastics might be used and state which of the material's characteristics makes it particularly appropriate.

i) Polythene
ii) Nylon
iii) Acrylic
iv) ABS
v) Melamine formaldehyde
vi) Epoxy resin

REMEMBER! Cover the answers if you want to.

ANSWERS

A1 The two main categories of plastic are thermoplastic and thermosetting plastic. Thermoplastic plastics can be heated and reformed a number of times whereas thermosetting plastics cannot. Thermosetting plastics tend to be harder than thermoplastics.

A2
i) Polythene – squeezy bottles – chemical resistant and flexible.
ii) Nylon – bearings – low coefficient of friction.
iii) Acrylic – signs – bright colours.
iv) ABS – kitchenware – tough.
v) Melamine formaldehyde – work surfaces – hard, scratch resistant.
vi) Epoxy resin – adhesive – bonds to unlike materials.

TUTORIALS

T1 *This is a fundamental aspect of plastics within design and technology. You will only have working experience of thermoplastic materials like acrylic but you must be aware of the thermosetting plastic. The term 'thermoset' is an alternative to 'thermosetting'.*

T2 *Clearly there is a range of answers to this question, but always answer within your knowledge area. The plastics here, and the applications are common in everyday life. Look down the chart of plastics and try to become familiar with at least one common place application for each material and the appropriate material property.*

In this answer it would have been acceptable to use 'melamine' rather than 'melamine formaldehyde'.

As part of your preparation for examinations within design and technology you should be looking at technological products and artefacts in everyday life. As you do this you will begin to notice an increase in the number of standard components that are being used; from door handles on cars to hinges on kitchen furniture.

There are a number of advantages for a manufacturer who uses '**standard components**' which are quite often '**bought in**'.

- The use of standard components can ensure a constancy of size and quality.
- Where the same component is used in more than one product there is a reduction in the amount of stock that has to be held. Stock represents money that is standing idle.
- Standard components are more likely to be available for replacement and maintenance over long periods of time.
- Components bought in from a specialist manufacturer will normally be cheaper than making your own because they specialise.

The most common application for components is within product assembly for fastening devices such as hinges, screws, nails and nuts and bolts. It is unlikely that you would consider making any of these things; you would use the standard components.

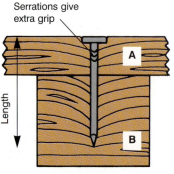

Figure 8.1 *Joining wood with nails.*

NAILS, PINS AND STAPLES

These are quick and permanent methods of joining wood and most wood-based materials. Nails grip by friction, the fibres are compressed and forced away from the head of the nail thereby holding and acting against withdrawal.

Nails are available in a wide range of lengths and are most commonly made from steel and are also available galvanised (zinc-plated) and made from brass and copper. Figure 8.4 shows a selection of the most common types:

(a) **Wire nails** are used for general carpentry, frames and pallets.

(b) **Lost-head wire nails** are used for work where it is necessary to punch the head below the surface.

(c) **Oval wire nails** are used where there is a danger of splitting the grain.

(d) **Panel pins** are used in fine work with thin materials.

(e) **Staples** are used as a quick method of fixing. Staples are used in furniture and upholstery work and are normally fired from a gun.

(f) **Corrugated fasteners** are used for simple cheap work.

Figure 8.2 *Staggered nailing avoids splitting the wood.*

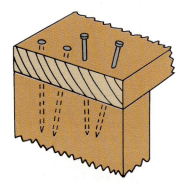

Figure 8.3 *'Dovetail' nailing provides extra strength*

Figure 8.4 *Nails, pins and staples.*

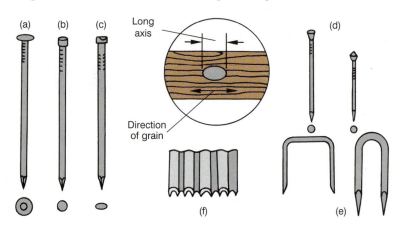

WOOD SCREWS

Wood screws provide a neat and strong method of fixing which can be either permanent or temporary. Screws are commonly made from steel which can be galvanised (zinc-plated), chrome plated or finished black (black jappaning).

Screws are specified by: length, gauge (4–10), material, head and type of slot, for example 50 mm, no.8, steel, countersunk, Phillips.

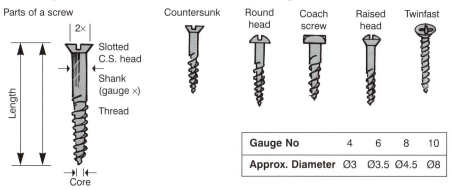

Gauge No	4	6	8	10
Approx. Diameter	Ø3	Ø3.5	Ø4.5	Ø8

Figure 8.5 *Wood screws.*

Figure 8.6 *Screwdriver slots: crossed slots reduce the chances of slipping.*

- **Countersunk screws** are used where a flush surface is required and for fixing hinges.
- **Round head screws** are used for attaching thin metal and plastic fittings.
- **Raised head screws** are decorative and are used for door fittings such as latch plates.
- **Twinfast screws** have a 'quick' thread and are made for materials such as chipboard.
- **Coach screws** are for heavy duty work and are turned using a spanner.

There is a proper sequence for fixing using a wood screw:
1) Select the appropriate screw.
2) Drill the clearance hole to the shank gauge size.
3) Drill a pilot hole to the core diameter.
4) In hardwood use a countersink.

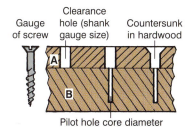

Figure 8.7 *Stages in preparing a hole for a screw.*

RIVETS

Riveting is a quick and convenient method of permanently fixing together two or more pieces of material, traditionally sheet metal. For many applications it is a cheap alternative to threaded fastenings. In addition to making rigid joints, rivets can also form hinge pins in moving parts. Rivets are classified by length, diameter, material and head pattern.

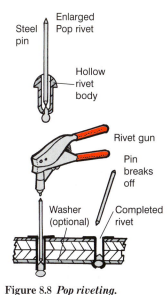

Figure 8.8 *Pop riveting.*

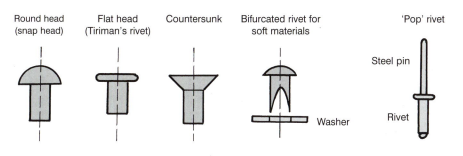

Figure 8.9 *Types of rivet.*

Pop rivets are a quick and easy alternative that was developed within the aircraft industry to enable riveting from just one side. Pop rivets are hollow and therefore not as strong as ordinary rivets.

MACHINE SCREWS, NUTS AND BOLTS

Figure 8.10 *Machine screws and bolts.*

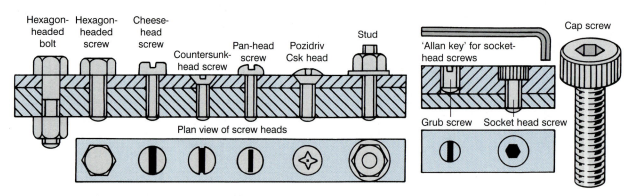

Figure 8.11 *Types of nut.*

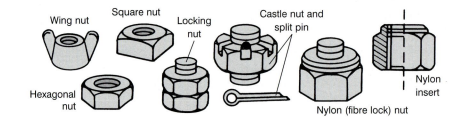

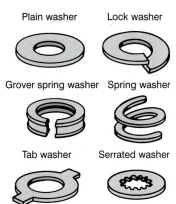

Figure 8.12 *Types of washer.*

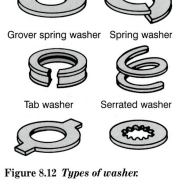

Machine screws, nuts and bolts are regarded as temporary fittings because they can easily be taken apart.

- **Machine screws** are available in a wide range of materials, diameters, lengths, head shapes and thread forms.
- **Bolts** are strong being made from high tensile steel. They have either square or hexagonal heads.
- **Nuts** must match, in size and thread form, the screw or bolt with which they are to be used. There are many forms of nut, from those that are designed to be easily removed (wing nuts) to those that resist removal, particularly through vibration (lock nuts).
- **Washers** are used to protect the surface when nuts are being tightened by spreading the load. They also help to prevent loosening through vibration.

Thread forms

The ISO standard thread form is metric-sized ISO coarse and ISO fine. There are however many other thread forms still in regular usage. In particular you may come across BA series threads and also BSF, BSW, UNC and UNF.

Self-tapping screws

Self-tapping screws are made from hardened steel and cut their own thread as they are screwed in. They are suitable for joining sheet metal and plastics. Preparation requires a clearance hole and a pilot hole equal to the screw's core diameter.

Figure 8.13 *Self-tapping screws.*

MECHANICAL JOINTING

There are many other devices used to join materials together within manufacturing. You need to have an awareness of these means of effecting mechanical joints. These may be permanent or temporary and may have fixed or moving parts.

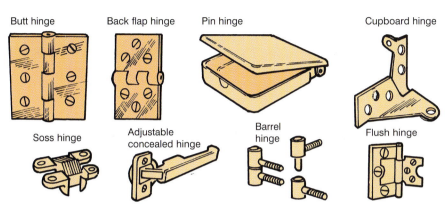

Butt hinge   Back flap hinge   Pin hinge   Cupboard hinge

Soss hinge   Adjustable concealed hinge   Barrel hinge   Flush hinge

Figure 8.14 *Hinges are flexible joining fittings. They can be made from steel, brass or nylon. Look at doors and cupboard doors for examples of hinges.*

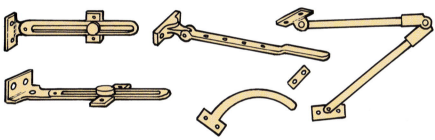

Figure 8.15 *Stays are used in bureaux and opening windows.*

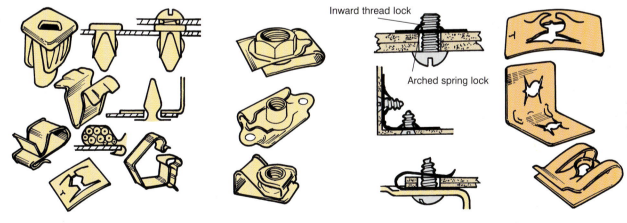

Inward thread lock

Arched spring lock

Figure 8.16 *Clips and threaded fasteners of this nature are very common within cars.*

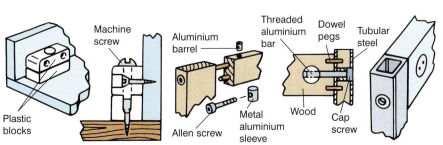

Machine screw

Aluminium barrel

Threaded aluminium bar

Dowel pegs

Tubular steel

Plastic blocks

Allen screw

Metal aluminium sleeve

Wood

Cap screw

Figure 8.17 *'Knock-down' (KD) fittings are used in many furniture applications, particularly in the kitchen.*

Figures 8.14, 8.15, 8.16 and 8.17 show only some of the vast range of joining methods that are in common use. Look at these and consider where you might have seen them before and where you might look in the future. Design and technology is about having an awareness of things technological and this body of knowledge will enable you to answer examination questions from your own experience.

OTHER MECHANICAL JOINTS, FIXINGS AND FITTINGS

Figures 8.18, 8.19 and 8.20 show a variety of fixings and fittings, many of which allow for disassembly.

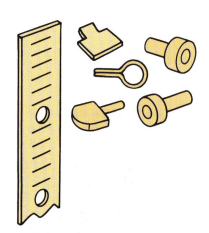

Figure 8.18 *Shelving fitments.*

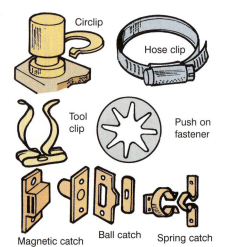

Circlip

Hose clip

Tool clip

Push on fastener

Magnetic catch   Ball catch   Spring catch

Figure 8.19 *Special fixings.*

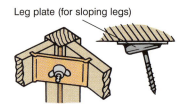

Leg plate (for sloping legs)

Figure 8.20 *Leg fastenings.*

Check yourself

QUESTIONS

Q1 Explain what is meant by the term 'standard components'. Give two ways in which the use of standard components could help a manufacturer save money.

Q2 Compare the use of nails and screws in respect of their holding strength in soft wood.

Q3 What particular aspect of modern furniture manufacture has made 'knock-down' fittings popular and cost effective?

ANSWERS

A1 A standard component is an item that has been standardised upon for a range of applications such as a hinge or a handle. Manufacturers can save money by using standard components because these reduce the amount of stock they hold. It is also normally cheaper to buy-in standard components than to make them yourself.

A2 Nails hold by friction and they can be extracted by pulling with sufficient force. Screws have a greater holding strength because they create a spiral thread that is enmeshed with the fibres of the wood.

A3 Knock-down fittings have enabled the development of 'flat-pack' furniture, particularly for kitchens and bedrooms. They are more cost effective because the manufacturer does not have to assemble them or store and deliver bulky items.

TUTORIALS

T1 The definition is not easy to state without the use of examples such as hinges and handles. It is important that you understand the concept here in order to answer the question.

If you take for example a manufacturer of table lamps, the fittings for the bulb and the electric plug will be standard components that the manufacturer 'buys in'. The manufacture of plugs is a very competitive market; you can buy them in a supermarket for less than 50p. To tool up and employ people to make your own would be very expensive and remember that the quantity that you sell would only be the same quantity as the quantity of lamps that you sell. A lamp manufacturer would not be able to make plugs as cheaply as they could be bought.

T2 Questions of this nature are testing your knowledge of commonplace items within design and technology, in this case nails and screws. Most people know that a nail can be pulled out using a claw hammer or pincers, but a screw can only be removed mechanically, that is by using a screwdriver. You need to be able to think through why that is the case.

T3 The development of knock-down fittings and flat-pack furniture was simultaneous, each depending upon the other.

For 'cost effective' you can usually read 'cheaper' and it is important to see things from the perspective of manufacturing industry. In this instance it is not really the assembly that would increase the price the most, it is the cost of storage and distribution for both the manufacturer and the retailer - consider how many flat wardrobes you can store in the space of one assembled wardrobe.

KEY WORDS

These are the key words. Tick them if you think you know what they mean. Otherwise check on them.

standard components	**rivets**	**washers**
nails	**pop rivets**	**thread**
pins	**machine screws**	**self-tapping screws**
staples	**bolts**	**mechanical fastenings**
screws	**nuts**	**mechanical fittings**

EXAMINATION CHECKLIST FOR THIS SECTION

After studying materials and components you should be able to:

- select the most appropriate material or component for a given task based upon your knowledge of that material or component's properties and its characteristics;
- recall how materials such as woods, metals and plastics are classified and in what forms they are commercially available;
- understand how the properties of materials can be improved by combining them and processing them;
- select and describe the most appropriate method of finishing for a range of materials within a variety of situations;
- understand the use of pre-manufactured standard components and the economic benefits in relation to manufacturing and industrial production.

EXAM PRACTICE

Sample Student's Answers & Examiner's Comments

EXAMINER'S COMMENTS

(a) 1. *This is a correct response but you should use terms such as 'stronger' with a degree of caution. In this case it is quite correct but students very often mix up terms such as 'strong' and 'tough'.*

2. *It is correct to say that manufactured boards will not warp but it would be more correct to say that they are more stable. Manufactured boards are more stable than solid timber because of their construction. They either have no grain like MDF and chipboard, or the effects of the grain movement are controlled by the structure, as in the case of plywood and blockboard.*
It would also be correct to say that you would choose manufactured board because solid timber is not available in wide enough planks. This is a point that students often miss; we all know that wood comes from trees but you must remember that trees only grow so wide.

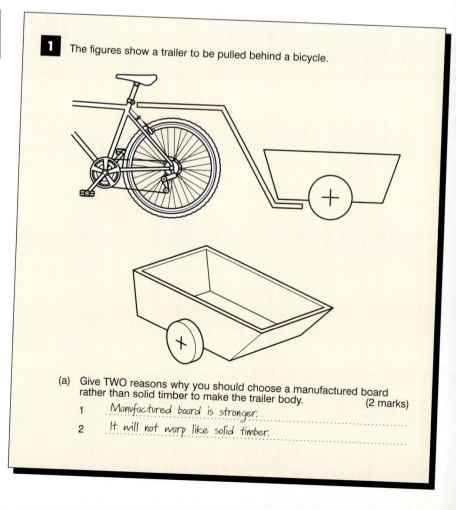

1 The figures show a trailer to be pulled behind a bicycle.

(a) Give TWO reasons why you should choose a manufactured board rather than solid timber to make the trailer body. (2 marks)

1   Manufactured board is stronger.

2   It will not warp like solid timber.

EXAM PRACTICE

Sample Student's Answers & Examiner's Comments

(b) The towing bar is made from a single length of metal tube.

Give TWO suitable metals that could be used for the tube and state the type of finish that each would require. (4 marks)

1 Metal _Mild steel_ Finish _Paint_

2 Metal _Aluminium_ Finish _No finish is needed_

(c) A manufacturer of cycle accessories has decided to make bicycle trailers with plastic bodies.

(i) Give THREE advantages of using a plastic material instead of wood-based manufactured board for the trailer body. (6 marks)

1 _Maintenance free._

2 _It will be lighter but still strong._

3 _The shape can be curved so it will be easier to clean._

(ii) Name a suitable plastic and manufacturing process for the manufacture of the trailer body.

Plastic _Acrylic_ (1 mark)

Process _Vacuum forming_ (2 marks)

(b) *These are correct answers and it is easy to gain maximum marks with recall questions of this nature. For material finishes always think of what you might see on real products. Another suitable finish for mild steel could have been plastic coating but do not suggest 'oil blacking' even if you have used this in the school workshop; it is not used commercially and is not at all hard wearing.*

(c) (i)
These are very good answers to this part of the question and show that the student has a sound understanding of the materials that are being compared. This is particularly true of point 3. You should be able to think around the issues and realise that when using a flexible plastic material, in comparison with a solid sheet material, you are able to re-examine the original design and improve upon the form of the trailer body.
(ii)
The answers in this section are correct but they are not good answers. Acrylic is rather hard for this application, it will scratch and break too easily. ABS or polypropylene would be better materials because they are tougher. Vacuum forming is a suitable process as is press forming. These processes are covered in Section 4 of this revision guide.

Question to Answer

The answer to Question 2 can be found in Chapter 21.

2 When selecting materials for kitchen products such as kettles and saucepans a designer needs to consider certain factors to be included within the design specification.

Identify three such factors and say how they relate to the particular application.

MEG, 1998

THE PROCESS OF DESIGNING

Designing is a very complex activity. It involves thinking and doing and taking time to reflect followed by more thinking and more doing. In reality these things take place continually throughout the process of designing and making. When you are making you still have to make decisions that could be regarded as designing. In order to try to understand this process and to structure it, designing is looked at as a process model. This is a way of visualising it, not a three-dimensional model, but a model like that shown in Fig. 9.1 or sometimes shown more simply as in Fig. 9.2.

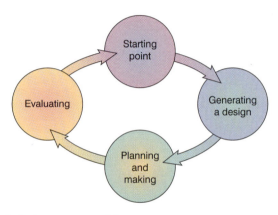

Figure 9.2 *A simple design process model.*

Look at these two design process models. Your coursework should also follow this pattern. The process of designing is the structure for your coursework as well as being a topic for your examination. You need to be familiar with the terms used within the process for both aspects of your GCSE. This section of the revision guide follows that same process model.

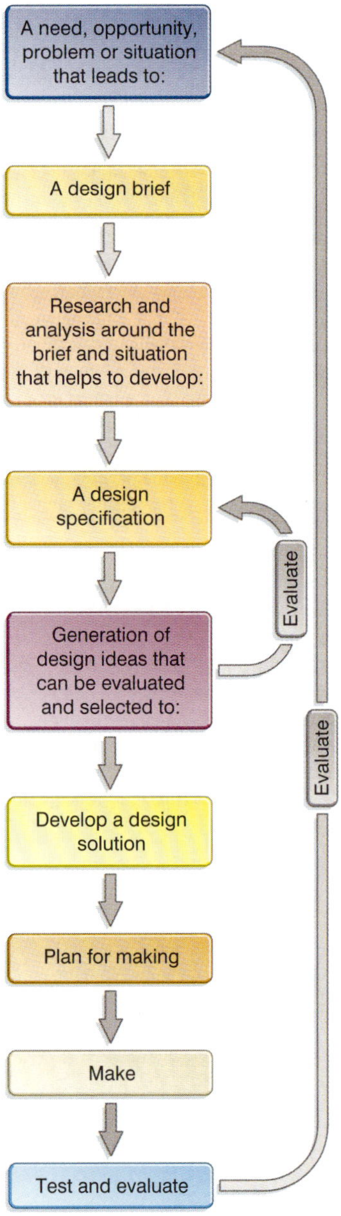

NEEDS AND OPPORTUNITIES FOR DESIGN ACTIVITY

NEEDS

All design must start somewhere. It often starts from an identified need that a person or group of people might have. Real basic human needs are food, water, warmth and shelter but many people have other additional and important special needs. People with disabilities, old people and small children all have special needs. Some people have needs related to the job they do, where they live, what they eat or how they like to spend their leisure time; all of these can provide a starting point for design activity.

CONTEXTS

In your examination or your coursework you may be presented with a context from which you will be asked to find a design opportunity. The context could

Figure 9.1 diagram (left column flowchart):

A need, opportunity, problem or situation that leads to:
↓
A design brief
↓
Research and analysis around the brief and situation that helps to develop:
↓
A design specification
↓
Generation of design ideas that can be evaluated and selected to:
↓
Develop a design solution
↓
Plan for making
↓
Make
↓
Test and evaluate

Evaluate

Figure 9.1 *A model of the process of designing.*

be a public place like a park or bus station or it could be closer to home such as your bedroom or kitchen. Look at the girl in Fig. 9.3. Within this bedroom context there are design opportunities related to storage of clothes, books and compact discs. There is a need for a desk, some improved display space, and possibly better lighting. Can you identify more?

Figure 9.3

PRODUCT ANALYSIS AND EVALUATION

It is unlikely that your coursework will take an existing product as its starting point although most real product design is actually about improving or remodelling existing products. Your examination however may present you with a familiar product such as a ballpoint pen to analyse or you may be asked about the actual process of product analysis and evaluation.

To be able to carry out product analysis you need to know:

- **The product's purpose** A product can only be evaluated against its original design intention or design specification.
- **How the product achieves its purpose** How does the product function or operate for it to do what is intended?
- **The materials used** Why has a particular material been chosen for a component? What are the properties that make it suitable?
- **The processes involved in the manufacture of the product** By discovering how a product has been made and assembled it is possible to understand much of why it is like it is.

INFORMATION GATHERING

There will be many times within a design-and-make activity when you need to gather information. This process begins when you gather information to get you started. You may call this process research or investigation and you will get information either by collecting it first hand yourself or by referring to information or data that already exists.

PRIMARY SOURCE INFORMATION

This is information collected directly from people through surveys or questionnaires or by holding discussion groups and brainstorming sessions.

Questionnaires are very useful but you must be sure to ask only those questions that you need to know the answers to: this makes it quicker to fill in and people are not put off by it. You should also consider how you will deal with the information that you collect. If you ask questions that have a tick box response then you can enter the results into a computer **database** which you can interrogate for information such as 'how many people like this' and 'what percentage of the whole sample is that'. Avoid asking questions that need a written response or comment. These cannot be sorted on a database and it is difficult to draw any conclusion from too many different responses to the same question.

Brainstorming is when a group of people all contribute their ideas about an issue; 'anything goes' and everything is noted down. Some good ideas can come out of brainstorming sessions.

Figure 9.4

SECONDARY SOURCE INFORMATION

With the advances in ICT (information and communication technology) over the last ten years there is more information that is easy to get at than ever before. Information that is stored for you to access – in books, charts, data sheets, CD ROMs and on the Internet – is called secondary source information.

Information from a secondary source can save you lots of time but you must be sure that it is correct. It is also important to be very selective when information is so easily available, and choose only that which is relevant to what you are doing.

Useful secondary sources include:

- Libraries;
- Books;
- Newspapers and magazines;
- Museums and exhibitions;
- Television and video;
- Computer databases;
- CD-ROMs;
- Internet / World Wide Web.

The British Standards Institution publishes BSI and ISO (International Standards Organisation) data about many aspects of technology such as signs and graphics, and tools and components. BSI also make available standard information on people, **anthropometric data**, and the way people use things such as controls and displays, **ergonomic data**.

Figure 9.5 is an extract from a BSI publication that gives information about seated men and women. It is the kind of information used when designing seating on public transport.

SORTING AND SELECTING INFORMATION

You need to be able to extract useful data from the information that you may gather. Study the data in Fig. 9.5 and read off the seat height (1) for the tallest man with shoes on. It is 465 mm + 25 mm = 490 mm. It is important to get at the data you need; this is always related to what you are designing. For the height of a seat you could use average data so that for some people it would be low and for some it would be high. If you needed data for a door opening, however, you would need maximum data, otherwise half of the population would knock their heads.

This data presents the 5th to the 95th percentile. These are not the absolute shortest or tallest people but the majority. The number of people that fall outside of this range are very few.

Anthropometric dimensions taken into consideration

References (see figure)	Dimensions unclad	Subjects	Averages	Standard deviations	Limits		Add for shoes and clothing
					Min. 5th percentile	Max. 95th percentile	
			mm	mm	mm	mm	mm
For information	Size standing	man	1753	66	1644	1861	
		woman	1626	66	1517	1734	
	Size sitting (natural)	man	919	36	860	977	
		woman	854	36	796	912	
(1)	Popliteal to floor (without shoes)	man	430	20	396	465	25
		woman	398	20	364	432	25 to 75
(2)	Popliteal to buttocks	man	489	25	447	531	
		woman	469	25	427	511	
(3)	Width of bitrochanter	man	358	23	321	396	15 to 28
		woman	379	23	341	416	15 to 28
(4)	Plane of vision to seat (natural)	man	807	31	756	858	
		woman	750	31	699	801	
(5)	Elbow to seat	man	228	28	182	274	
		woman	205	28	160	251	
(6)	Elbow to shoulder	man	371	29	323	419	
		woman	341	29	293	389	
(7)	Maximum height of thigh	man	145	16.5	118	172	
		woman	137	20.3	104	170	

Figure 9.5

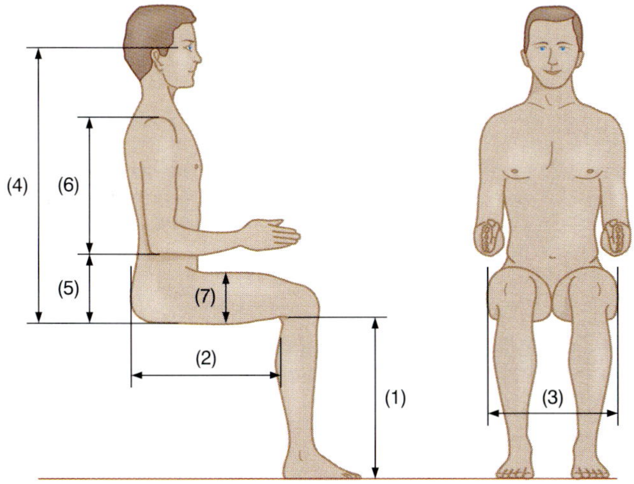

Figure 9.6

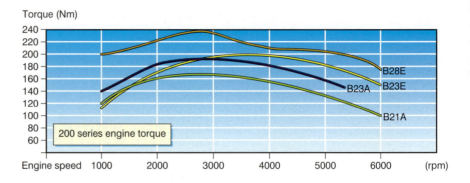

Figure 9.6 shows a graph that enables you to compare the performance of engines (the 200 series). It compares four engine types and shows how much torque (rotational force) they produce at a range of speeds (revolutions per minute). To extract information you read off the axes. For example, the B21A engine and the B23E engine both produce 150 Nm torque at 1700 r.p.m.

The Internet is an excellent source of easily available information. The main problem that most people have is getting the information that they want without spending time going through lots of information that they don't want. It is too easy to gather useless information. If you use search engines be precise.

ANALYSING INFORMATION

You have to be intelligent in your use of information. How reliable is it? Never assume that because something is in a book or newspaper that it is necessarily correct. Factual information such as that stored in the BSI data charts will be objective. Other information that you get may be subjective.

- **Objective information** is based upon factual information.
- **Subjective information** is based upon people's opinions or comments.

VALUE JUDGEMENTS AND CONFLICTING DEMANDS

Much of the information used within design and technology will be subjective because much of what you design will be to satisfy the needs of people. You need to apply value judgements. Value is not just about value for money, although this is, of course, an issue. There will be many instances when the values of different types of people will conflict, particularly those between young people and adults. For example, what would you do with a piece of waste ground near to your home: turn it into a skate board park, a play area for toddlers, or a sitting out area for old people? Clearly your opinions will vary according to your age and particular needs.

Conflicts can arise for a variety of reasons.

- **Moral** There are issues that some people may find offensive because of their views and the values that they hold, for example in the use of animal products.
- **Economic** Designs may result in products that are too expensive to sell or be used. All designs have a cost implication that must be resolved.

- **Social** Designs for housing, public areas and transport involve groups of people and how they react with each other. Over-crowding and discomfort can lead to many social problems.

- **Cultural** People have differing cultural backgrounds and needs that designers need to be aware of and to which they should be sensitive. This is particularly true in respect of religion and lifestyles. Cultural issues are often related to moral and social considerations.

- **Environmental** Designers are becoming increasingly aware of their responsibility towards the environment. In the past little regard was paid to this issue resulting in the over-use of non-renewable resources such as oil, and industrial processes that create pollution and waste.

Designers need to make judgements about how to resolve conflicts and find a compromise solution. It is very difficult to satisfy the demands from all sides. Society is increasingly demanding and consumes an increasing amount of resources. We all want to be able to move around more easily and quickly, and more families than ever in the developed world own several cars, keep their houses warm instead of wearing warmer clothes and have entertainments and gadgets in their home that were not invented 60 years ago.

Consumers blame fashion and trends, manufacturers say that they are responding to market demands and yet everybody agrees that we should conserve the environment and not create so much waste. The designer's role is to balance the conflicts by being responsible in:

- designing energy efficient products;
- designing for long product life and not fashion trends;
- reducing waste during production;
- using few non-renewable resources;
- using recyclable materials;
- reducing packaging requirements.

DESIGN BRIEFS AND SPECIFICATIONS

DESIGN BRIEF

A design brief is a clear statement of intent. It should do no more that set out clearly what you intend to design, for example:

To design and make a pull-along toy for a pre-school child.

Professional designers usually start at this point, with a brief that has been provided by their company, a customer or a client. From the brief it is possible to develop a design specification.

DESIGN SPECIFICATION

A design specification sets out the criteria that you want your product to achieve. It is important to think of the criteria for design in terms of the checklist or test that you can apply to your finished product when you come to evaluate it. A simple design specification for a design and technology project in school might look like that shown in Fig. 9.7. This one has the criteria defined as essential and desirable; this gives you some relative value of the criteria listed.

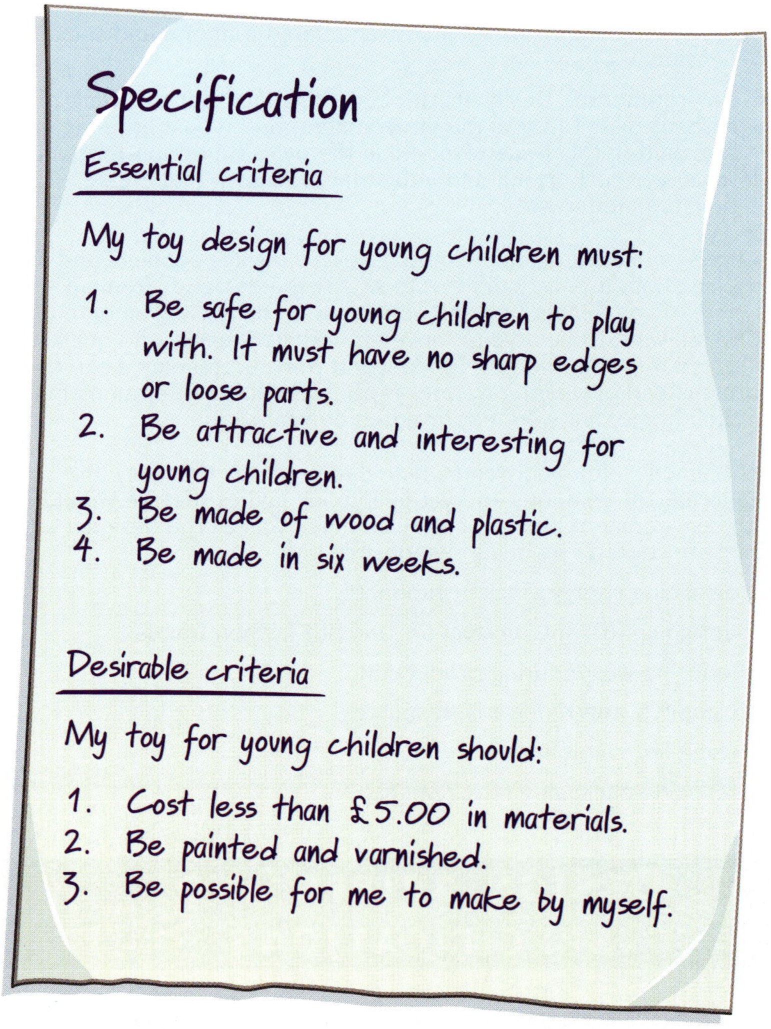

Specification

Essential criteria

My toy design for young children must:

1. Be safe for young children to play with. It must have no sharp edges or loose parts.
2. Be attractive and interesting for young children.
3. Be made of wood and plastic.
4. Be made in six weeks.

Desirable criteria

My toy for young children should:

1. Cost less than £5.00 in materials.
2. Be painted and varnished.
3. Be possible for me to make by myself.

Figure 9.7 *Simple design specification.*

A more detailed product design specification will address all of the following points:

- **Function** What the product should do and how it should work.
- **Ergonomics** Who is to use the product and react with it? Will it be suitable within its intended environment?
- **Appearance** How important is the appearance and what finishing process should be applied?
- **Manufacture** What are the options for manufacture and how are these effected by the possible quantity required?
- **Materials** What will be the most appropriate materials to use for the product and for the manufacturing process being considered?
- **Environmental considerations** Are there issues that need to be addressed such as material usage, energy consumption and waste?
- **Time** How long is available before manufacture needs to begin? What other deadlines need to be met?

Check yourself

QUESTIONS

Q1 Figure 9.8 shows an ordinary plastic clothes peg. Carry out an analysis of this product as though it were the first stage of a re-design exercise.

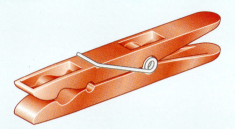

Figure 9.8

Q2 Devise a questionnaire to find out about the type of toys Key Stage 3 pupils (Years 7, 8 and 9) in your school like to play with. Your questionnaire should be suitable for entry in a computer database so that you can interrogate it later.

Q3 Outline the conflict and the responsibility that a designer will need to consider when working on a new sign for a public house in a small rural village.

REMEMBER! Cover the answers if you want to.

ANSWERS

A1 Purpose:
The peg is designed to:
> hold clothes to the washing line;
> withstand rain and wind;
> be easy to use with one hand;
> be light and easy to store.

How it works: The peg uses a single spring to store energy and a simple lever system to operate it.

Materials: The body is made from a weather resistant plastic material and the spring is steel that has been galvanised to resist the wet.

Manufacturing: The body is injection moulded in large quantities and the spring is made on a shaped former.

TUTORIALS

T1 *By learning the principle points needed to carry out product analysis it is possible to structure your answer and be concise. The examiner will be looking for the key points and the presentation is assisted by using a structured rather than an essay type of answer.*

The answer would have been improved by the addition of a simple line diagram to show how the peg works.

ANSWERS

Name ....

Boy ☐   Girl ☐   Y7 ☐   Y8 ☐   Y9 ☐

How often do you play with toys?

Everyday ☐   More than once a week ☐

Not often ☐   Never ☐

Tick the type of toys that you like to play with

Action toys ☐

Outdoor toys ☐

Computer games - 'shoot em up' ☐

Computer games - 'adventure' ☐

Construction kits ☐

Dolls and soft toys ☐

Board games ☐

A3 The main conflict will be between the interests of the pub owner and the local community. The owner will want to promote the pub as much as possible and may want a large bright sign with lights in it. The local community and people wishing to protect the countryside will want a sign that blends in rather than stands out.

The designer will be aware of the issues but his customer is the pub owner. The designer has a responsibility to point out to the owner that he should consider other people's interests.

TUTORIALS

T2 *The key point to remember is to get people to fill it in with responses that you can deal with. The easiest way to deal with responses is to use a database. This answer will do that because it is all tick box responses.*

T3 *Always be aware that these issues are never simple. The important point to remember however is that designers act on behalf of clients and customers and that in the end it is their wishes that must come out on top.*

KEY WORDS

These are the key words. Tick them if you think you know what they mean. Otherwise check on them.

design	**database**	**moral**
design process	**Internet**	**economic**
need	**anthropometric**	**social**
context	**ergonomic**	**cultural**
product analysis	**standard data**	**environmental**
primary source information	**analysis**	**design brief**
secondary source information	**objective information**	**design specification**
brainstorming	**subjective information**	**function**
questionnaire	**value**	
data	**conflict**	

GRAPHIC TECHNIQUES

Graphic techniques and examples are covered within the coursework section of this revision guide. The principle difference to be aware of is the time element. Your coursework will benefit from time taken to present your ideas and from presentation drawings. The techniques that you must employ within the examination must be those that you can carry out with speed.

'DESIGNING' WITHIN THE EXAMINATION

In your coursework and throughout your design and technology GCSE course you will have come to regard designing as a process or activity that can often take a long time. In your GCSE examination you may be asked to carry out small parts of this activity or produce designs for small component parts of a product. You will not have time to carry out complex design drawings. It is important to remember this and always be guided by the number of marks that are allocated to the question. The marks are a guide to the amount of time to spend on the question.

SKETCHES AND GRAPHICS

Examiners will expect you to use the space provided and the time available sensibly. You should use whatever graphics instruments that you are comfortable using.

Be prepared and take with you into the examination:

- Sharp pencils, HB and 2H. Take a few pencils then you won't need a pencil sharpener, but take one just in case.
- An eraser, a good quality soft one is best, and make sure that it is clean!
- A ballpoint or fine fibre tip pen. Take whichever you are accustomed to sketching with.
- Crayons or highlighter, again it must be whichever you are used to. Never use a wide range of bright colours, use subtle shading to good effect; greys with an occasional colour will bring out the detail in your work.
- A 300 mm rule. Use this to assist you in getting the proportions of things correct. Do not use it for drawing, it is better to draw freehand if you can. Practice using the exercises shown below.

PRACTICE!

Use plain A4 paper and hold the pencil lightly between your thumb and first two fingers. Do not consider using a rule, you should try to work as quickly as you can.

- Begin with horizontal lines about 80 mm long. Keep them as straight as possible and try to draw with your arm and not your wrist. Then try vertical lines, without turning the paper round!
- Now try lines at right angles to each other and build these up into rectangles and squares.

● Circles and ellipses are not as hard as you may think. A circle will fit into a square and an ellipse will fit into a rectangle, so start with a square or rectangle. Then mark a halfway point along each side. Now draw your circle as four arcs to join the points together. Take care to avoid circles with points where they touch the square.

Figure 10.1 *Drawing horizontal and vertical lines.*

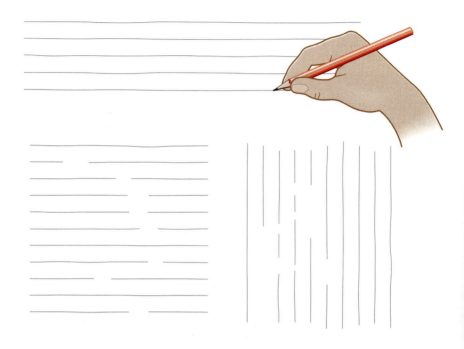

Figure 10.2 *Drawing right angles.*

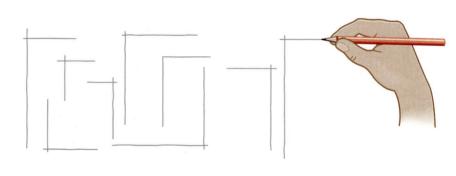

Figure 10.3 *Drawing rectangles and squares.*

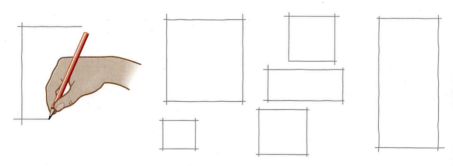

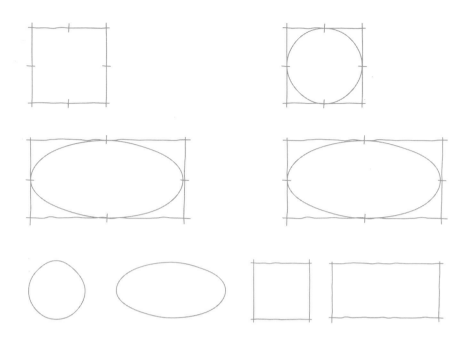

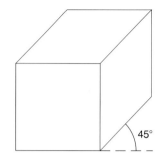

Figure 10.4 *Drawing circles and ellipses.*

Draw lines at 45° to the horizontal

45°

Then draw those lines half their true length to make the cube look more realistic, like this:

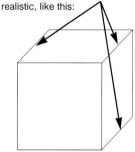

Figure 10.5 *Constructing an oblique drawing.*

3D DRAWING

All sketches that you will need to do within an examination will be of small items or components. This means that you need to be familiar with isometric drawing and oblique drawing.

Oblique drawing

Objects are drawn with a flat front view and the depth of the drawing is then added. Figure 10.5 shows an oblique drawing of a cube. To make the drawing look more 'real' all of the lines that go back are drawn at half their true length. Try sketching an oblique cube without using a rule or protractor.

Isometric drawing

Here the object is drawn tipped forward at 30° to the horizontal plane. This looks realistic and all of the sides are the correct length, but all of the angles are in fact wrong. Now try sketching an isometric cube.

Crating

Complex objects can be simplified by looking for the simple geometric shapes that make them up. When you have identified the simple shape then you can use the above techniques to draw them, to form circles and arcs and to link them together. Think of objects within a see-through box or crate then draw the lines that you need on the surface of the crate. Look at Fig. 10.7 and practice drawing the cylinder in the three steps.

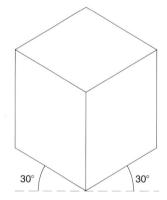

30°   30°

Figure 10.6 *An isometric cube.*

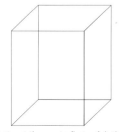
Construct the crate first – faintly

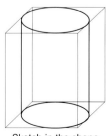
Sketch in the shape

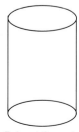
Rub out the crate

Figure 10.7 *Crating.*

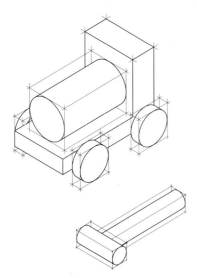

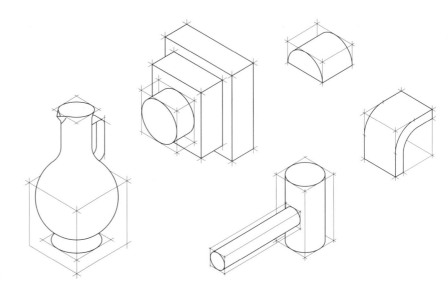

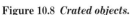

Figure 10.8 *Crated objects.*

Now practice by copying the objects shown in Fig. 10.8. They are all constructed using crating; look for the simple shapes that make up the more complex one.

RESPONDING TO A DESIGN SPECIFICATION

The generation of any design proposal or idea must be in response to the design specification. Examination questions that ask you to respond to a specification or to comment upon one will not be trying to catch you out or trip you up. You must read very carefully what it is that you are presented with and you need to think before responding.

If you are presented with a situation within a question followed by a design need then make sure that your solution is appropriate for the situation. For example, you could be asked to sketch or comment upon a catch for the side of a child's play pen. How would this differ from a catch for a rabbit's cage? It is still a catch and of a similar size. Consider how the criteria for safety and for appearance are to be satisified – the expectations would be quite different.

DEVELOPING AND MODELLING DESIGN SOLUTIONS

Within an examination you may be asked to develop an idea further through the use of sketches. Always look for the simple solution and the elegant solution. Complex ideas will consume too much examination time and they are rarely the best.

It is not possible within an examination to be asked to demonstrate any three-dimensional modelling, also called **prototyping**, but it is necessary to know about the materials and processes that could be used, and why it is often appropriate to model design solutions in three dimensions.

Three-dimensional modelling is used to:

- test if mechanical devices and systems work;
- determine if parts of a product will fit together;
- try out assembly procedures;
- visualise what things might look like from different perspectives and alongside other things;
- clarify the designer's thinking and ideas;
- refine the ergonomics and determine whether a solution works with the people for whom it was intended;
- present principles and show how things work;
- present possible design solutions to customers and clients.

THREE-DIMENSIONAL MODELLING MATERIALS

Modelling needs to be quick and cheap and use materials that can be altered with relative ease so that designs can be modified and further developed. The following materials can be used when modelling design solutions that will later be realised using resistant materials.

- **Card** Stiff card can be easily cut, formed, joined with adhesives and painted.
- **Plastic sheet materials** Foam board, Plasticard and Corriflute are examples of modelling plastics that are made light and easy to work specifically for modelling, and they are available in different colours.
- **Wood** Thin plywood, balsa wood and MDF are often used by model makers. They can be joined with PVA glue, hot melt glue, pins, nails and staples.
- **Styrofoam** This is a high density expanded foam material that is light, clean and easy to cut and work using a hot wire cutter or band saw. It can be finished with glass paper and brush or spray painted. Figure 10.10 shows a design model for a glue gun made using Styrofoam.
- **Clay, plaster and plasticine** These are the traditional modelling materials that have largely been overtaken by the use of materials such as Styrofoam. However, car manufacturers still make full size clay models of new designs.

COMPUTER MODELLING

Many software packages are available to assist the designer. These are aspects of 'Computer-aided Design' (CAD). Virtual models can be created on the screen that can be trialled and tested. This process is known as simulation. It has most of the virtues of 'real' 3D modelling but is much cheaper once the capital costs of equipment and the training costs have been met.

Computer models can be used to visualise, fit components together, clarify thinking, demonstrate and test. Software can also simulate mechanical failure and the breakdown of systems and be used to model chemical and biological systems that would otherwise be impossible.

Figure 10.9 *A model used to demonstrate how a solar-powered water heating system works.*

Figure 10.10 *Styrofoam model of a glue gun.*

COMPUTER-AIDED DESIGN (CAD)

COMPUTER-AIDED DESIGN AND DRAUGHTING (CADD)

Computer-aided Design is about using ICT (information and communication technology) to assist the designer during any number of stages within the process of design. Real design software is more complex than computer draughting (drawing) packages that only support engineering drawing. The term CADD, Computer-aided Design and Draughting, is becoming more common and refers to software that includes design software and engineering drawing software.

The process of designing is a process of communicating ideas, visualising and making decisions. It is important to appreciate that if a design exists then it is not economic to start again. Designs can always be modified, reworked and developed and if they exist on a computer then the process can be fast and very economic.

Figure 10.11 shows a simple engineering component that has been given five different interpretations by CADD software. This process is called **solid modelling**.

While the solid model is the easiest to visualise because it is closest to reality, it is expensive on computer memory and processing time; this makes it slow to manipulate on the screen. Designers often stop at the wire frame stage and wire frame modelling as a language of communication is very popular. It also has the advantage of being able to show features behind and on the rear

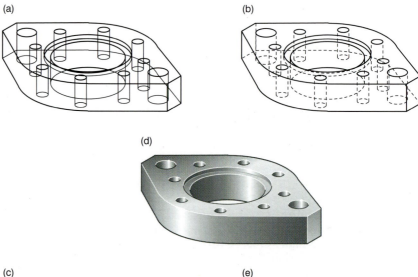

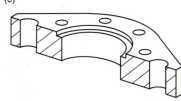

Figure 10.11 *Simple engineering component given five different interpretations by the computer*
(a) *wire frame model*
(b) *solid model with hidden detail*
(c) *solid model with hidden line removal*
(d) *rendered model*
(e) *section view.*

surface of components. By using colour to identify different components wire frame assemblies become easy for the trained designer to interpret.

CAD can assist the designer in many ways:

- Drawings can be generated three times faster than by conventional drawing.
- The quality and accuracy of 'hard copy' (paper-based drawing) is better than conventional drawing.
- Drawings can be stretched, rotated, duplicated and flipped over.
- Existing designs can be modified and reworked.
- Libraries of standard features and components speed the process and help in making decisions.
- It is easier to visualise design outcomes quickly and make changes to help in making decisions.
- The paths of moving parts for clearance and collision detection can be simulated.

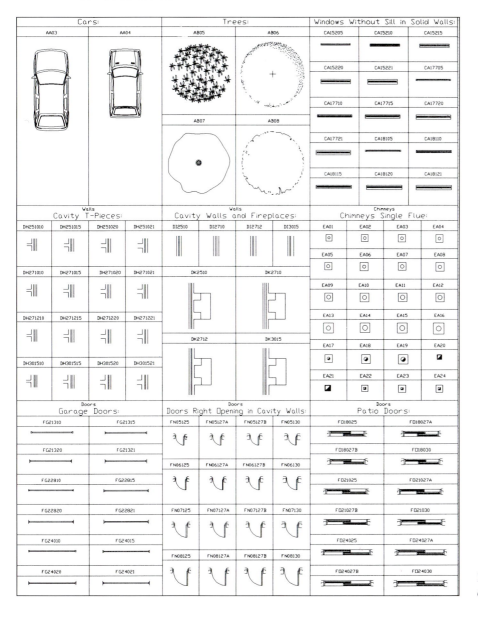

Figure 10.12 *Library symbols for architectural drawing using CADD.*

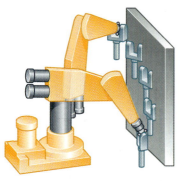

Figure 10.13 *Example of computer simulated clash detection.*

• Engineering analysis of components subject to stresses and fatigue can be carried out through simulation.
• Designs can be shared electronically via communication networks such as 'e'-mail, Internet and video conferencing.

Figure 10.12 shows a library of standard components used in architectural drawing. By using standard components from a library file like this, designs can be created much faster and the designer knows that the components used actually exist. The library file can also be used to show the stock that is available and which components might be preferred.

Parametric design is another aspect of CADD. This software enables the design engineer to plot the path of moving parts to see how they could potentially interfere with other aspects of the design. Software of this nature is also used to design manufacturing cells to avoid clashes between robot operations. Figure 10.13 shows a virtual robot 'clashing' with a wall.

PRESENTING TO AN AUDIENCE

The presentation of design proposals to a customer or client is an important part of the process of design and manufacture. Designers must consider how to 'sell' their idea over that of the competition. There are a number of presentation options:

Figure 10.14 *An airbrushed drawing.*

• Three-dimensional models;
• Airbrushing;
• Spirit marker drawings;
• Crayon rendering;
• Pastel rendering;
• Poster paints.

Some of the above techniques are covered in the previous chapter on coursework. You will not be asked to carry out any of these during your examination but you do need to be aware of them and consider which would be appropriate for a particular audience. Look at the three presentation drawings in Figs.10.14, 10.15 and 10.16. The wacky style associated with the fashion drawing is quite different from the solid style of the drill and the sleek style of the car. They are intended to appeal to different audiences.

Figure 10.15 *Fashion drawings.*

Figure 10.16 *Ideas rendered with markers.*

Check yourself

QUESTIONS

Q1 Produce pencil sketches of the following commonly used components:
door hinge;
hexagonal headed M10 bolt;
countersunk wood screw;
compression spring.

Q2 Under what circumstances might you use a three-dimensional model rather than a presentation drawing?

Q3 Identify the main disadvantages with CADD systems.

ANSWERS

A1

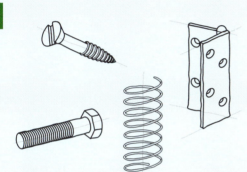

A2 A three-dimensional model would be used rather than a drawing under the following circumstances:
- If it was a mechanical product, it would then be an advantage to demonstrate how it worked.
- It may be necessary to show how the product needed to fit together or fit with other things.
- To be able to handle the product and look at the ergonomic factors.
- To walk around and look at the product from different angles that all must look good as in the case of a car or a building.

A3 There are three main disadvantages with CADD systems:
1 They are expensive to install and keep up to date.
2 People have to be trained how to use them.
3 All existing drawings need to be changed to CADD files in order to fully take advantage of the system.

TUTORIALS

T1 *This question is more than just a sketching exercise. You should know what these and many other similar components look like. Practice isometric drawing techniques on a range of common design and technology bits and pieces and notice the details.*

For example:
A door hinge is countersunk on the inside of the flaps.
A bolt has a plain section without a screw thread.
Wood screws are pointed just at the end.
A compression spring is open, unlike a tension spring.

T2 *Without you having to draw or make models this question is testing your knowledge of both. Make sure that you know about the applications of processes and not just the techniques.*

T3 *This is a good answer to this question. Do not be tempted to respond in terms of needing less people and therefore saying that it is a disadvantage because companies lose staff. Companies make investments to be competitive and stay in business so it is also an advantage to pay less in wages. Most aspects of modern technology need fewer people who are better qualified.*

KEY WORDS

These are the key words. Tick them if you think you know what they mean. Otherwise check on them.

design	CAD
graphics	CADD
oblique	simulation
isometric	solid modelling
crating	wire frame
specification	library files
model	parametric design
prototype	presentation drawing
computer-aided design	

EVALUATING DESIGN PROPOSALS

The key to any evaluation or test is what you evaluate it against. Evaluation should be **objective** rather than **subjective**. This means evaluating against some criteria rather than using bland statements such as 'I like this because it looks nice'. Earlier in this section we covered the need for a detailed design specification that could be used as a checklist or criteria for evaluating the finished product. The same applies to the evaluation of design proposals. They should be evaluated against the design specification because this reflects that intention of the design-and-make activity. It is appropriate to ask certain questions:

- **Function** Will it work?
- **Ergonomics** Can it be used as intended?
- **Appearance/aesthetics** Will it look good and fit in?
- **Manufacturing** Can it be made economically?
- **Materials** Are the materials appropriate?
- **Environmental** What about energy and waste?
- **Time** Can it be made in the time available?

It is possible to draw up a checklist from the design specification to check your design proposals against when evaluating them and then score each idea. Try this with your own coursework.

Figure 11.1

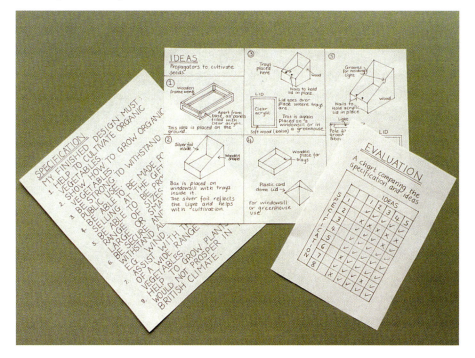

WORKING DRAWINGS

A working drawing does not have to be a formal engineering drawing. A working drawing is a means of communicating between the designer and the manufacturer. A manufacturer should be able to make what appears on a

ORTHOGRAPHIC DRAWING

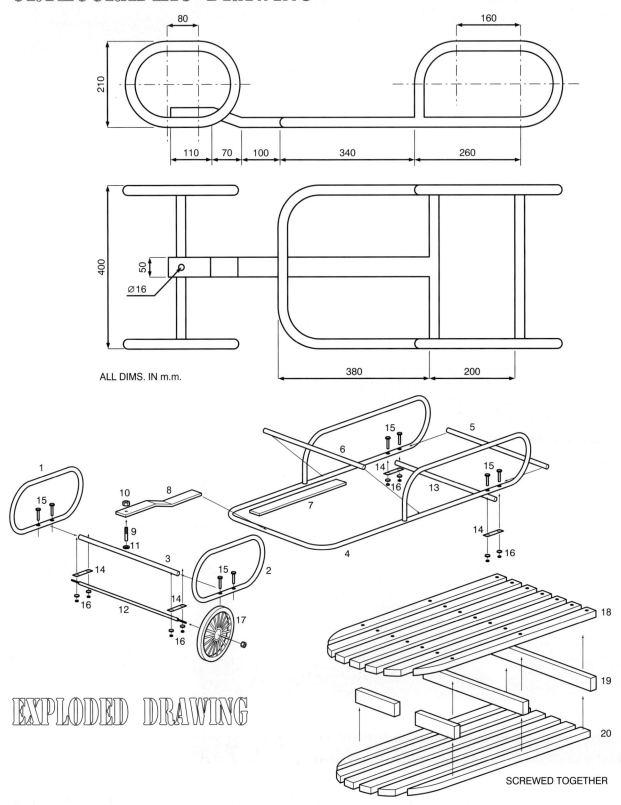

ALL DIMS. IN m.m.

EXPLODED DRAWING

SCREWED TOGETHER

Figure 11.2

76

working drawing without having to refer back to the designer and ask questions about the detail. It should have all of the information about size, position and materials to use. Figure 11.2 is a working drawing from a pupil's design and technology coursework folder.

It is quite clear, without a photograph, that this is a play cart. There are two drawings: a **detail drawing** that provides all of the information for the manufacture of the tubular framework and an **assembly drawing** that shows how it is put together (assembled). The numbers on the assembly drawing are part numbers. The project folder contains a parts list with these numbers and gives details of the materials and the material sizes.

Within your examination you may be asked to read information from a formal drawing or add features to the drawing. You should therefore understand orthographic drawing and the conventions that are used.

ORTHOGRAPHIC DRAWING

The style of drawing known as orthographic drawing has become the standard language of working drawings. Orthographic drawing is really only about the way that views of an object are arranged.

Figure 11.3 is an isometric drawing of a pencil sharpener. In Fig 11.4 the same pencil sharpener is shown as an orthographic drawing. The plan which is drawn looking down on the sharpener is positioned above the front view (called an elevation). The plan is above because this is where it is being viewed from. The two end views are positioned at the ends from which they are being viewed. Imagine yourself standing in those positions above and at each end of the pencil sharpener and ask yourself, 'What view could I see from here?'

Notice how the elevations line up with each other, and how the 45° sloping line also links the positions of the elevations; this relationship is important.

This type of orthographic projection is called 'third angle orthographic projection'. There is another type that you may come across known as 'first angle'. This positions the views on the opposite side from the viewing position. The cart shown in Fig. 11.2 is drawn in first angle and the plan is positioned below the front elevation. Third angle projection is the most commonly used.

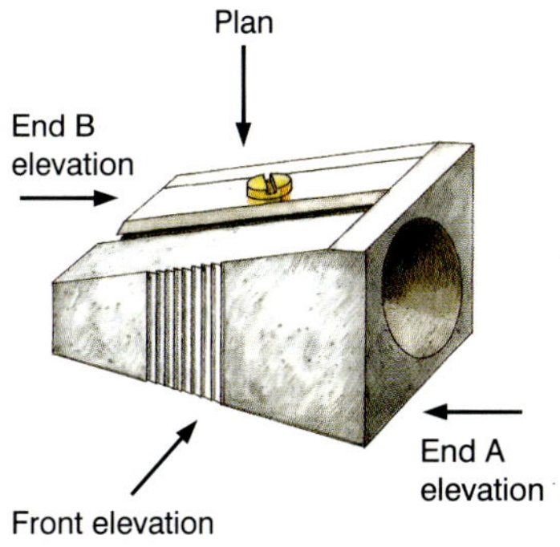

Plan

End B elevation

End A elevation

Front elevation

Figure 11.3 *Isometric drawing.*

Plan

End B elevation

Front elevation

End A elevation

Figure 11.4 *Orthographic drawing (third angle).*

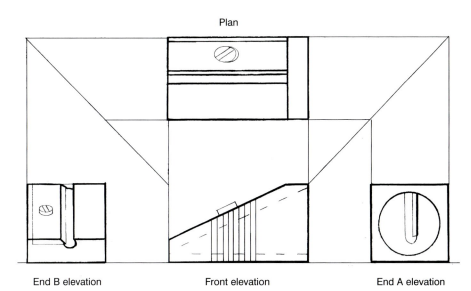

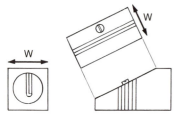

Figure 11.5 *Auxiliary view.*

OTHER VIEWS

Sometimes objects are viewed from other positions to show specific details: auxiliary views; they may be drawn cut through to show internal details: sectional views. Let's look at the pencil sharpener again.

Figure 11.5 is an auxiliary view to show the true shape of the sloping surface of the sharpener. The dimension W is taken from the end elevation because this is a true size.

To show the internal details the sharpener has to be 'cut' along an imaginary cutting plane. The cutting plane is indicated with arrows which also show the viewing direction. The surfaces that are 'cut' are 'hatched' on the sectional view with 45° sloping lines. Figure 11.6 shows two separate sectional views of the pencil sharpener.

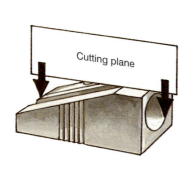

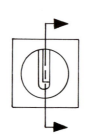

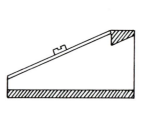

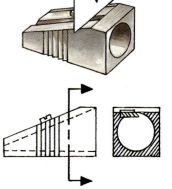

Figure 11.6 *Sectional views.*

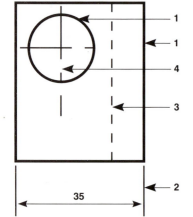

Figure 11.7 *Types of line and where they are used.*

CONVENTIONS USED IN ORTHOGRAPHIC DRAWINGS

Figures 11.7, 11.8, 11.9 and 11.10 show some of the conventions that are used in orthographic and engineering drawings. You need to be able to recognise these when they appear in drawings and in the case of the dimensioning and line types you should be able to use them correctly.

1 ——————————————————————————
CONTINUOUS THICK – Visible outlines and edges

2 ——————————————————————————
CONTINUOUS THIN – Dimension lines, projection lines, hatching and outlines of adjacent parts

3 – – – – – – – – – – – – – – – – – –
THIN DASHES – Hidden outlines and edges

4 ———— — ———— — ————
THIN, LONG CHAIN – Centre lines

Figure 11.8 *Dimensioning correctly.*

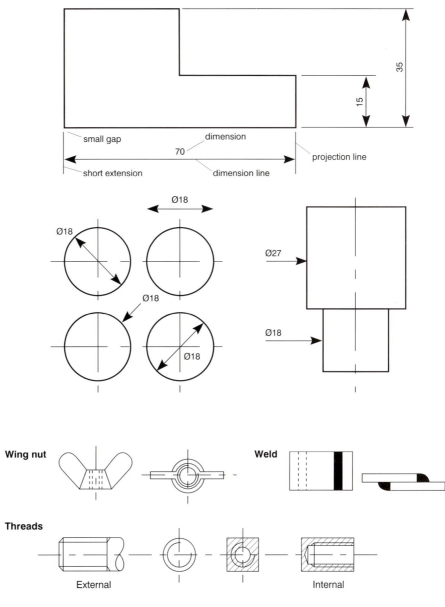

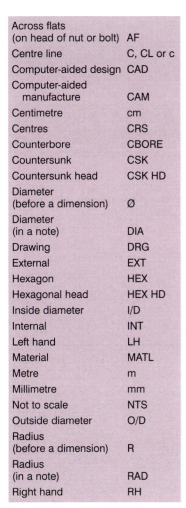

Figure 11.9 *Commonly used abbreviations.*

Across flats (on head of nut or bolt)	AF
Centre line	C, CL or c
Computer-aided design	CAD
Computer-aided manufacture	CAM
Centimetre	cm
Centres	CRS
Counterbore	CBORE
Countersunk	CSK
Countersunk head	CSK HD
Diameter (before a dimension)	Ø
Diameter (in a note)	DIA
Drawing	DRG
External	EXT
Hexagon	HEX
Hexagonal head	HEX HD
Inside diameter	I/D
Internal	INT
Left hand	LH
Material	MATL
Metre	m
Millimetre	mm
Not to scale	NTS
Outside diameter	O/D
Radius (before a dimension)	R
Radius (in a note)	RAD
Right hand	RH

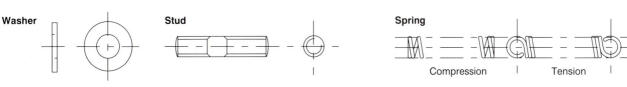

Figure 11.10 *Commonly used drawing conventions.*

SEQUENCING MANUFACTURING

Sequencing manufacturing deals with ordering events logically to avoid delays and over-production. In order to be able to plan a sequence of operations, you need to be aware of the actual processes and the availability of materials and machine and assembly processes.

WHAT ARE THE FIXED PARAMETERS?

There will be things that are determined by the design and the specification that cannot be changed at this stage. Planning must begin with a parts list that sets out the manufacturing requirements and should provide:

- Part name;
- Part number referenced to the drawing;
- Material or source of supply;
- Number required (No. off).

Figure 11.11 *Assembly drawing and parts list.*

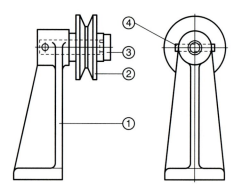

PARTS LIST			
4	TAPER PIN	1	HRD STEEL
3	PIN	1	MILD STEEL
2	PULLEY	1	ALUMINIUM
1	BRACKET	1	CAST IRON
PT	DESCRIPTION	NO. OFF	MATERIAL

WHERE IS THE FLEXIBILITY?

Within industrial manufacturing components can be made on-site (in-house) or they can be 'bought in' from suppliers or sub-contractors. Suppliers will provide standard components such as nuts, bolts, hinges and fixings. A sub-contractor is somebody who makes things on your behalf. These factors must be considered commercially to avoid people waiting for components or the manufacturer not being able to achieve the targets and delivery dates. There will always be choices that have to be made in order to ensure a smooth production flow. Within your own experience you will be aware that you can 'buy in' rather than make components such as screws, plastic boxes and wheels. This has been mentioned in Chapter 8 'Components'.

Figure 11.12 shows a flow chart used to sequence operations in the manufacture of a small battery powered clock. The manufacturer actually produces only the clock housing and the packaging. The hands and face are bought in as components and the mechanism is bought in as a sub-assembly. A sub-assembly is an item that forms part of a larger product.

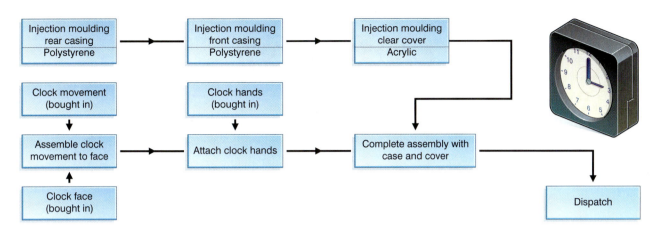

Figure 11.12 *Sequencing manufacturing operations.*

Within your project work an important feature has been time management – getting things finished on time. This becomes even more critical when you have to rely upon other people to supply you with components before you can carry on. The clock is an example of this. Return to the examples of time planning and management within Chapter 2.

EFFICIENT USE OF MATERIALS

When designing products there are often decisions that can be made with little reference to other aspects of the design. For example, a rack for CDs has some dimensions determined by the CD such as the height and the depth. The length of the rack will be determined by how many CDs it is required to store, but this is an estimate and there is room for flexibility. Considerations of this nature should be made with reference to the economic use of material. If the material for the rack is available in 2 metre lengths then the length of the rack needs to be in parts or multiples of this. It would be poor use of resources to specify that the rack should be 1.1 metres long.

This consideration also applies when cutting from a sheet. Some shapes will fit together or tessellate to make efficient use of a sheet of metal or plywood. Computer software is used industrially to determine how material can be used efficiently. The component size is entered along with the stock size of the material. The computer then determines how to arrange the shapes.

Figure 11.13 *Efficient use of materials.*

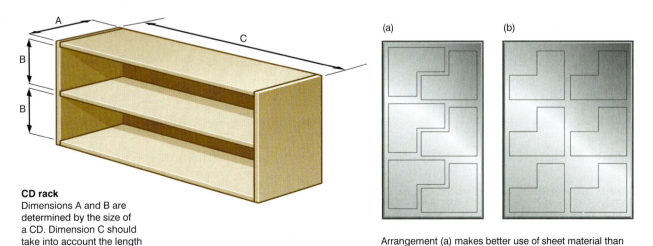

CD rack
Dimensions A and B are determined by the size of a CD. Dimension C should take into account the length of the material available.

(a) (b)

Arrangement (a) makes better use of sheet material than arrangement (b). But! it could be difficult to cut out.

Check yourself

QUESTIONS

Q1 Discuss the relationship between the design specification and the ability to fully evaluate design proposals.

Q2
i)   Outline the principle function of a 'working drawing'.
ii) Name and describe the purpose of the two types of drawing that combine to make a complete working drawing.

Q3 Within your own experience of planning for making, explain how it is possible to reduce the manufacturing time and provide some flexibility. Identify also the potential problems that this may cause.

REMEMBER! Cover the answers if you want to.

ANSWERS

A1 Evaluation of the design proposals should be carried out against the criteria that is set out in the design specification. This enables the evaluation to be carried out objectively.

A2
i)   The working drawing is used to make the product that you have designed.
ii) The detail drawing which has all the sizes so that the parts of the product can be made, and the assembly drawing which shows how the parts of a product fit together.

A3 It is possible to buy in parts for products that are being made. This can be fittings like catches and handles or they may be plastic boxes to hold electronics or control parts. This gives you more time to work on other parts of the product and the bought in parts can give a really professional finish.

This can have problems because you may need to adjust your design to suit the things that you buy in; also there can be delays in getting the components so it is important to plan and place orders in good time.

TUTORIALS

T1 *The important point to remember about carrying out any evaluation at any time during the design process and within your coursework, is to carry it out against some criteria. This enables you to be objective. When making judgements objectivity is important.*

T2
i)   *The working drawing is the method of communicating between the designer and the manufacturer. It doesn't have to be a formal engineering drawing but it must have enough information for manufacturing to take place.*
ii) *Working drawings for any product that has more than one component part should have these two aspects, although, again, they do not have to be presented in a formal way.*

T3 *Examination questions often expect you to draw upon your own designing and making experience and relate this to industry and manufacturing. You must be aware that companies and individuals can buy in components and services depending upon economics, time and quality.*

KEY WORDS

These are the key words. Tick them if you think you know what they mean. Otherwise check on them.

evaluation	first angle projection	parts list
design specification	third angle projection	bought in
working drawing	auxiliary views	supplier
detail drawing	sectional views	sub-contractor
assembly drawing	drawing conventions	sub-assembly
orthographic drawing	sequencing operations	

EXAMINATION CHECKLIST FOR THIS SECTION

After studying designing you should be able to:

- recognise design needs and opportunities taking into account the considerations of other people and recognising conflicting needs and demands;

- gather, organise and present research data;

- develop a design specification;

- generate a range of ideas whilst recognising constraints;

- develop, model and test ideas using a variety of graphical means including CAD systems;

- communicate design proposals appropriate to the needs of an audience;

- evaluate design proposals and develop working drawings and plans for scheduling manufacture.

EXAM PRACTICE

Sample Student's Answers & Examiner's Comments

1 A playgroup for 3 to 4 year old children is based at your school. The group leaders have asked the Design & Technology department to design and make a see-saw that can be taken outdoors.

(a) After some research it was decided that the overall length of the see-saw should be 2 metres (2000 mm).

    (i) Name two other important dimensions of the see-saw. (2 marks)

       1 *The height of the child's seat.*

       2 *The distance from the seat to the handles.*

    (ii) Explain how these two dimensions have been decided upon. (2 marks)

       These sizes could be gathered by visiting the playgroup and measuring a group of children of that age and finding out which sizes will be the best to use.

(b) Safety is another consideration. Name three other areas of research that would need to be considered before finalising ideas. (3 marks)

    1 *The materials to use.*

    2 *The overall cost of the see-saw.*

    3 *How to make sure that the see-saw does not topple over; it must be stable.*

EXAMINER'S COMMENTS

(a) *These are correct responses to the question but not sufficient to gain full marks. In determining the sizes of people it is best to use anthropometric data tables. These have been compiled from a far wider sample of people than could be carried out by first hand research and they relate to seating and reach positions that are difficult to determine without first modelling the product.*

(b) *These are correct answers and three good points, particularly point 3. This shows the examiner that the student is thinking about areas that are relevant to that particular situation.*

EXAMINER'S COMMENTS

(c) *This is a good method of answering this question. The student has used an assembly drawing and then an auxiliary drawing to cover the details of the pivot. There are a few details missing that will lose marks; it is not clear how the steel bar that acts as a pivot is fixed into the side plates, neither is it clear how the seat back and handle are attached. It is, nevertheless, a good answer with sufficient detail to fully communicate the design proposal and to meet most of the requirements of the question. In this type of question marks will be added for the notes that supplement the design ideas and for the quality of the presentation. Clear sketches are required. Only add shading or colour to sketches if you can do it well and are certain that you have time, it may gain a few marks but it will not be many; clarity of communication is the most important consideration.*

(c) Using materials you are familiar with, sketch ideas that would be suitable for a see-saw.

Your ideas must show you have considered the following points:
- a safe and secure sitting position (5 marks)
- stability of the see-saw (4 marks)
- materials and finishes (4 marks)
- ideas for pivoting (5 marks)
- methods of joining parts together. (4 marks)

Presentation and annotation of ideas.
(4 marks)

Add notes to explain your ideas.

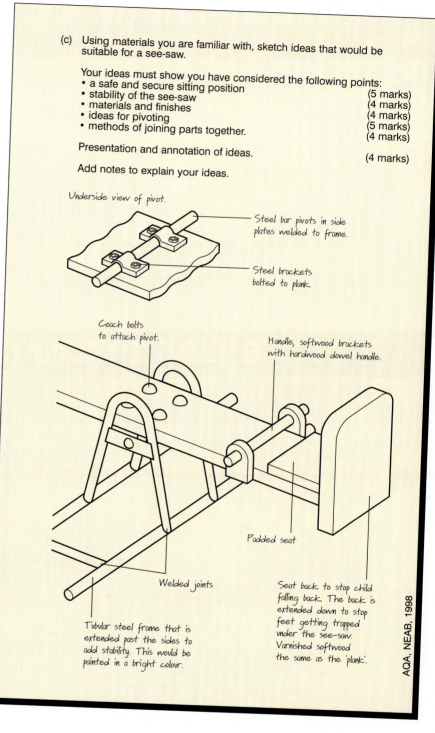

Underside view of pivot.

Steel bar pivots in side plates welded to frame.

Steel brackets bolted to plank.

Coach bolts to attach pivot.

Handle, softwood brackets with hardwood dowel handle.

Padded seat

Welded joints

Seat back to stop child falling back. The back is extended down to stop feet getting trapped under the see-saw. Varnished softwood the same as the 'plank'.

Tubular steel frame that is extended past the sides to add stability. This would be painted in a bright colour.

AQA, NEAB, 1998

Question to Answer

The answer to Question 2 can be found in Chapter 21.

2 The simple stand shown in Fig. 1 is used to hold a roll of wire ready for use.

The stand and arm are made from mild steel.

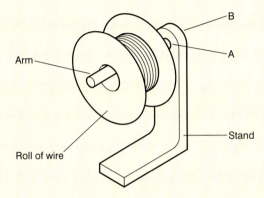

Fig. 1

(a) Look carefully at the stand. It has two serious design faults.

Sketch a possible solution to each fault. Show all design details.

(i) Fault 1: the roll of wire falls off the end of the support arm. (3 marks)

Fig. 2

(ii) Fault 2: the stand falls over when the wire is pulled off. (3 marks)

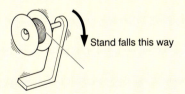

Fig. 3

(b) Two design features of the stand in Fig.1 are given below.

Give one reason for each feature.

(i) Design feature 1: the stand has a rounded top at B. (2 marks)

(ii) Design feature 2: the roll of wire is a 'loose fit' on the arm. (2 marks)

MEG, Specimen 1997

CHAPTER 12

PREPARATION

SAFETY

There can be no doubt that the most important aspect of manufacturing is safety, whether in a school workshop or a large manufacturing industry. Safety is also a subject that is picked up without fail in GCSE examinations. You must be aware of the particular safety issues that surround manufacturing processes, especially those about which you will be expected to be knowledgeable. Safety is always about being sensible, responsible and mature; these aspects can be grouped together under a few headings and a few commonsense rules.

BEHAVIOUR

- Behave in a sensible manner and report other people's foolish behaviour – it could be you that they are putting at risk.
- Always walk around workshops; never run.
- Carry tools and equipment in a safe manner and get help with heavy or long materials.

DRESS

- At all times wear overalls or an apron and stout shoes. Remove or tuck in loose clothing, jewellery and ties, and tie back or cover long hair.
- Wear the appropriate additional protective clothing for processes such as casting and welding.
- Wear eye protection when in designated eye protection areas or when operating any machine tool or powered hand tool.

WORKING PRACTICE

- Keep your work area and work areas around machine tools clean and tidy.
- Check the condition of all tools and machines regularly and report any damage or breakages.
- Keep gangways and emergency exits clear at all times.
- Report any accidents, however small, to your teacher or a responsible adult.
- Read and follow all safety instructions on chemical-based substances such as adhesives and solvents, and pay particular attention to skin contact and ventilation.
- Always tidy up and wash your hands thoroughly after work.

Figure 12.1 *Safety symbols – be aware of them.*

MEASURING

The preferred unit of measurement is the millimetre, this is an SI (International Standard) unit of measurement. Do not use centimetres; 3 centimetres, for example, should be shown as 30 mm. Parts of millimetres should be expressed in a decimal form; use 0.5 mm and not half a millimetre. The type of measuring instrument that is used for any application is determined by the accuracy required. You should be familiar with:

- steel rules ('rules' not 'rulers');
- steel tape measures;
- vernier calipers;
- micrometers.

Figure 12.2 *Electronic digital micrometer.*

Increasingly calipers and micrometers have direct digital electronic read-outs that can be zeroed at any point and the device used as a comparitor. A comparitor is any instrument that will compare one size with another rather than measure it, and will give a reading that is the difference between the sizes. It is beyond the scope of any book to cover all of the variations but you do need at least to be familiar with the measuring devices within your own school sufficiently well to be able to describe their operation.

Combination square

The combination square is a very versatile and useful tool. It is a combined rule, square and protractor. It can be used to measure sizes like a rule, and also distances from edges and corners. It can also be used to measure angles, depths from faces, and to check for squareness of corners.

Figure 12.3 *Using a combination square.*

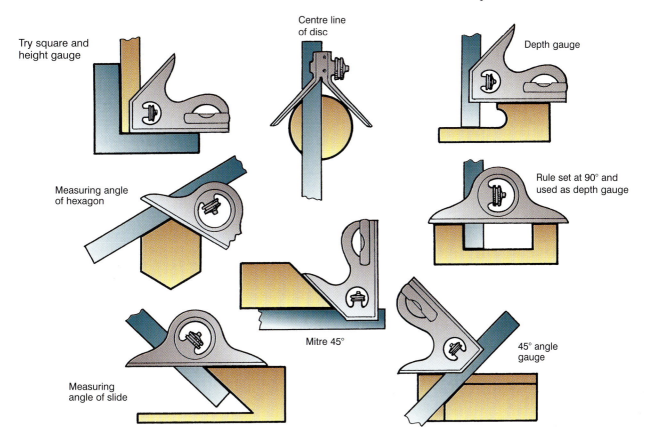

Try square and height gauge

Centre line of disc

Depth gauge

Rule set at 90° and used as depth gauge

Measuring angle of hexagon

Mitre 45°

45° angle gauge

Measuring angle of slide

MARKING OUT

The tools and techniques used for marking out are determined by the degree of accuracy required by the finished product. (Refer also to tolerances and quality control in Chapter 18.)

Templates

Templates are prepared shapes that can be cut or drawn around. It is often appropriate to use a template made from card or paper that has been developed during the modelling stage of your design process. Templates are especially useful when you need to cut out the same shape a number of times. Card or paper may not be appropriate for a template that is used repeatedly therefore templates can be made from any thin material that is easy to work such as aluminium, ABS plastic or plywood.

Datum faces and surfaces

You should always mark out from a known datum face or surface. This is a face that is flat and straight. When all measurements are made from the same face or faces the risk of **cumulative errors** is reduced. Cumulative error happens when measurements are taken from one point to the next and from there on to the next, etc. Any slight mistakes that are made get added on to each other and get bigger and bigger.

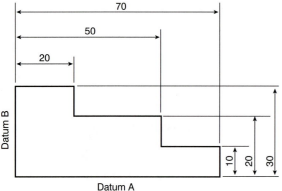

Figure 12.4 *All measurements taken from the two datum faces.*

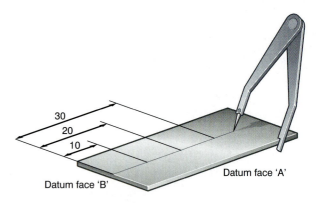

Figure 12.5 *Marking out a series of holes using odd leg calipers.*

Figure 12.6 *Marking out using a try square and marking knife.*

When marking out with wood it is equally important to always work from the same faces. These datum faces on wood are often referred to as the face side and face edge and they are traditionally given a mark to identify them. Figure 12.6 shows four stages in marking a line around a piece of wood using a **marking knife** and a **try square**. Notice that the stock of the square is always against a datum face. When marking out on metal surfaces an **engineer's square** and a **scriber** should be used.

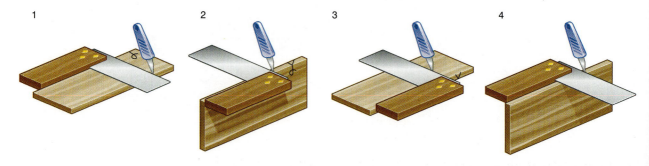

1   2   3   4

Centre punch

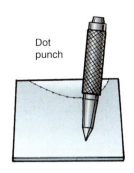
Dot punch

Compasses

Dividers

Figure 12.7 *Tools for marking holes and curves.*

Holes and circles

The positions of hole centres on metal surfaces are marked using a hammer and **centre punch**. The punch mark leaves an indent that stops the drill from wandering. **Dot punches** are lighter versions of the centre punch and are used to highlight lines. Dot punches are also used to provide a location for divider points when **dividers** are being used to draw arcs and circles. An ordinary pencil compass can be used on wood and some plastics.

Marking gauges

Marking gauges are used to mark straight lines on wood parallel to an edge. The spur on the gauge is set with a rule. **Mortise gauges** are marking gauges with two spurs and these are used for marking out before cutting joints.

Precision marking out

Very accurate marking out requires a range of marking out tools that all operate from a **surface plate**. The surface plate provides the flat datum surface from which all measurements are taken. Flat objects are held against an angle bracket and cylindrical objects are clamped using **vee blocks and clamps**. (See Fig. 12.9.)

Figure 12.8 *Using gauges for wood.*

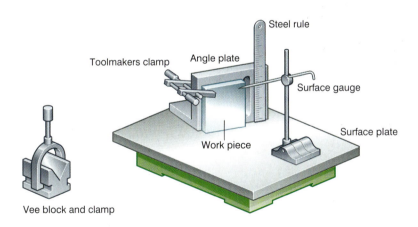
Vee block and clamp

Toolmakers clamp
Angle plate
Steel rule
Surface gauge
Surface plate
Work piece

Figure 12.9 *Precision marking out.*

WORK HOLDING

Holding work is about resisting the forces associated with cutting materials. Movement of any object can take place in any combination of the six ways shown in Fig. 12.10 and this movement can be resisted by:

- Positive location – being against a solid object;
- Frictional resistance – being gripped.

It is always best to resist cutting forces by positive location where possible.

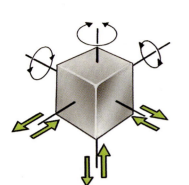

Figure 12.10 *Six ways in which movement can take place.*

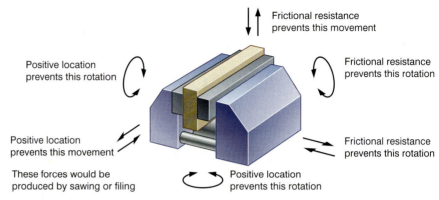

Frictional resistance prevents this movement

Positive location prevents this rotation

Frictional resistance prevents this rotation

Positive location prevents this movement

Frictional resistance prevents this rotation

These forces would be produced by sawing or filing

Positive location prevents this rotation

Figure 12.11 *Movement restricted by jaws of vice.*

Cutting force

Bench stop

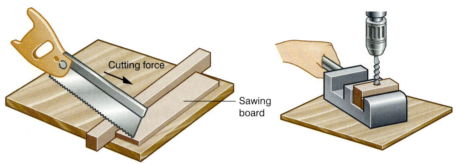

Cutting force

Sawing board

Figure 12.12 *Positive location acting against cutting forces.*

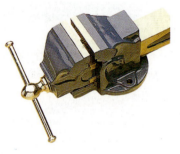

Figure 12.13 *An engineer's vice.*

Figure 12.16 *Workmate.*

HOLDING DEVICES

Vices are made from cast iron, often with quick release mechanisms. Engineer's vices are often fitted with fibre jaws to protect work being held whilst woodwork vices have wooden (plywood) faces fitted. Both are bolted to the bench. Machines vices, for use on drilling and milling machines are loose but can be bolted down as required.

Figure 12.14 *A woodworking vice.*

Figure 12.15 *Machine vices.*

A **bench hook** or **sawing board** provides positive location and resistance to cutting forces when using a tenon saw. (See Fig. 12.12.)

A **workmate** is a portable bench that provides very flexible holding features enabling awkward shapes to be held firmly.

G-cramps and **sash cramps** are available in a wide range of sizes and typically used for clamping together work whilst adhesives are allowed to set.

Jigs are work-holding devices that are made specifically for a single or small range of components. A jig will provide location and clamping for the component to facilitate small batch production. The holding of components within a jig often relies upon fast acting toggle clamps so that components can be quickly clamped and released.

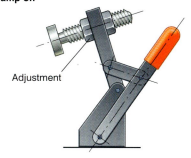

Clamp off

Adjustment

Clamp on

Workpiece

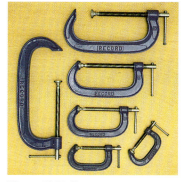

Figure 12.17 *G-cramps.*

Figure 12.18 *The holding action of a toggle clamp.*

Check yourself

QUESTIONS

Q1 Identify four different aspects of safe working practice for school workshops.

Q2 Explain why it is important to work from reliable datum faces when marking out the position of a line of holes to be drilled.

Q3 Show with sketches how you would mark a line parallel to the edge of:
a) a piece of wood
b) a strip of mild steel

REMEMBER! Cover the answers if you want to.

ANSWERS

A1
1 Wear an overall or apron
2 Wear eye protection
3 Check the condition of tools and report damage
4 Get help when carrying large or heavy objects

A2 Working from a datum is particularly important when marking out the position of a number of features such as holes. By taking each measurement from the datum the risk of cumulative error is reduced.

TUTORIALS

T1 *This is a correct answer which would have gained four out of four marks. However, the first two points both relate to clothing and the question does ask for 'different aspects'; if a further point within the answer had also been about clothing then it is possible that a mark could have been lost.*

T2 *This is the correct answer; remember that cumulative error will only occur in marking out when progressing in steps away from a datum.*

ANSWERS

A3 a)

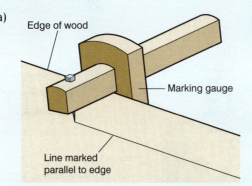

Edge of wood

Marking gauge

Line marked
parallel to edge

b)

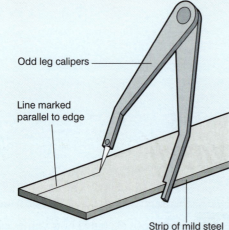

Odd leg calipers

Line marked
parallel to edge

Strip of mild steel

TUTORIALS

T3 *Sketch answers should be clear and not too small. Make sure that you always take the opportunity to show that you know the correct name(s) of the tools being used.*

KEY WORDS

These are the key words. Tick them if you think you know what they mean. Otherwise check on them.

safety	cumulative error	angle bracket
SI units	marking knife	toolmaker's clamp
steel rule	try square	positive location
steel tape measure	engineer's square	frictional resistance
vernier caliper	scriber	engineer's vice
micrometer	centre punch	woodwork vice
comparitor	dot punch	bench hook
combination square	dividers	workmate
template	marking gauge	G-cramps
datum	surface plate	sash cramps
datum faces	vee block	jigs

WASTING

The term wasting is used to describe those processes that produce waste by cutting bits out or cutting bits off. For example, sawing will produce saw dust. Waste is not always something that is discarded, it is increasingly more cost effective and responsible to look at waste material as a recyclable commodity.

Wasting processes include:

- planing;
- chiselling;
- sawing;
- filing;
- drilling;
- centre lathe turning
- wood turning;
- milling;
- screw cutting.

Understanding cutting

The action of cutting is in fact the same for all wasting processes. It can be likened to driving a wedge into the material causing the waste to split off. Tool cutting angles are important, tools work by tearing and then cleaning up the surface of the material that they are cutting. This is achieved by a combination of **rake**, **cutting** and **clearance** angles. This applies to all of the above wasting processes. Figure 13.1 could be an illustration of a chisel, a tooth on a saw or file, a turning tool on a lathe or the cutting point of a drill.

Shearing

It is worth noting that shearing, like when cutting with scissors, is a cutting action that is an exception to the above rule. With shearing the material required is separated from the surplus material without any waste being created. This applies to scissors, tin snips, guillotines and bench shears.

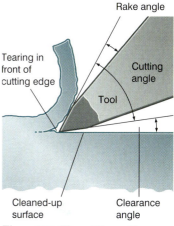

Figure 13.1 *The cutting action.*

Figure 13.2 *Tin snips shearing sheet metal.*

CHISELLING AND PLANING

It is convenient to look at chiselling, of both wood and metal, and planing at the same time. The single edge cutting action of these processes is very similar. Metal cutting chisels are called **cold chisels**; they have a hardened and tempered cutting edge and the other end is left soft to withstand hammer blows. Wood chisels are used for:

- **paring** – the removal of small shavings using hand pressure;
- **chopping** – driving the chisel with blows from a mallet to remove large quantities of waste.

Planes are used to work wood; their action is like that of a chisel. There are many types of plane but these are the most important.

- **Jack planes** are 350 mm long and used for planing wood flat and to size.
- **Smoothing planes** are 250 mm long, lighter and used for finishing and cutting end grain. Smoothing planes are easier to handle.

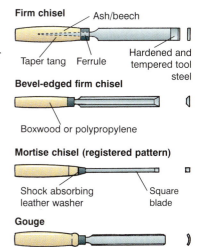

Figure 13.3 *Wood chisels.*

Figure 13.4 *The cutting action of a plane.*

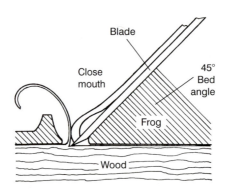

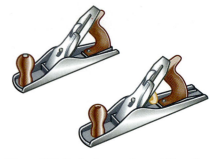

Figure 13.5 *Jack plane and smoothing plane.*

SAWING

There are many types of saw. The choice of saw is governed by the material to be cut and it is important to get the choice right. Saws intended for wood are not hard enough to cut metal and saws for metal do not cut wood effectively. Plastics can be cut with either type but not large wood handsaws such as rip saws and panel saws.

The kerf, or cut, that the saw makes, must be wider than the blade to avoid it jamming and getting stuck. This is achieved by the saw's teeth having a 'set' which creates clearance as it cuts. They are bent out in alternate directions or, as with hacksaws, the blade has a wavy edge.

Sawing curves

Sawing curves requires a saw with a narrow blade, the disadvantage of which is that the blade can break very easily. All narrow-bladed saws have replaceable blades.

- **Coping saws** are used for wood and plastic. The blade has backward facing teeth that cut on the back stroke.
- **Piercing saws** are similar to coping saws but have finer blades suitable for fine curves in metal and plastic.
- **Abrafiles** are toothed circular blades, for metal and plastic, that fit into hacksaws frames.

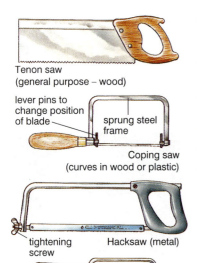

Tenon saw
(general purpose – wood)

lever pins to change position of blade

sprung steel frame

Coping saw
(curves in wood or plastic)

tightening screw

Hacksaw (metal)

Junior hacksaw

Figure 13.6 *Types of saw.*

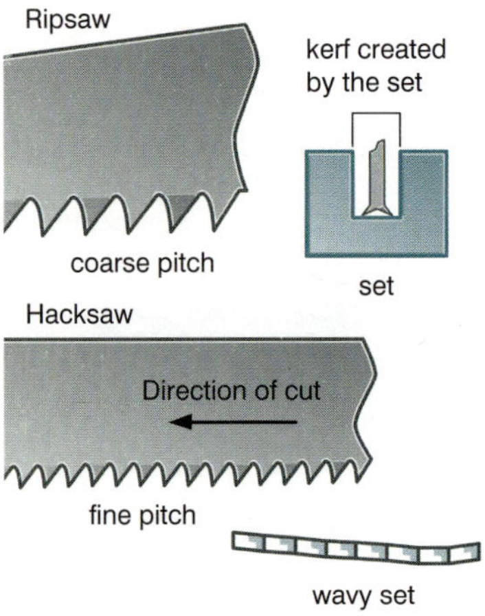

Ripsaw

kerf created by the set

coarse pitch

set

Hacksaw

Direction of cut

fine pitch

wavy set

Figure 13.7 *Saw set.*

FILING

Filing is a versatile process. Files are made from high-carbon steel which is hardened and tempered. Cutting is achieved by rows of small teeth which remove particles of material called 'filings'.

Files are classified by:

- length;
- shape;
- cut.

Files are normally double cut, with small diamond teeth. There are various grades of cut:

- **rough and bastard cuts** for course work and soft materials;
- **second cut** for general use;
- **smooth and dead smooth** for finer cuts before finishing and polishing.

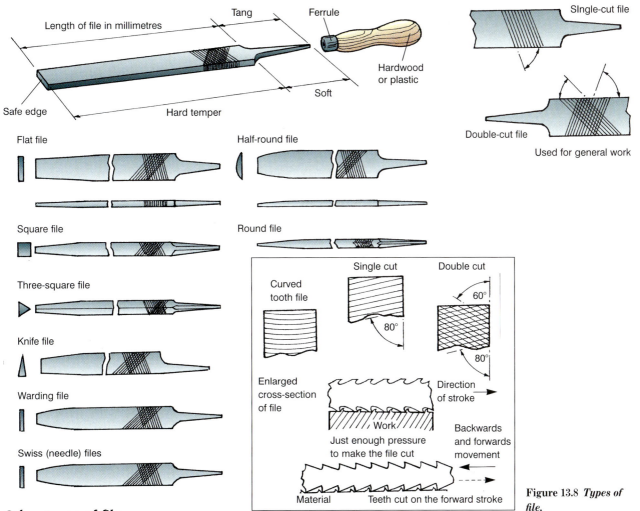

Figure 13.8 *Types of file.*

Other types of file

- **Warding files** are used for thin narrow slots.
- **Needle files** (Swiss files) are small files in a wide range of shapes with dead smooth cuts.
- **Dreadnought files** have course curved cuts for roughing out on soft and fibrous materials.
- **Rasps** have individual teeth instead of a true cut and are used for working wood.
- **Surforms** have replaceable blades with many cutting edges. There are many shapes and types of cut to suit a wide range of applications and materials.

Figure 13.9 *Surform tools.*

DRILLING AND CUTTING HOLES

Twist drills made from HSS (High Speed Steel) are the most commonly used tool for making holes in wood, metal and plastic materials. Twist drills use the same basic 'wedge' cutting action as chisels and saws by using two rotating cutting edges. Most drills have straight shanks and are held in drill chucks but larger drills may have morse tapered shanks (taper shanks) that locate directly into the spindle of drilling machines or lathe tail stocks (see 'Centre lathes' later in this chapter).

Figure 13.10 *Twist drills.*

Figure 13.11 shows a range of bits for making holes in wood. Wood boring bits are better suited to larger holes because they have a small spur that cuts through the wood fibres in advance of the actual cutting edge. This avoids tearing of the surface.

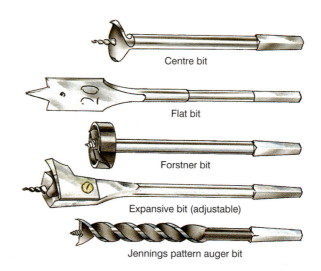

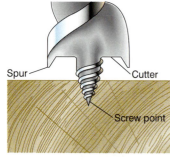

Figure 13.11 *Wood boring bits.*

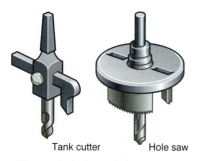

Tank cutter   Hole saw

Figure 13.12 *Large hole cutters.*

For large diameter holes in thin sheet materials it is best to use an adjustable tank cutter or a hole saw which has interchangeable toothed cutting rings ranging from 20–75 mm diameter.

Countersinks and counterbores

When it is required to have screw heads that finish flush with the surface, countersink bits and counterbores are used to provide the 'seating' for the screw head.

Countersinks have a 90° point angle for countersunk wood screws.

Counterbores create a flat bottom recess for cheese head screws or bolt heads.

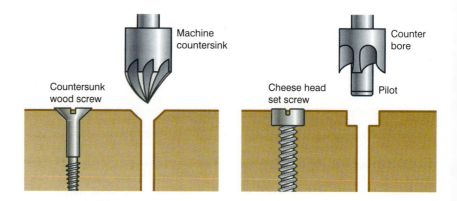

Figure 13.13 *Countersinks and counterbores.*

Hand drills and drilling machines

Portable electric power drills and hand drills can be used for straight shank drills up to 13 mm diameter. Machine pedestal and bench mounted machines have larger capacity chucks and can also accommodate taper shank drills. A carpenter's ratchet brace should be used for wood boring bits that have a square shank.

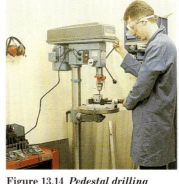

Figure 13.14 *Pedestal drilling machine.*

CENTRE LATHE TURNING

Centre lathes are used to make cylindrical components from metals and plastic materials. The process is called **turning** – never use the term 'lathing'. The principle of turning is straightforward. Work is held firmly and is rotated whilst a single point cutting tool, located in the tool post, cuts the work using the familiar wedge cutting action. The shape of the work produced depends upon the path taken by the tool, the two principle shapes being cylindrical and flat, produced by parallel turning and facing.

Centre lathes, like the one shown in Fig. 13.17, have four main elements:

- **Lathe bed** – very rigid and usually made from cast iron. The bed keeps the other parts in alignment.
- **Headstock** – containing the gearbox, controls and the means of holding the work, most commonly a 3- or 4-jaw chuck.
- **Tail stock** – for location of drills and drill chucks and for supporting long work.
- **Saddle** – travels along the bed and carries a cross slide upon which is mounted the tool post.

Figure 13.15 *Hand drills and carpenter's braces.*

Headstock   3-jaw chuck   Tool post   Compound slide   Cross slide   Tail stock   Lathe bed

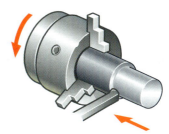

Parallel turning producing a cylindrical form

Facing producing a flat surface

Figure 13.16 *Parallel turning and facing.*

Figure 13.17 *Centre lathe.*

Figure 13.18 *4-jaw chuck.*

Figure 13.19 *A face plate, used for mounting irregular shapes.*

Work holding

When turning, the cutting forces are considerable so work must be held securely. The method of holding work will depend upon the shape and size of the material and the turning operation that is to be carried out. The methods of holding work are:

- **Self-centering 3-jaw chuck** – the most common device for holding cylindrical and hexagonal work. The jaws are stepped so that work can also be held from the inside; a second set of jaws, that step in the opposite direction, can be used to hold larger diameters.
- **Independent 4-jaw chuck** – used to hold square, rectangular and irregular shapes and for 'off centre' turning. Each jaw is adjusted independently.
- **Face plate** – for clamping awkward shapes, often in conjunction with an angle bracket.
- **Between centres** – for long pieces of work. Work must first be prepared by facing and centre drilling.

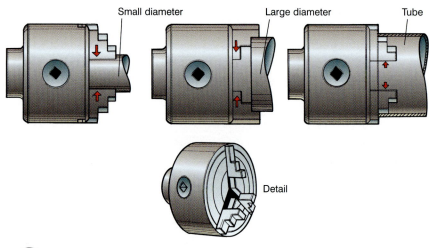

Figure 13.20 *3-jaw chuck.*

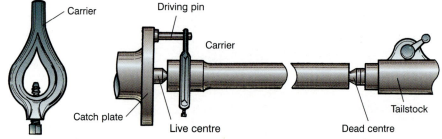

Figure 13.21 *Turning between centres.*

Turning tools

Turning tools need to be both hard and tough. They are made from high carbon steel, high speed steel or have replaceable tungsten carbide tips. The shape (profile) of the tool is determined by the turning operation being carried out.

- **Roughing tools** normally have a broad radiused point for strength and are used to reduce work to within 1 mm of the finished shape.
- **Finishing tools** are used for fine cutting, normally with a small radiused point.
- **Knife edge tools** in left- and right-hand forms are used to finish turning sharp internal corners.
- **Parting-off tools** are used to produce grooves and to cut the work off from the material remaining in the chuck.

The geometry of turning tools is important to ensure efficient cutting. The tool's clearance and rake angles must be correct and the tool must be set on the centre line height of the workpiece as shown in Figs. 13.23 and 13.24.

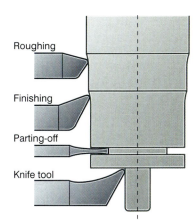

Figure 13.22 *Tool profiles (plan view).*

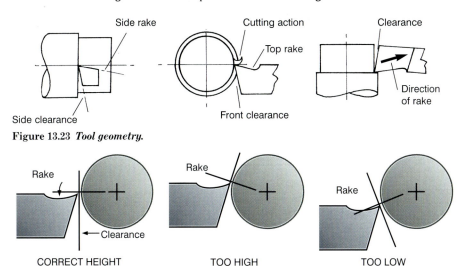

Figure 13.23 *Tool geometry.*

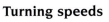

CORRECT HEIGHT

TOO HIGH
Clearance lost, result in rubbing

TOO LOW
Rake lost, tool will not cut

Figure 13.24 *Setting tool to the right height.*

Turning speeds

The speed at which a lathe rotates is determined by the material and the diameter of the work. The speed is calculated using the formula in Fig. 13.25. The formula may be provided in your examination paper.

Cutting lubrication

Most turning operations benefit from the use of a cutting lubricant that acts as a coolant and lubricant for the operation, reducing friction and heat and assisting the waste removal.

$$N = \frac{1000\,s}{\pi d}$$

where N = Speed in revs per minute
s = Cutting speed (metres per minute)
d = Diameter of work

Example – the turning speed for ø40 mm mild steel bar
$$N = \frac{100 \times 25}{\pi \times 40} = 200 \text{ rpm}$$

Figure 13.25 *Cutting-speed formula.*

The table in Fig. 13.26 shows the rake angle, cutting speeds and recommended cutting lubricant for a range of materials.

Material	Rake angle	Cutting speed M/min with HSS tool	Cutting lubricant
Aluminium	40°	200	Paraffin
Brass	2°	90	None needed
Cast iron	2°	20	None needed
Hard steel	6°	18	Soluble oil
Mild steel	20°	25	Soluble oil
Nylon	30°	170	None needed
Acylic	40°	200	Paraffin

Figure 13.26

Drilling

Drilling on the centre lathe is undertaken using a drill in a **Jacob's chuck** held in the tailstock of the lathe or using a taper shank drill. It is necessary when drilling on the lathe to start the process with a centre drill to create a small location to start the drill.

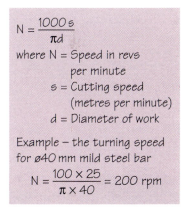

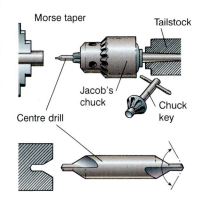

Figure 13.27 *Jacob's chuck and centre drill.*

Boring

Boring is internal turning. The process must start with a drilled hole to enable the boring tool to enter. It is a process that requires great care as it not possible to see what is happening.

Figure 13.28 *Boring.*

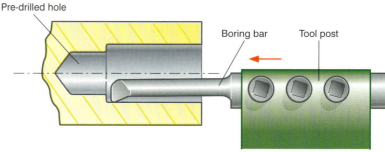

Taper turning

Short tapers, or chamfers, can be created by using a tool that is shaped, by grinding, to the required chamfer angle. Longer tapers are turned using the compound slide of the lathe that is set over at the required taper angle and the slide hand wheel is used to move the tool along the work.

Figure 13.29 *Taper turning.*

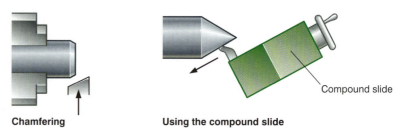

Chamfering   **Using the compound slide**

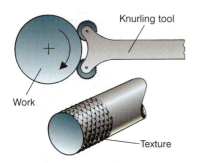

Figure 13.30 *Using a knurling tool.*

Knurling

Knurling is a means of creating a 'diamond' or 'straight line' textured surface on cylindrical work by using a special wheeled knurling tool.

WOOD TURNING

Wood lathes are used for turning wooden products such as bowls, dishes, spindles, legs and lamps. The process is carried out with work mounted on the headstock for bowl-type products or between centres for long thin products.

There is a very wide range of wood turning tools including scrapers, gouges and chisels. The tools are hand held against a rest that must be adjusted close to the work and at a height that suits the tool being used.

MILLING

Milling uses rotating multi-toothed cutters to work metal, plastic and composite materials. The two main types of machine are horizontal milling machines and vertical milling machines; so named because of the way that the cutters are mounted.

Figure 13.31 *A wood turning lathe*

Milling processes

These are shown in Figs. 13.32, 13.33 and 13.34.

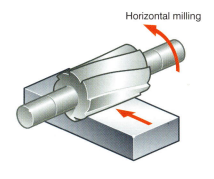
Horizontal milling

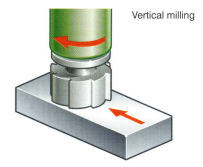
Vertical milling

Figure 13.32 *Horizontal and vertical milling of horizontal flat surfaces.*

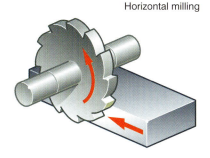
Horizontal milling

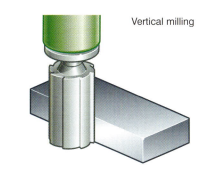
Vertical milling

Figure 13.33 *Horizontal and vertical milling of vertical flat surfaces – the horizontal machine is using a side and face cutter which cuts on its side and on its diameter.*

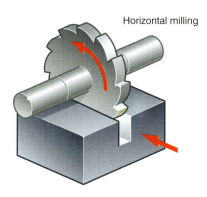
Horizontal milling

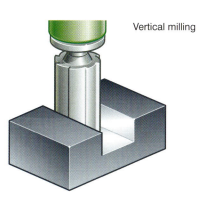
Vertical milling

Figure 13.34 *Horizontal and vertical milling of slots.*

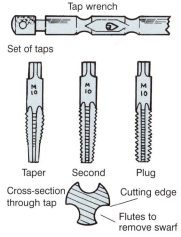
Figure 13.35 *Taps and tap wrench.*

SCREW CUTTING

Screw cutting is appropriate for metal and plastic materials.

- Tapping is the process of cutting internal screw threads using a set of three taps in sequence: taper, second and plug. The hole must first be drilled to the correct tapping size; the taps are held in a tap wrench.

- Threading is the process of cutting external threads using a split die held in a die stock.

When screw cutting by hand it is important to remember to use a cutting sequence that involves half a turn clockwise followed by a quarter turn anti-clockwise, this breaks off the swarf (waste) and stops the tap or die from getting jammed or breaking.

Figure 13.36 *Split die and die stock.*

Using a centre lathe

Screw threads can also be cut using a single point tool on a centre lathe. This is a very precise process requiring a tool that is ground to the exact profile of the screw thread and very accurate setting up of the lathe to achieve the correct pitch of the thread.

COMPUTER-AIDED MANUFACTURING (CAM)

Many manufacturing processes are able to be computer controlled, the more sophisticated of which are covered in greater detail in Chapter 19.

Some commonly used terminology and abbreviations are explained below:

- **CNC – Computer Numerical Control** Numerical Control (NC) simply means control by numbers. CNC therefore refers to systems that use a computer to generate, process and store the number systems that control a machine tool. All computer controlled machines are, in fact, CNC machines because all control is numerical.

- **CAM – Computer-Aided Manufacturing** This means any aspect of manufacturing that uses a computer system to assist in a calculation or in the provision of data for other processes such as designing (CAD). CAM can also be part of a total Computer Integrated Manufacturing system (CIM) that includes: marketing, stock control, quality control, robot assembly systems, etc.

- **CAD and CADD** – refer back to Chapter 10.

- **CAD/CAM – Computer-Aided Design and Manufacture** This describes the process of linking computer-aided designing with the process of computer-aided manufacture. This link actually involves processing the numerical data that makes up a design or drawing and converting this into machine data that can be used to provide the instructions for a machine to carry out the process of manufacture.

Machine axes

The numerical instructions for any machine movement must have a number of elements within it. In the case of a CNC centre lathe these will include as a minimum:

- Work rotation – on or off;
- Work rotation – speed in r.p.m.;
- Tool movement – direction: plus or minus 'X' or 'Z';
- Tool movement – distance in mm;
- Tool movement – speed in mm/min;
- Cutting lubrication – on or off.

The axes for all machines follows an ISO convention; this is shown for the lathe in Fig. 13.37. Many other machines, including the milling machine, also have a 'Y' axis of movement.

Programming

Part programming is the term used for the process of programming a 'part' or component. With the advent of CAD/CAM the process of writing codes to send to the machine via the computer is no longer required within examination syllabuses at GCSE. You should however be aware of the two

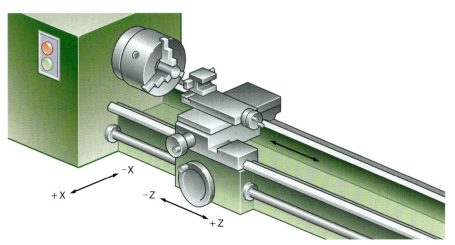

Figure 13.37 *Centre lathe machine axes.*

methods of instructing directional movement: incremental and absolute, both shown in Fig. 13.38.

- **Incremental programming** relates each movement to the final position of the previous movement.
- **Absolute programming** relates each movement to a single datum point.

Incremental programming

X	Z
−3	0
0	−2.5
1	0
0	−1.5
2	−2

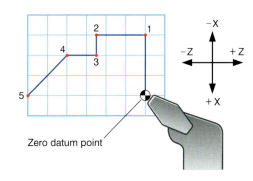

Zero datum point

Absolute programming

X	Z
−3	0
−3	−2.5
−2	−2.5
−2	−4
0	−6

Figure 13.38 *Incremental and absolute programming applied to the same sequence of movements.*

KEY WORDS

These are the key words. Tick them if you think you know what they mean. Otherwise check on them.

wasting	hacksaw	boring
rake angle	twist drill	knurling
cutting angle	taper shank drill	horizontal milling
clearance angle	countersink	vertical milling
shearing	counterbore	tapping
paring	turning	threading
chopping	headstock	CNC
kerf	tailstock	CAM
saw set	3-jaw chuck	CAD/CAM
tenon saw	4-jaw chuck	
coping saw	face plate	

Check yourself

QUESTIONS

Q1 Explain why some processes are known as 'wasting processes' and why this is not necessarily a good description?

Q2 Explain why it is necessary for saw teeth to be 'set' and describe how this is achieved in the case of a hacksaw.

Q3 Give the most appropriate tool for cutting the following holes:
a) 10 mm diameter hole in mild steel
b) 12 mm diameter hole in soft wood
c) 50 mm diameter hole in 3 mm hardboard

Q4 Figure 13.39 shows an aluminium control knob for an electronic product. Set out step by step the stages required to make the knob using a centre lathe.

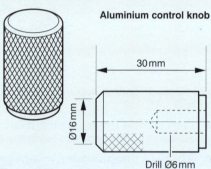

Aluminium control knob

30 mm

Ø16 mm

Drill Ø6 mm

Figure 13.39

REMEMBER! Cover the answers if you want to.

ANSWERS

A1 Wasting processes produce waste in the form of bits cut off or removed. This is not a good description because often the waste that is cut off can be re-cycled and it is therefore not actually wasted.

A2 Saw teeth are set so that the slot that they cut out is wider than the blade and the blade does not get stuck. With a hacksaw this is achieved by making the saw blade 'wavy'.

A3
a) 10 mm twist drill
b) 12 mm auger bit
c) Hole saw set to 50 mm diameter

A4

Stage	Operation
1	Locate the bar in the lathe chuck
2	Face off the end
3	Knurl the bar
4	Chamfer the end
5	Groove and part off
6	Reverse knob and hold with packing
7	Face off
8	Centre drill and drill

TUTORIALS

T1 *This is a good concise answer. Always be aware of the environmental issues associated with any form of manufacturing.*

T2 *This answer is correct but could very easily have been enhanced with a sketch of the hacksaw blade.*

T2 *A straightforward question requiring short responses, part (b) could have also been a 'flat bit' or a 'forstner bit'.*

T4 *Questions of this type are very common at GCSE and test your ability to carry out manufacturing processes. The sequence of operations is extremely important. Study this answer and visualise each stage to make certain that you understand it. Look also at the terminology: face off, part off, knurl, chamfer.*

- **Deforming processes** bring about a change in shape such as bending, without the loss of material that is associated with the wasting processes.
- **Reforming processes** involve a change of material state such as solid to liquid and return to solid.

DEFORMING PROCESSES

Deforming processes rely upon materials being in a malleable condition (see Chapter 4) to allow the material to be deformed by the application of force without any fracture taking place. The deforming processes often require the application of heat to bring about a 'softening' of the material concerned.

The deforming processes include:

- bending and forming thermoplastics;
- hot and cold forming metals;
- bending and laminating wood;
- GRP – Glass Reinforced Plastic (glass fibre).

BENDING AND FORMING THERMOPLASTIC

Figure 14.1 *A strip heater.*

Thermoplastic materials such as acrylic are very easy to bend and form with the application of a moderate amount of heat, only 160°C. This makes acrylic particularly suitable for school project work as this is a temperature that can be achieved easily and safely.

Figure 14.1 shows a strip heater, sometimes called a line bender, that is used to provide local heating for line bending acrylic sheet. When forming more that one bend it is a good idea to use card to work out the sequence of bends. The position of the bends should be marked out on the acrylic using a fibre-tipped pen. Have all necessary formers or bending jigs to hand before applying heat and apply the heat equally to both sides of the sheet; this will avoid blistering the acrylic.

With any process that involves heating plastics it is difficult to judge the time required. This is because darker coloured material will absorb the heat more quickly than light coloured materials.

Figure 14.2 *Formers and jigs are used to make accurate bends in acrylic.*

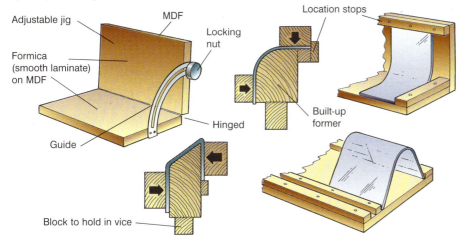

Adjustable jig

MDF

Formica (smooth laminate) on MDF

Locking nut

Location stops

Hinged

Guide

Built-up former

Block to hold in vice

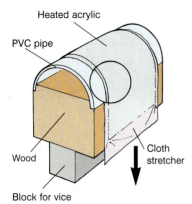

Figure 14.3 *Creating a curved form in acrylic.*

For more complex forms it may be necessary to heat the sheet all over using an oven. The oven temperature should be set to 170°C. Figure 14.3 shows how a curved form can be achieved using a former made from PVC pipe. The softened acrylic is pulled over the former using a cloth stretcher. This process is called **drape forming**.

More complex forms, such as trays and dishes, can be made from thin acrylic sheet using a **plug and yoke press forming** technique. For this process a two-part former as in Fig.14.4 is needed. The male half, the **plug**, needs to have tapered edges and rounded corners to assist the flow of material and removal. The female part, the **yoke**, needs to be slightly larger to allow for the material thickness.

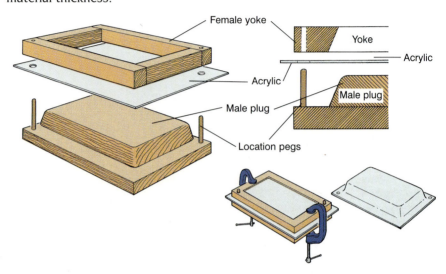

Figure 14.4 *Deforming acrylic using a plug and yoke technique.*

Vacuum forming

Vacuum forming is a popular school workshop process and examination topic. It is a process that you should make a point of seeing or preferably experiencing.

Vacuum forming works by removing air, creating a partial vacuum, from underneath soft and flexible thermoplastic sheet and allowing atmospheric pressure to push the plastic down onto a mould.

Figure 14.6 shows a typical mould. Moulds must be made with care and should have regard for the following:

- Sides should all be tapered towards the top so that the formed plastic can be removed. This taper is called a draft.

- Deep 'draws' should be vented to ensure that air does not get trapped.

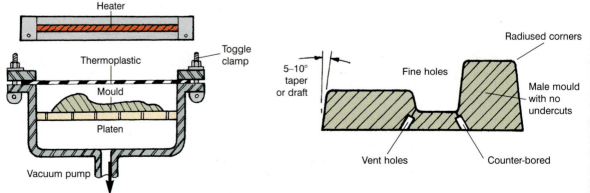

Figure 14.5 *A vacuum former.*

Figure 14.6 *A vacuum forming mould.*

- Corners should be radiused so that the material flows and does not become thinned on the corners.

- There must be no undercuts where plastic could get drawn in so preventing the formed shape from being removed.

- The mould should have a smooth finish so that the material flows easily.

The vacuum forming process may start with a 'blow' that stretches the plastic all over or it may be started by raising the mould, on the platen, to create a drape forming. On some machines a combination of these processes is used. The aim is always to create a high definition outcome without any excessive thinning having taken place.

Blow moulding

In its simplest form blow moulding forms flexible hot plastic material into a dome shape as in Fig. 14.8.

More complex forms are achieved by using a hollow mould. The industrial version of this process is very common for the production of bottles, bowls and containers; see Chapter 18.

Figure 14.7 *This mask was produced by vacuum forming.*

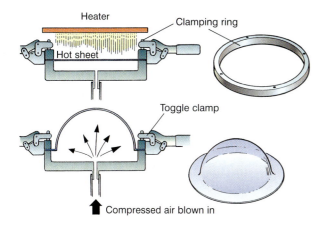

Figure 14.8 *The blow moulding process.*

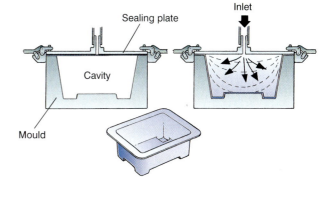

Figure 14.9 *Blow moulding.*

HOT AND COLD FORMING METALS

Forging

Hot forging is one of the oldest techniques for working metal. It is however a process that has been considerably developed within manufacturing industry, see also Chapter 18. Hammering hot metal improves the structure of the material by refining the grain flow. Strength is increased because the grain flow follows the shape rather than being cut into.

The basic tools for forge work are a hammer and an anvil although there is a wide range of tools such as flatters, swagers and fullers that have been developed for all of the various tasks (see Figs, 14.11 and 14.12).

Beaten metal work

It is important that metal for beaten metal working is **malleable**. As metal is worked it becomes harder, this is known as **work hardening**, and it needs regular **annealing** to restore its malleability, see Chapter 6. Silver is an ideal metal for beaten work but it is very expensive. Other commonly used metals are: copper, brass, gilding metal and aluminium. Beaten metal working

Forged crank with uninterrupted grain flow

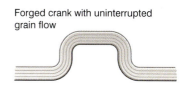

Crank produced by a wasting process Grain flow cut into

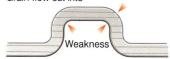

Figure 14.10 *Hot forging a crank.*

107

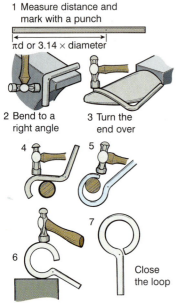

1 Measure distance and mark with a punch

πd or 3.14 × diameter

2 Bend to a right angle

3 Turn the end over

4

5

6

7

Close the loop

Figure 14.11 *Forming a loop.*

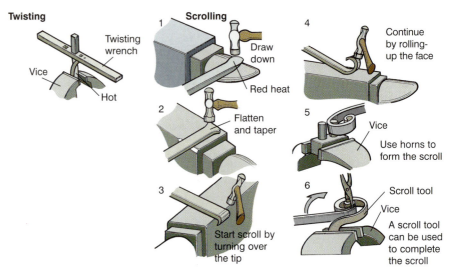

Twisting

Twisting wrench

Vice

Hot

Scrolling

1 Draw down

Red heat

2 Flatten and taper

3 Start scroll by turning over the tip

4 Continue by rolling-up the face

5 Vice — Use horns to form the scroll

6 Scroll tool — Vice — A scroll tool can be used to complete the scroll

Figure 14.12 *Twisting and scrolling.*

processes tend to be rather specialised and it is not necessary to know all of the detail. The most common processes are:

- **Hollowing** is a process of thinning the metal to produce shallow bowl shapes typically using a boxwood bossing mallet and a sand-filled leather bag.

- **Sinking** is similar to hollowing but the centre is beaten down leaving a rim with surplus material to be beaten out flat.

- **Raising** is the process used for deep bowls and tall-sided forms. Unlike the previous processes, raising the metal increases its thickness.

- **Planishing** is a final process that removes blemishes and produces an accurate finish. Planishing also work hardens the material giving it mechanical strength.

Sheet metal working

Boxes, trays, pipework, cylinders and cones can all be made from sheet metal such as mild steel, tin-plate, aluminium, brass and copper. Sheet metal can be folded cold using a mallet and folding bars but it is much better to use a folding machine is order to achieve sharp and accurate corners.

Before carrying out any sheet metal work it is best to make a full size or scaled card model or prototype. Card is easy to work and this enables you to work out the position of flaps for joining and the sequence of bends. The card can then also be used as a template for the **net** or **development** of your product. Safe edges are used to prevent exposed sharp edges.

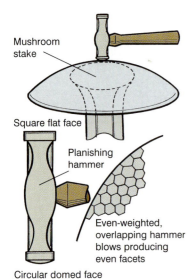

Mushroom stake

Square flat face

Planishing hammer

Even-weighted, overlapping hammer blows producing even facets

Circular domed face

Figure 14.13 *Planishing.*

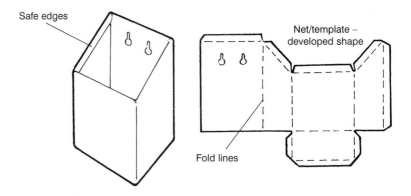

Safe edges

Net/template – developed shape

Fold lines

Figure 14.14 *A wall pamphlet holder – development and final form.*

Press work

Pressing a form from a sheet of material produces a strong **monocoque** (shell-like) structure. Many products ranging from kettles to car bodies are made in this way. In its simplest form a channel section can be produced by using a two-part press tool with pressure exerted by a vice or fly press. The channel section in Fig.14.15 has much greater strength than the sheet materials from which it was made.

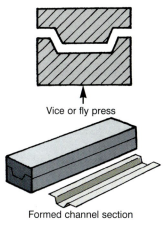

Vice or fly press

Formed channel section

Figure 14.15 *Simple two-part press tool.*

BENDING AND LAMINATING WOOD

Bending wood

Wood will only bend by a limited amount before it fractures and breaks. One way to overcome this problem is to make a number of cuts in the surface so that in effect only a thin surface layer of the wood is actually bending. This process, called '**kerfing**' is used in the manufacture of musical instruments such as guitars.

Another way to assist bending is to use a steam chest where wood is made to absorb moisture so that it behaves like a live or 'green' stick.

Laminating

Thin layers of wood are called **lamina** or **veneers**, and because they are thin they bend more easily. Laminating is like constructing plywood. Using strong adhesive, forms can be built up that stay in shape once the adhesive has hardened.

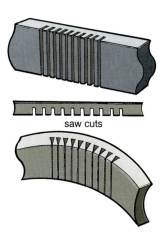

saw cuts

Figure 14.16 *Kerfing.*

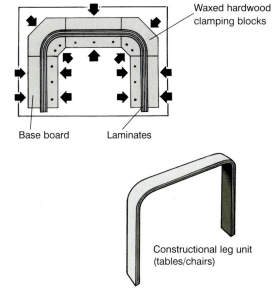

Waxed hardwood clamping blocks

Base board   Laminates

Constructional leg unit (tables/chairs)

Figure 14.17 *Laminating using clamp pressure and formers to shape veneers.*

GRP – GLASS REINFORCED PLASTIC (GLASS FIBRE)

GRP is a popular manufacturing process for cars, caravans and boats, etc. It is also a process that lends itself easily to school project work. GRP involves bonding together flexible glass fibre (stranded glass) mat using a polyester resin.

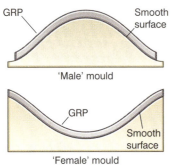

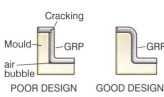

Figure 14.18 *GRP mould design features.*

The product made takes its form completely from the mould. The finished surface of the product is the surface that is in contact with the mould. Moulds therefore must be made to the highest standard and have a good quality surface finish. It is also necessary to apply a release agent to the mould surface to assist removal.

REFORMING PROCESSES

Reforming processes involve a change of material state such as solid to liquid and return to solid, like making a jelly in a mould. The change in state is brought about by heat energy.

CASTING

Aluminium sand casting is the only metal casting process that is commonly available for school use. This is because the material (aluminium) is cheap and the temperature required for casting 750°C is not hard to achieve. The process involves six distinct stages:

1 Making a pattern for the required workpiece

2 Encasing the pattern in moulding sand

3 Removing the pattern thereby leaving a sand mould

4 Pouring the molten metal into the mould

5 Removing the sand from around the solidified workpiece

6 Cleaning up the workpiece

Pattern making

The quality of the casting depends upon the quality of the pattern. The requirements are similar to those for vacuum forming moulds:

- radiused corners;
- drafted sides (tapered);
- good surface finish.

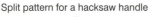

Figure 14.19 *Split pattern.*

Most moulds are made from wood and they may be flat backed for simple forms or split as in Fig. 14.19. Notice that the two halves are pegged together for location.

Mould making

The moulding must be sieved to get rid of lumps and any foreign matter, and damp enough to hold its shape. The mould box to contain the sand is a two-part construction with pins to locate the halves together.

The mould is built up in stages:

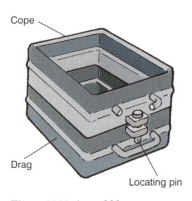

Figure 14.20 *A mould box.*

1 The lower half, the drag, is placed on a flat board around the lower half of the pattern. Parting powder is dusted onto the pattern and the mould is then filled with sand.

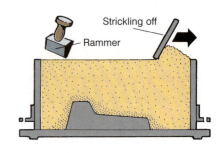

Figure 14.21 *Stage 1.*

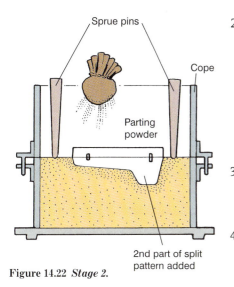

Figure 14.22 *Stage 2.*

2 The drag is turned over and the cope and top half of the pattern are put in place. The sprue pins are then added and the mould box filled with sand.

3 Pouring basins are made in the sand and the sprue pins are carefully removed.

4 The mould box is opened, the pattern is removed, and gates are made in the sand to allow the molten metal to flow into the cavity. The mould is re-assembled ready for pouring.

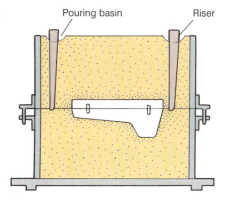

Figure 14.23 *Stage 3.*

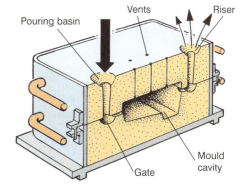

Figure 14.24 *The mould box ready for pouring.*

Pouring

Aluminium melts at 600°C but needs to be at 750°C for pouring. Pouring should be slow and continuous into the pouring basins until a pool forms at the top of the riser. Great care is needed, the safety issues are important:

- Always have adult supervision.
- Wear protective clothing; gloves, apron, leggings, stout shoes and a full face mask.
- Ensure that there is fume extraction and good ventilation.

Fettling

Fettling is the term used to describe the process of finishing off the work by removing the runners and risers with a hacksaw and file, and cleaning up the casting.

Lost pattern casting

Patterns for casting can be made from expanded polystyrene of the sort commonly used for packaging. This can be embedded in the sand and when the molten aluminium is poured in the pattern is totally burnt away. The main advantage is that the pattern can be made as complex as required because it does not have to be removed from the sand, but this does mean that is can only be used once. The disadvantage is that when the polystyrene is burning it gives off dangerous toxic fumes. This process must therefore only be carried out where the ventilation system is designed to safely take these fumes away.

Figure 14.25 *Casting in a commercial foundry.*

Check yourself

QUESTIONS

Q1 Identify the forming processes that enable acrylic to be a useful and versatile material for project work. Explain why acrylic is so popular.

Q2 Vacuum forming and blow moulding both rely upon air pressure to deform plastic sheet.
a) Describe these two processes making particular reference to use of air pressure.
b) With the aid of a sketch show the design features that must be included in a vacuum forming pattern.

Q3 Give two reasons why planishing should be carried out on beaten metalwork.

Q4 Produce an annotated sketch of a section through a sand casting mould that has been prepared for casting a flat backed house name plate from aluminium.

REMEMBER! Cover the answers if you want to.

ANSWERS

A1 Acrylic can be used for any heat forming processes such as line bending using a strip heater, vacuum forming and blow moulding. It is a popular material because it softens at a low temperature. It is also available in a wide range of colours and is not too expensive.

A2 a) The vacuum forming process evacuates the air from under the softened plastic material and allows air pressure to push the plastic onto the mould.
Blow moulding uses the pressure of compressed air to force the plastic onto the mould.

b)

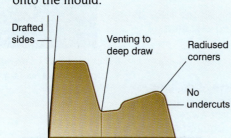

Drafted sides
Venting to deep draw
Radiused corners
No undercuts

Section through vacuum forming pattern

TUTORIALS

T1 *This answer is not altogether correct. Acrylic is not the best material for vacuum forming although it is sometimes used for this. High density polystyrene, ABS and forming grade PVC are better materials. Acrylic has only a short range of temperature within which it remains plastic so it tends to cool too fast for high definition forming.*

It is good to pick up on the wider points regarding the material: the colours and the cost.

T2 *It is important to remember that with a process like vacuum forming the vacuum does not suck the plastic down onto the mould; it allows air pressure to push it down. This is a correct answer and the sketch picks up all of the important points.*

ANSWERS

A3 Planishing should be carried out on beaten metalwork to:
1 Provide the work with a good finish. This could be very flat or with a pattern on the surface.
2 Work harden the surface to make the product stronger.

A4

Runner Pouring basin Riser Mould cavity for name plate
Cope
Drag
Moulding sand

TUTORIALS

T3 *This is correct answer that picks up the key points. Examination papers do not expect a detailed knowledge of the beaten metal working processes.*

T4 *Questions about casting are common and it helps if you are able to use some of the correct terminology; i.e. drag and cope (the drag is the one at the bottom, it 'drags on the floor') runner and riser (run down the runner and rise up the riser).*

KEY WORDS

These are the key words. Tick them if you think you know what they mean. Otherwise check on them.

deforming	forging	laminating
reforming	forge	lamina
thermoplastic	malleable	veneers
strip heater	beaten metal work	GRP – glass reinforced plastic
formers	work hardening	fibre glass
jig	annealing	casting
drape forming	sheet metal work	pattern
plug and yoke	net	drag
vacuum forming	development	cope
draft	press work	fettling
blow moulding	monocoque	

CHAPTER 15

FABRICATION AND ASSEMBLY

Manufactured products are not often made using only a single piece of material. Most products are built up (fabricated) and joined together (assembled). These processes often make use of the components such as screws, nails, nuts and bolts etc. that are covered early in this book.

Study this chapter alongside Chapter 8 'Components'.

ADHESIVES FOR FABRICATION AND ASSEMBLY

There are many adhesives (glues) available that have been developed over recent years. Some adhesives such as wood glues are for specific materials, whilst others like epoxy resin will bond dissimilar materials. Adhesives may be rigid or they may be flexible. Some will allow time for repositioning and adjustment whilst others bond instantly on contact. You must check instructions and if you are not certain then try a test join.

It is important to select the correct adhesive to suit the application and to ensure that the correct preparation is carried out and that clamping or curing time instructions are followed. Adhesives will not normally bond to greasy, dusty or wet surfaces. Adhesive bonds often fail because the surface has been handled without care and a layer of natural oil from your skin is left deposited on the surface.

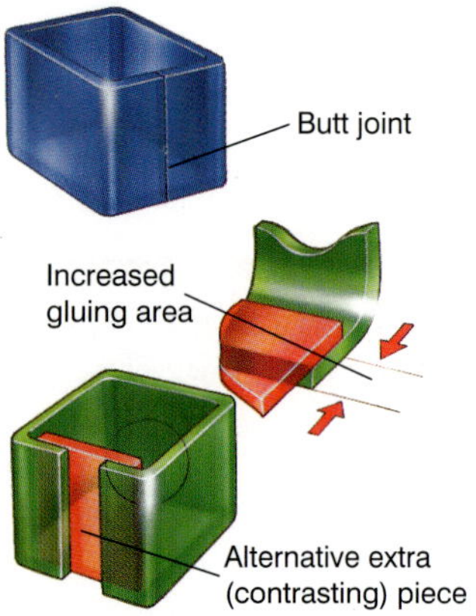

Figure 15.1 *Adhesives.*

- **PVA glue (polyvinyl acetate)** is the most popular wood glue; it is white in colour and comes ready mixed. PVA glue is strong and does not stain, excess glue can be wiped off with a damp cloth. It requires only light clamping and sets within 2–3 hours depending upon temperature.

- **Tensol cements** are a range of solvent-based adhesives for joining thermoplastics. It is important to have the correct adhesive, the most popular for acrylic is Tensol 12. In an examination it is sufficient to know that 'Tensol cement' or 'a solvent-based adhesive' is used. The size of surface gluing area will effect the strength of the joint: use an overlap where possible and position butt joints away from corners.

- **Epoxy resin** is a two-part adhesive for unlike materials. It will bond glass, ceramic, wood, metal and hard plastics. Mixing the two parts, resin and hardener, triggers a chemical reaction that begins the setting process. A popular brand is Araldite.

- **Contact (impact) adhesive**, such as Evostik, is used for fixing plastic laminates (melamine) and other sheet and strip materials. Surfaces are coated and left until 'touch dry'. Correct positioning is essential as bonding is immediate.

- **Hot-melt glue** comes in glue stick form and is used in conjunction with a glue gun. It is popular for modelling and temporary work. It tends to be messy, is not very strong and gives a poor quality finish.

- **Double-sided tape** is used increasingly for large flat areas of metal and plastics. Clean surfaces are essential for effective joining.

Butt joint

Increased gluing area

Alternative extra (contrasting) piece

Figure 15.2 *Surface areas for gluing thermoplastics.*

JOINTS IN WOOD

Wooden structures are either of a frame or box type of construction and they always require joining at the corners or where pieces cross over each other.

FRAME CONSTRUCTION

There are a number of joints used in frame construction for:

- corners;
- 'T' joints for joining rails to frames;
- cross joints where pieces cross over.

Figure 15.3 shows some of these but there are many more that are associated with traditional wood working. The current trend in construction is for joints that can be machine made such as dowel joints.

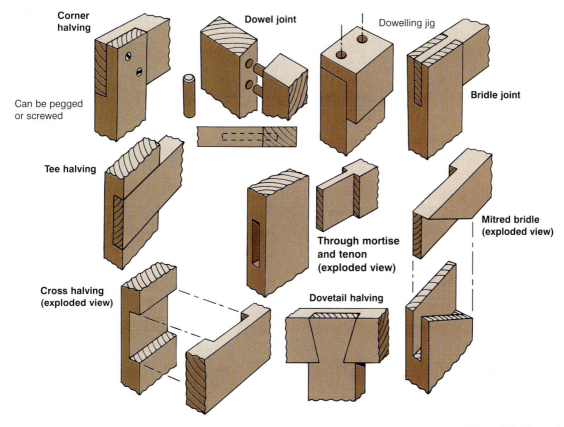

Figure 15.3 *Frame joints.*

BOX CONSTRUCTION

Box construction methods are for joining wide pieces of solid timber and some manufactured board. They are used for boxes and shelves, etc. The aim of this construction is to provide mechanically strong joints such as dovetails or large gluing areas such as dowels and comb joints. The latter are more popular because they lend themselves to machine manufacture and they take advantage of the advances in modern adhesives.

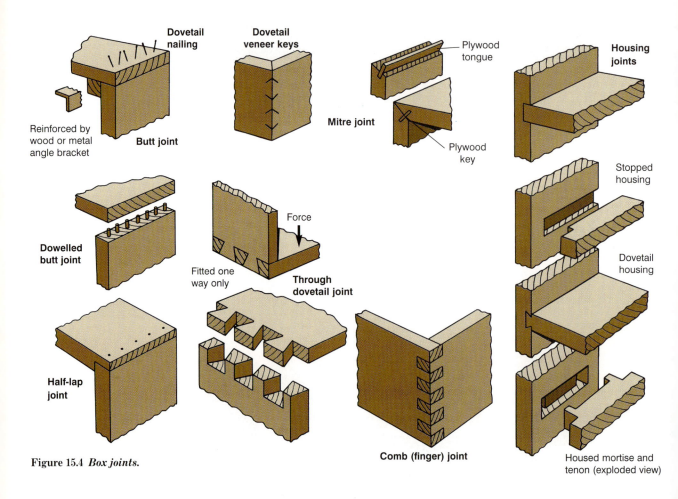

Figure 15.4 *Box joints.*

JOINING METAL

Joining metal to itself or to other materials by mechanical means is covered in Chapter 8 'Components'. The components used include rivets, nuts and bolts, and a range of other threaded fasteners. These are called mechanical fixing devices because they rely upon mechanical forces to fix and hold the joint in place. Nuts and bolts and screw type fixings are regarded as temporary fixings as they can always be taken apart.

HEAT PROCESSES – SOLDERING AND BRAZING

Soldering is a process that effects a joint by introducing another metal to the surface of the metal to be joined; this is called 'local alloying'. The solder actually becomes a part of the surface of the material and forms a permanent joint. There are a wide range of solders that have different strengths and melting points. For all soldering processes joints must be prepared and cleaned, and the correct flux used. Flux is a chemical cleaning agent.

● **Soft solder** is the weakest solder and has the lowest melting point. It is used mainly for electrical work and joints in tin-plate. Soft soldering can be carried out using either a flame or a soldering iron. It is an alloy of tin and lead. Use resin flux for soft soldering.

- **Silver solders** are hard solders and have melting points in the range 625°C–800°C. They are used for many beaten metal work applications. Silver soldering is carried out using either a brazing hearth or an Oxy-acetylene flame. Silver solders are alloys of copper and zinc with some added silver. Use 'easy-flo' flux for silver soldering.

- **Brazing** is the hardest form of hard solder and melts at the highest temperature, 875°C. This is too hot for brass and copper work but ideal for mild steel. Brazing spelter, the rod used for brazing, is an alloy of copper and zinc. Use borax flux for brazing.

Making soldered joints

Joints must be prepared and held securely in place for all soldering processes. Joints will always be stronger if they have a mechanical strength built into them such as interlocking or slotting together. Fire bricks should be used around joints to retain and concentrate the heat from the flame.

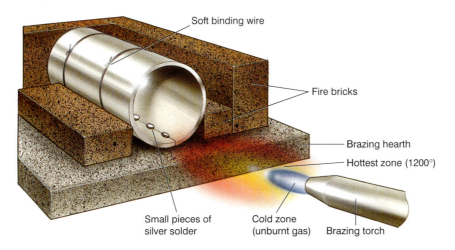

Figure 15.5 *Silver soldering.*

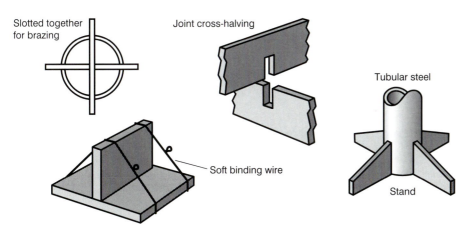

Figure 15.6 *Joint preparation for brazing.*

WELDING

Welding joins materials together by the process of melting the parent metal and allowing it to fuse together as it solidifies. It is a permanent joining process best suited to steel but can also be applied to aluminium provided that the surface is shielded from oxidisation by an inert gas or a controlled atmosphere. With all welding preparation is necessary to ensure a sound joint. This is particularly true with thick material.

117

There are three welding processes common to school workshops although familiarity with any one of these should ensure competence when answering examination questions.

- **Oxy-acetylene welding** uses a mixture of the two gasses to produce a very hot flame (3500°C) that is used to melt the metal. The molten pool is moved along the joint line and additional material is introduced to it from a filler rod of the same metal.

- **Electric arc welding** makes use of a flux coated filler rod that acts as an electrode. A low voltage, high electrical current is struck between the electrode rod and the workpiece. The heat produced by the resulting electric arc melts both the rod and the material to be joined. The rod acts as a filler for the joint and so is consumed in the welding process.

- **Metal Inert Gas (MIG) welding** is another electric arc welding process. In this instance a continuous wire electrode is fed from a coil through the welding torch. The process is shielded by an inert gas enabling it to be used for aluminium welding. MIG welding has developed into a very controllable process and is now one of the most popular applications for robots.

Figure 15.7 *The oxy-acetylene welding process.*

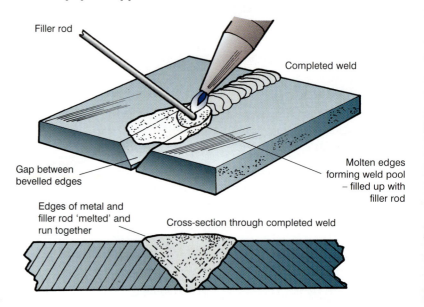

Filler rod

Completed weld

Gap between bevelled edges

Molten edges forming weld pool – filled up with filler rod

Edges of metal and filler rod 'melted' and run together

Cross-section through completed weld

SAFETY

Remember the safety issues associated with heat processes.

- Eye protection;
- Clothing;
- Overcrowding of the work area;
- Care with the placing of hot materials after the process.

Check yourself

QUESTIONS

A

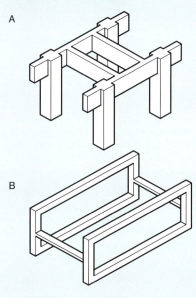

B

Figure 15.8 *Two designs for the underframe of a coffee table.*

Figure 15.8 shows two design ideas for the underframe of a coffee table.

Design A is to be made from hardwood, and design B is to made from square section steel tube.

The questions below relate to the coffee table designs shown.

Q1 Produce sketches of the joints that are involved in the construction of the two different frames. There are two different joints associated with each frame.

Q2 Suggest a sequence of assembly for each of the frames.

Q3 The coffee table top is to made from hardwood. One of the problems with wood is that some degree of movement with time is always encountered. With this in mind sketch a method of attaching both of the frames to a hardwood top.

REMEMBER! Cover the answers if you want to.

ANSWERS

A1

Design A

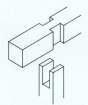

This joint would be used to join the legs to the long rails.

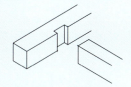

This joint would be used to join the cross pieces to the rails.

Design B

This joint is used for the corners; it is bent round then brazed or welded.

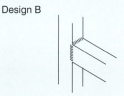

This is used for the cross members; it is a butt joint that is brazed or welded all round.

TUTORIALS

T1 *This is a good answer but it could have been improved had the joints for design A been given a name. The first is a bridle joint and the joint between the cross piece and the rail is a housing joint.*

The joints for design B are very appropriate, to bend the mitre joint on the corner is much better than cutting it off completely.

ANSWERS

A2 Design A the wooden frame: The long rails and the cross pieces should be assembled first so that they can be clamped together laying flat. The legs can then be attached.

Design B the tubular steel frame: The rectangular side frames should be welded up square first and then joined together by the cross members.

A3

Design A

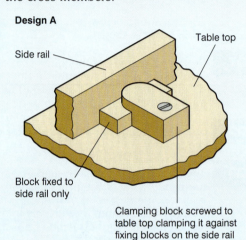

Side rail

Table top

Block fixed to side rail only

Clamping block screwed to table top clamping it against fixing blocks on the side rail

Design B

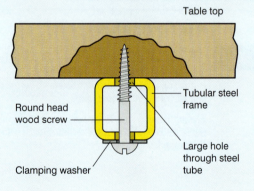

Table top

Round head wood screw

Clamping washer

Tubular steel frame

Large hole through steel tube

TUTORIALS

T2 *This is the correct sequence but an answer of this type will always benefit from the use of sketches.*

T3 *Both of the ideas are good and will do the job but there are other equally good alternatives that would satisfy the requirements of the design. The methods of illustrating the designs are well suited to the solutions. Design A is an isometric sketch but design B needs to communicate the internal detail so a sectional view is used.*

Note *Movement with wood is always a problem. If wooden boards panels are secured firmly then they tend to split: you may have seen this in old cupboards and doors. The solution is to accommodate the movement not to try and restrict it.*

KEY WORDS

These are the key words. Tick them if you think you know what they mean. Otherwise check on them.

fabrication	frame construction	soldering
assembly	halving joints	silver soldering
adhesive	dowel joints	brazing
PVA	dovetail joints	oxy-acetylene welding
Tensol cement	butt joint	electric arc welding
epoxy resin	lap joint	MIG welding
contact adhesive	comb joint	
hot-melt glue	housing joint	

EXAMINATION CHECKLIST FOR THIS SECTION

After studying making you should be able to use and demonstrate understanding of a range of tools, skills and techniques for:

- marking out and the correct preparation of materials;
- hand tool and machine tool manufacturing, including the use of CAM (computer-aided manufacturing);
- hot and cold deforming and reforming, as appropriate, of wood, metal and plastic materials;
- the fabrication and assembly of products.

EXAM PRACTICE

Sample Student's Answers & Examiner's Comments

1 (a) Complete the table by matching the fixing component with the correct tool.

State the correct name for each tool.

The first example is done for you.

FIXING COMPONENT	SELECTED TOOL	NAME OF SUITABLE TOOL
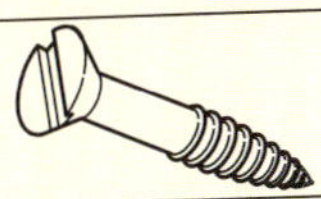	F	Screwdriver
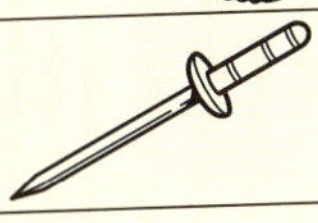	G	Pop rivet gun
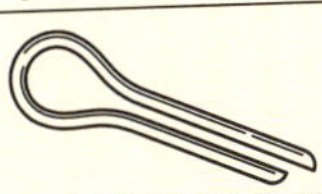	A	Hammer
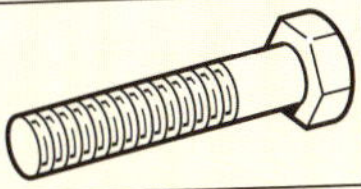	E	Spanner
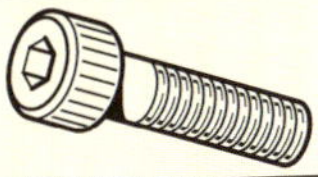	C	Allen key

(8 marks)

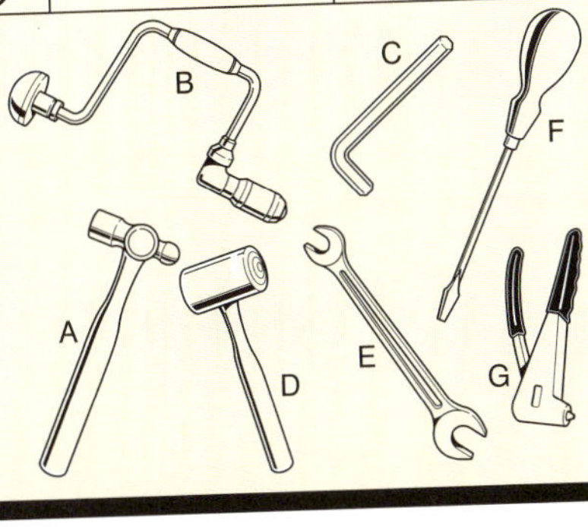

EXAMINER'S COMMENTS

(a) *These are correct responses to this question. Quick questions of this type are common at the beginning of the examination. The split cotter pin may be unfamiliar but it is a common fixing device to hold wheels and pulleys onto shafts. The hammer is used to tap it into place.*

121

MAKING

EXAMINER'S COMMENTS

(b) *Safety is an important issue and questions about safety are very popular on examination papers. They are usually straightforward to answer.*

(c) *This question is testing your understanding of a simple assembly process that you should be familiar with through your own project work. If you make sure that you carry out your practical work to the highest standard then you will be equipped to answer questions of this nature.*

(d) *This is another question testing knowledge of good practice. You should not place plastic sheet on a heater and just leave it because it will overheat in a small area and blister. The cause of the blistering is actually moisture trapped within the plastic. Once blistering has taken place the appearance is spoilt and it cannot be corrected.*

(b) State **two** safety precautions which need to be taken before switching on a drilling machine. It is set up to drill 6 mm diameter holes in a flat piece of 9 mm thick 100 square of mild steel.

1 *Wear goggles*

2 *Make sure that the work is held securely*

(4 marks)

(c) **Wood** is joined to **wood** using this type of screw.

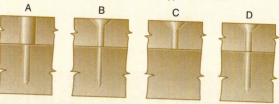

A   B   C   D

Complete the following statements. The first has been done as an example.

A is incorrect because *there is no countersink for the head of the screw.*

B is correct because *there is a countersunk clearance hole in the top piece and a pilot hole in the bottom piece of wood.*

State a reason why C and D are incorrect.
C is wrong because there is no pilot hole.
D is wrong because the clearance hole goes too deep and the screw would just drop in without fixing them together.

(5 marks)

(d) The drawing shows the outside of a right-angled bend made from a piece of 3 mm thick plastic. During heating, the plastic gave off a distinct smell and made a crackling sound. The surface of the plastic was filled with tiny holes and bubbles.

(i) State what caused this problem.
The plastic became too hot.

(2 marks)

(ii) State how it might be prevented.
This could be prevented by taking more care, not having the plastic too close to the strip heater and remembering to turn it over regularly as it is heating up.

(2 marks)

(e) A piece of aluminium of 9 mm diameter cracked when it was bent cold.

(i) State what caused this problem.

The problem is likely to be caused by work hardening.

(2 marks)

(ii) State how it might be prevented.

Work hardening can be prevented by annealing or by bending the metal hot.

(2 marks)

(f) The drawing below shows a corner bracket cut from solid wood. During fixing it snapped at point X.

X ←

(i) State what caused it to snap at point X.

It snapped due to the short grain.

(2 marks)

(ii) State how it might be prevented from snapping.

It could be prevented from snapping by having the grain going across the corner or by replacing the solid wood with plywood.

(2 marks)

EDEXCEL, London, 1997

EXAMINER'S COMMENTS

(e) The marks for this question will be awarded for the use of the correct terminology. 'Work hardening' is a key concept as is 'annealing' or 'normalising' which would also have been acceptable.

(f) This is a common accident to happen when working with solid wood. Short grain is a weakness and the answer given benefits from the suggestion that the solid wood could be replaced by plywood, a much better design solution.

Question to Answer

The answer to Question 2 can be found in Chapter 21.

2 Jewellers need to hold delicate items such as rings and brooches firmly without damage when working on them. Figure 1 shows a small jeweller's vice that is used for this purpose.

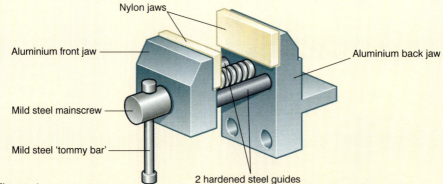

Figure 1

(a)   The aluminium back jaw is to be made by casting followed by machining.

    (i)   Sketch a pattern that could be used to make the back jaw.

          Indicate on your sketch the faces that will require finish machining.   **(4 marks)**

    (ii)   Sand casting is a potentially dangerous process.

          List four safety precautions that must be taken when carrying out
          sand casting.   **(4 marks)**

(b)   Figure 2 shows the 'tommy bar' and mainscrew assembly.

    The main screw has a hole at one end through which the 'tommy bar' fits.

    When assembled the 'tommy bar' is held in place but is free to slide
    through the hole in the mainscrew.

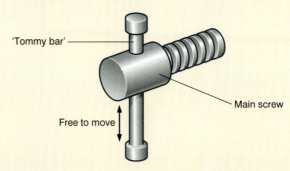

Figure 2

    (i)   Name three tools needed to set up accurately and clamp the
         mainscrew to a drilling machine table for drilling.   **(3 marks)**

    (ii)   Use an exploded sketch and notes to show how the 'tommy bar'
         could be made and assembled so that it is attached to the
         mainscrew and is still free to slide.   **(6 marks)**

MEG, 1998

SYSTEMS AND SUB-SYSTEMS

A system is a concept that exists within technology and technological design. This means that it is a way of looking at things; it is a way of trying to understand how they work so that you are more able to make design decisions.

A system is a group of components or parts that work together to perform a task. Systems can be based on mechanisms, pneumatics, electronics, structures or be combinations of any of these. The key point about systems is that it is not always necessary to know how each part of a system works in order for you to assemble the system and be able to use it. It does, however, help if you understand what is happening for these occasions when you want to add to or improve the system to make things work better, and for those occasions when things go wrong.

A bicycle is a good example of a system. It has a frame, wheels, peddles, gears, brakes and often lights. These things together make up a bicycle, they can be regarded as parts within the 'bicycle system'. An analysis of this system will reveal that it is in fact made up of other systems. These are called **sub-systems**.

Analysis of a bicycle system:

- Frame – a structural sub-system;
- Wheels – a structural sub-system;
- Drive system (peddles and gears) – a mechanical sub-system;
- Braking system – a mechanical sub-system;
- Lights – an electrical sub-system.

By understanding the bicycle as a system that is made up of sub-systems, it is possible to look at any problem or redesign associated with a bicycle and break it down so that you consider only the appropriate sub-system. For example, if the bicycle does not stop efficiently the problem must be within the braking sub-system.

Systems are sometimes shown as 'block diagrams' where an **input**, often in the form of energy, goes through a **process** within the system in order to produce a desired **output**. In our bicycle example the effort of pushing down on the peddles is converted into forward movement by the bicycle.

CHAPTER 16
SYSTEMS AND SUB-SYSTEMS

Examination requirements

All of the examination boards require some knowledge of mechanical and structural systems and their applications, but you should check your particular syllabus to determine the level of detail needed.

For D&T Resistant Materials examinations none of the examination boards require any detailed knowledge of electronic systems. They do, however, require an awareness of the application of electronic and microprocessor controlled systems and this is provided in sufficient detail through the systems examples in this chapter. You should also refer to computer-aided design and computer-aided manufacturing systems in Chapters 10, 13 and 19.

Figure 16.1

Figure 16.2 Energy input to the pedals is converted into forward motion.

Figure 16.3 *System block diagram.*

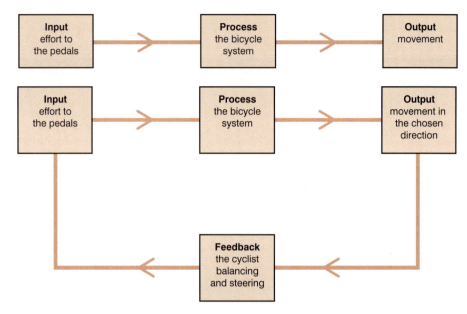

Figure 16.4 *System with feedback control loop.*

Figure 16.3 shows the bicycle in the form of a block diagram. The problem here however is that this is a system out of control. It needs somebody to steer it to make it go where you want it to. Look at Fig. 16.4: this block diagram has **feedback** in the form of a **control loop**. Having somebody in control enables the output movement to be in a controlled direction.

Control doesn't always have to be provided by a person. In a heating system control is often provided by a thermostat; this is an example of electronic control. A thermostat is a device that tells the heating boiler that the room is hot enough and it can stop providing more heat. A thermostatically controlled heating system saves valuable energy resources and reduces running costs. Figure 16.5 shows a heating system and how the system can be represented in the form of a block diagram.

Figure 16.5 *A controlled heating system.*

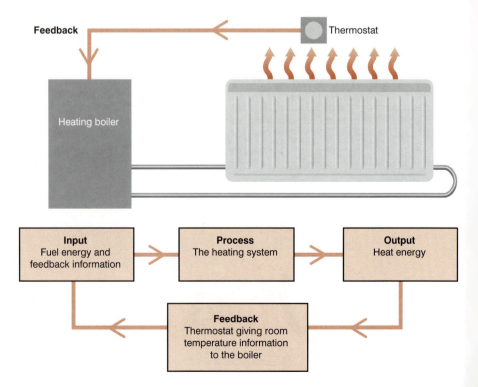

ELECTRONICS AND MICROPROCESSOR CONTROL

Microprocessors are at the heart of most control systems. The cost of such devices is reducing so dramatically that it is far cheaper to use only a fraction of their potential within a simple system than to construct a dedicated electronic circuit. A microprocessor is the part of a computer that does all of the processing and calculating. It is important to think beyond the normal view of a computer (in a large box connected to a keyboard and monitor) and see the microprocessor as the process within an 'input-process-output' model as in Fig. 16.6.

Figure 16.6 *Microprocessors are at the heart of many control systems.*

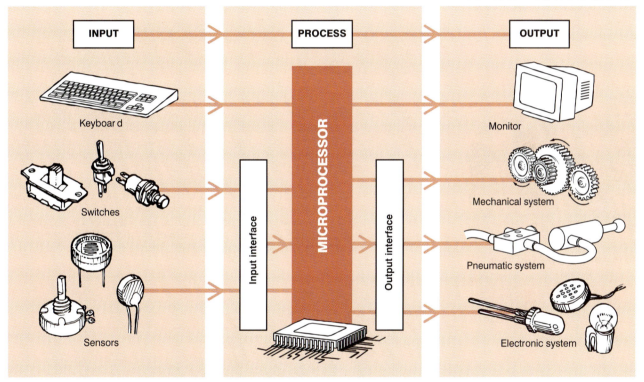

Microprocessor control **input** devices include:

- **Switches** that provide a digital input to the system; they are either on or off. Switches can be manual in operation or tilt switches and proximity switches. They can be normally open or normally closed, latching or push button.

- **Sensors** that can sense light, heat, moisture, sound, movement, infra red or changes in voltage. Sensors can be processed to provide a digital signal or an analogue input signal that provides a range of input levels.

Microprocessor control **output** devices include:

- **Lights and indicators** to show what is happening within the system;

- **Motors** to drive machines, robots vehicles, etc;

- **Displays** to provide information from the time on a watch to the score at a football match;

- **Relays, switches and solenoids** to interface with other systems such as hydraulic and pneumatic systems.

Figure 16.7 *Industrial robots are controlled by microprocessors.*

Figure 16.8 *A modern office environment is dependent upon computer systems.*

Increasingly within everyday life microprocessors are taking control of systems. Whole buildings and offices can be controlled by a microprocessor control system in order to support the human activities that take place within it. Such a system will continually monitor activity in order to make efficient use of energy and resources. The sub-systems could include:

- Heating, lighting and ventilation – all saving energy when areas are not in use;
- Security – monitoring movement in and around the building;
- Electronic mail and Internet links – sorting and downloading when the office systems are not in use;
- 'Smart' lifts – learning the habits of occupants so that they can anticipate demand and be waiting at the appropriate floors.

SYSTEM ANALYSIS AND PERFORMANCE

As systems become large and complex it becomes more important to be able to recognise and analyse the system and its sub-systems. Within a system such as a car there are many sub-systems that require different skills and materials to produce them. For example, the design and production of a car seat is very different from that of a gear box. The seat manufacturer does not need to know any details of the gearbox of the car.

Whole factories can be viewed as systems in order to plan and understand the way that complex manufacturing processes relate to each other and rely upon communication and the movement of components; see Chapter 19. Systems analysis is the process of breaking the system down to understand how it works so that you are in a position to be able to improve its performance.

Check yourself

QUESTIONS

Q1 Explain why a 'systems' approach to electronics is a better way of being able to understand complex electronics.

Q2 Draw a block diagram of an audio system of the type shown in Fig. 16.9.

Q3 Think of a microprocessor as the heart of a computer system.

List five input devices and five output devices that could be connected to the microprocessor.

Figure 16.9

ANSWERS

A1 A systems approach enables you to more easily understand complex systems.

A2

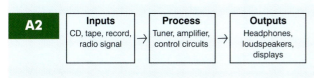

Inputs		Process		Outputs
CD, tape, record, radio signal	→	Tuner, amplifier, control circuits	→	Headphones, loudspeakers, displays

A3 Input devices – keyboard, mouse, switch, temperature sensor, scanner.

Output devices – monitor, printer, robotic arm, concert lighting system, CNC machine tool.

TUTORIALS

T1 *Correct. The whole point of a systems approach is so that you can understand how systems function without having to get involved with all of the detail. This enables you to 'interact' with the system. This means that you are able to design, develop, update or maintain elements of the system without having to interfere with all of it.*

T2 *An audio system is a good example of a system whose parts you can change if you understand it. In a system like this you can add or take away a CD player or tape player without doing anything to the process or output parts of the system. Equally you could change the output from loudspeakers to headphones and the system would continue to operate from any of the inputs.*

T3 *This is a good range of examples; there are of course many more. Be sure to think broadly when asked questions of this type. Think in terms of your own experiences: keyboard, monitor, etc. and also in industrial contexts: robot and CNC machine.*

KEY WORDS

These are the key words. Tick them if you think you know what they mean. Otherwise check on them.

system	**output**	**sensor**
sub-system	**feedback**	**system analysis**
input	**control loop**	**system performance**
process	**microprocessor**	

CHAPTER 17

MECHANICAL AND STRUCTURAL SYSTEMS

MECHANISMS AND MECHANICAL SYSTEMS

Mechanical systems are systems that use mechanisms to perform a particular function. All mechanisms have moving parts and mechanical systems always involve movement and energy.

Can openers and door handles are all examples of simple mechanisms. Complex mechanisms such as washing machines, sewing machines, lawn mowers and cars are examples of **mechanical systems**. They are made up of many simpler mechanisms, sub-systems, that all work together.

MECHANICAL ADVANTAGE

Mechanical systems are always designed so that people gain some advantage from using them. They enable you to do something that you could not otherwise do because it would be too hard or too slow. A vice enables you to grip tighter than you could with your hands and a bicycle enables you to get from one place to another quicker than you could by walking. Both mechanical systems give you an advantage. This is called **mechanical advantage**.

Mechanical advantage is an important concept. The mechanical advantage (MA) of a system can be given a value. If the effort that you put into a mechanical system results in an output that is greater than that effort, then the value of the MA will be greater than 1. For example, consider the vice shown in Fig. 17.1. You might apply a force of 10 Newtons (10 N) and be able to grip something with a force of 80 Newtons (80 N), the MA will be 8 : 1 or 8. This is calculated by dividing the output (80 N) by the input (10 N).

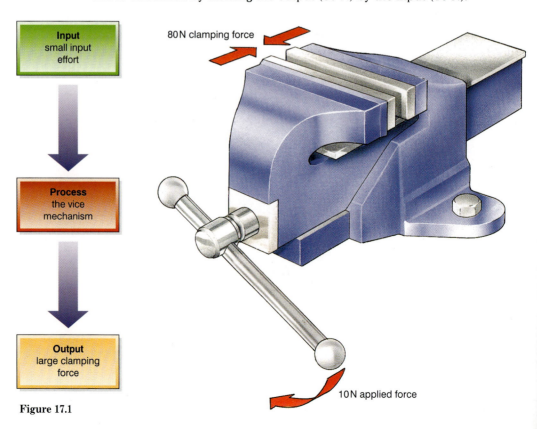

Input
small input effort

Process
the vice mechanism

Output
large clamping force

80 N clamping force

10 N applied force

Figure 17.1

MOVEMENT

The four types of motion (movement) associated with mechanical systems are:

- **Rotary motion** like a wheel or the hands of a clock;
- **Linear motion** meaning in a straight line;
- **Oscillating motion** like a clock pendulum;
- **Reciprocating motion** meaning backwards and forwards or up and down, like the needle of a sewing machine.

The function of many mechanisms is to change the motion in some way either by making it faster or slower, or by changing its nature, for example from rotary to linear. A lock mechanism will change the rotary motion of the key to the linear motion of the lock. A hand whisk is an example of a mechanism that changes rotary motion in one plane into rotary motion in another.

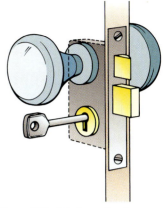

Figure 17.2 *A lock mechanism.*

LEVERS

Levers are amongst the oldest form of mechanical system. At its simplest a lever consists of a rigid bar that **pivots** on a fixed point. The input to this system is called the **effort** and the output is called the **load**.

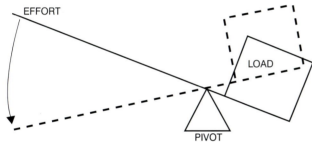

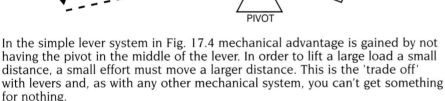

Figure 17.3 *A hand whisk.*

Figure 17.4

In the simple lever system in Fig. 17.4 mechanical advantage is gained by not having the pivot in the middle of the lever. In order to lift a large load a small distance, a small effort must move a larger distance. This is the 'trade off' with levers and, as with any other mechanical system, you can't get something for nothing.

Velocity ratio

The relationship between how far the effort and load move within mechanical systems is known as the velocity ratio (VR).

If the effort moves 500 mm and the load 100 mm then the ratio is 500 divided by 100. This gives a VR of 5 : 1 or 5.

Figure 17.5 shows a simple lever system that involves a crowbar lifting a box. The effort moves 600 mm to raise the box 150 mm.

The mechanical advantage of the system is

$$\text{MA} = \frac{\textbf{Load}}{\textbf{Effort}} = \frac{50\text{ N}}{10\text{ N}} = \frac{5}{1} = 5 : 1 \text{ or } \textbf{5}$$

The velocity ratio of the system is

$$\text{VR} = \frac{\textbf{Distance moved by Effort}}{\textbf{Distance moved by Load}} = \frac{600\text{ mm}}{150\text{ mm}} = \frac{6}{1.5} = 4 : 1 \text{ or } \textbf{4}$$

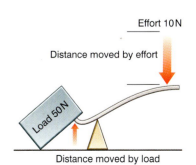

Figure 17.5

Figure 17.6 *Three classes of lever.*

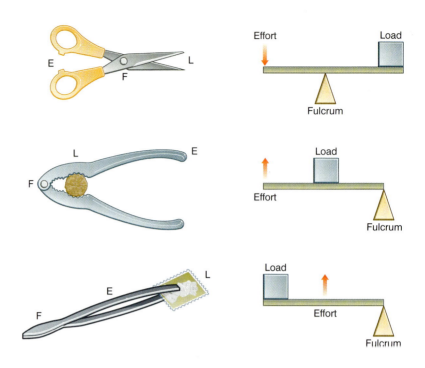

Classes of lever

The lever system in Fig. 17.5 is that of a Class 1 lever. Figure 17.6 shows the other classifications of lever.

- **Class 1** Crowbar and scissors. (Scissors are two levers acting around the same pivot.)
- **Class 2** The load is nearer to the pivot or fulcrum as in nut crackers and a wheel barrow.
- **Class 3** Tweezers and similar lever systems where the forces involved are small. Class 3 levers have a mechanical advantage that is less then 1.

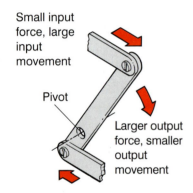

Small input force, large input movement

Pivot

Larger output force, smaller output movement

Figure 17.7 *The linkage in this example has one side of the pivot longer than the other so that it will have mechanical advantage.*

LINKAGES

Linkages are the connecting elements within mechanical systems. They transfer forces and can be used to bring about changes in direction.

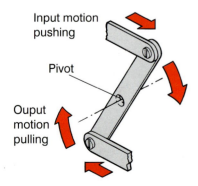

Input motion pushing

Pivot

Ouput motion pulling

Figure 17.8 *This linkage is used to transfer the direction of the input force.*

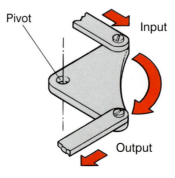

Pivot

Input

Output

Figure 17.9 *This linkage, called a bell crank, is used to transfer a force through 90°.*

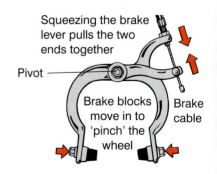

Squeezing the brake lever pulls the two ends together

Pivot

Brake blocks move in to 'pinch' the wheel

Brake cable

Figure 17.10 *The linkages within a bicycle brake.*

CAMS AND CRANKS

Cams are used in many reciprocating mechanisms to change rotary motion to up and down or backwards and forwards motion. In car engines they are used to open and close valves and contact breaker points and to operate fuel pumps.

Figure 17.11 *Cams within a car engine.*

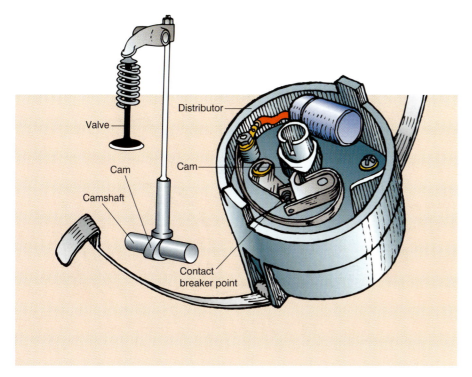

Valve

Distributor

Cam

Cam

Camshaft

Contact breaker point

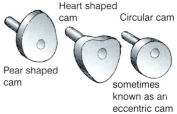

Heart shaped cam

Circular cam

Pear shaped cam

sometimes known as an eccentric cam

Figure 17.12

Rotary cams are the most common type of cam. They are often made from hardened steel to reduce wear but they can be made from acrylic or wood.

The cam is fitted to a rotating shaft and has a **follower**, which rests on it and moves up and down as the shaft rotates. Cams vary in profile according to the output movement required.

Cranks are used in a similar fashion to cams but the output motion is always reciprocating and uniform. Cranks are useful to gain a large rotational output from a smaller rotational input as in a child's tricycle and the 'pop-up' pull along toy in Fig. 17.14 where the cranked axle provides reciprocating motion.

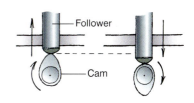

Follower

Cam

Figure 17.13

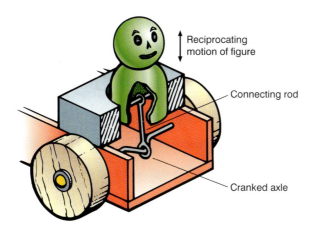

Reciprocating motion of figure

Connecting rod

Cranked axle

Figure 17.14

133

PULLEY SYSTEMS

Pulley systems use a belt or belts to transmit power and motion from one part of a mechanical system to another. When the pulley on the input shaft (driver) is larger than the pulley on the output shaft (driven) then the output speed will be faster than the input speed; see Fig. 17.15.

Stepped pulleys like those used on a drilling machine are used to effect changes of speed by moving the belt between the different pairs of pulleys.

Figure 17.15

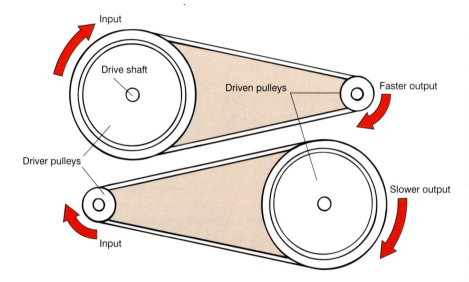

Figure 17.16 *A drilling machine with stepped pulleys.*

GEAR SYSTEMS

Gear systems are also used to transmit power and motion around mechanical systems. A system of gears is known as a gear train, the input gear of the system is known as the driver and the output gear is called the driven. The other gears are called idler or intermediate gears. Do not call gears 'cogs'.

Figure 17.17 shows some gear systems; notice the way that the direction of rotation changes throughout the system. The idler gears effect the direction of rotation but they have no effect upon the output speed. The ratio of the gear system is the relationship between the number of teeth on the driver gear and the number of teeth on the driven gear.

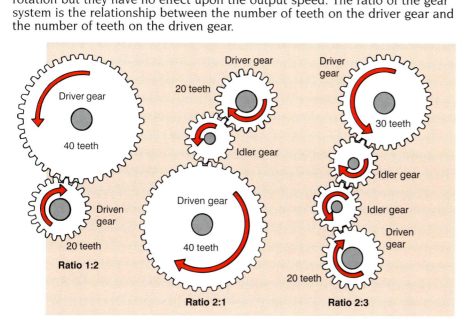

Figure 17.17 *Gear ratios.*

Figure 17.18 *Bevel gears.*

In the first example there is a 40 teeth driver gear and a 20 teeth driven gear; for every turn of the driver gear the driven gear will turn twice. The formula is:

$$\text{Gear ratio} = \frac{\text{driver}}{\text{driven}} = \frac{40}{20} = \frac{2}{1}$$

This is written as gear ratio 1 : 2 (1 turn of the driver = 2 turns of the driven)

In the second example the opposite is the case: a 20 teeth driver and a 40 teeth driven. Remember to ignore the idler gears. The ratio is:

$$\text{Gear ratio} = \frac{\text{driver}}{\text{driven}} = \frac{20}{40} = \frac{1}{2}$$

This is a gear ratio of 2 : 1 (2 turns of the driver = 1 turn of the driven)

This is a speed reducing gear system.

Special types of gears

- **Bevel gears** are used in pairs to change the rotation through 90°.
- **Worm and wormwheel** also change rotation through 90°. The ratio of this system is very low as the worm actually has only 1 tooth. The worm must be the driver; the wormwheel is not able to drive the worm.
- **Rack and pinion** change rotary to linear motion. The rack is really a flattened-out gear.

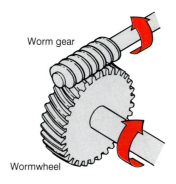

Figure 17.19 *Worm and wormwheel.*

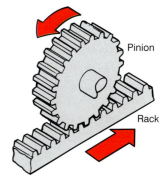

Figure 17.20 *Rack and pinion.*

135

ENERGY AND EFFICIENCY

All mechanical systems transfer energy from the input to the output of the system. If all of the energy that goes in was able to come out at the end, the system would be said to be 100% efficient. Unfortunately no systems are anywhere near this efficient. Energy is used up and effectively lost by the system itself. Energy is lost in the form of generated heat, noise, and unwanted wear. Mechanical systems can be made more efficient if the components are well-made, lubricated and properly maintained.

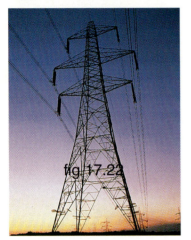

Figure 17.21 *Shell structure.*

Figure 17.22 *Frame structure.*

STRUCTURAL SYSTEMS

There are two principal types of structure:

- **Monocoque** or **shell structures** such as eggs, cans and car bodies;
- **Frame structures** are systems made up of members that work together such as a skeleton or an electricity pylon.

All structures must be capable of withstanding the loads and forces for which they are designed. This does not however mean that they must always be rigid; some structures are designed to be flexible. Flexible structures are often more able to withstand **dynamic forces**. These are forces that change direction and quickly become more intense. Car body shells are able to flex because this improves the road-holding capability; even buildings, such as those built in earthquake regions of the world, can be made flexible.

Structures are subject to the following types of forces:

- **Compression** A pushing force that tries to squash or shorten;
- **Tension** A pulling force that attempts to stretch or lengthen;
- **Bending** Forces that attempt to cause bending deformation;
- **Shear** 'Sliding' forces that act in opposite directions;
- **Torsion** Forces that cause twisting;
- **Centrifugal** Outward forces that result from a rotating action.

Figure 17.24 *Types of forces.*

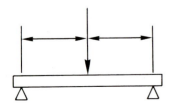

Figure 17.23 *This type of chair combines a tubular steel frame structure with a polypropylene shell structure.*

BEAMS AND BRIDGES

The simplest way of supporting a load across a gap is to use a beam. This is the simplest form of bridge, like using a tree trunk to span a stream. What is actually happening is that the forces that act upon the beam or bridge, caused by any load upon it and the weight of the beam itself, are being transferred to the support either side, as in Fig. 17.25.

If the beam has a force that acts in the middle or one that is spread equally across it, like its own weight, then the forces at either end are equal. Together they are also equal to the total force acting downwards. These are said to be equal and opposite reactions. If the force is moved towards one end then that end needs to react more, and subsequently the other end reacts less, but together they are always equal to the total downwards force.

Figure 17.25 *A beam.*

Look at the two examples shown in Fig. 17.26. In A the reactions at X and Y will be 250 N each. In B the reactions will be 333.3 N at X and 166.6 N at Y.

In practice the major design issue with beam construction is making the beam as light as possible without reducing its strength and risking it failing in use. This is called the '**strength-to-weight ratio**'. The cross-sectional shape of modern beams have enabled them to become lighter without compromising strength. Figure 17.27 shows a range of beam sections. Some beams are castellated to reduce the weight still further.

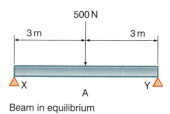

Beam in equilibrium

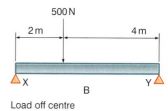

Load off centre

Figure 17.26

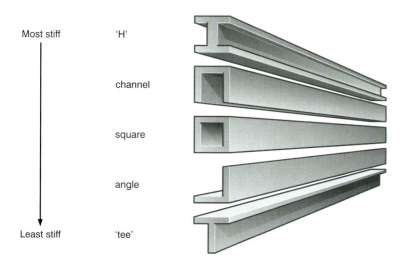

Figure 17.27 *Beam sections.*

When beams bend the top surface is compressed and the bottom surface is stretched as in Fig. 17.28. You can see, therefore, that the important areas for a beam to be strong are the top and bottom. The strength at the centre line is not important. This is why castellation and hollowing, etc. make little difference to the strength of a beam.

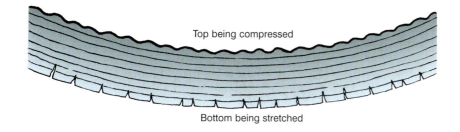

Top being compressed

Bottom being stretched

Figure 17.28 *A beam bending.*

Cantilevers

Cantilevers are beams that are held and supported at one end only, like a shelf bracket. Bridges that look like beam bridges or arched bridges are often two cantilevers that meet in the middle. Many motorway bridges are built like this.

Arched and suspension bridges

Arched and suspension bridges have been used for many centuries. Like a simple beam bridge they transfer the load to the bank of the river or side of the valley. With an arched bridge, the load is transferred through the structure of the arch to the bridges supports (abutments). The suspension bridge transfers the load through cables or ropes to the anchor points on the bank.

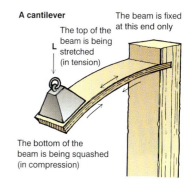

Figure 17.29 *A cantilever.*

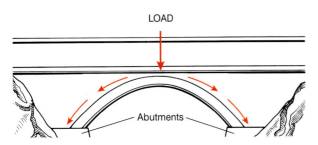

Figure 17.30 *In arched bridges the load is transferred to the bridge supports (abutments). This is a compressive force.*

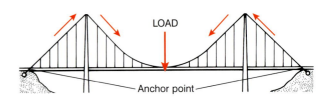

Figure 17.31 *In suspension bridges the load is transferred to the anchor points of the cables. This is a tensile force.*

STABILITY

A stable structure is one that is safe and will not fail under the conditions for which it is designed. Stability in many fabricated products is dependent upon them being well made with sound joints, etc. Structures often gain stability from having a triangulated structure. There are many examples of triangulated structures such as house roofs, bicycle frames, electricity pylons, and girder bridges.

Figure 17.32 *Triangulated structures.*

Check yourself

QUESTIONS

Q1 a) Give examples of mechanical systems that change:
    i)   rotary motion to linear motion;
    ii) linear motion to rotary motion;
    iii) rotary motion to oscillating motion.
   b) In terms of motion changes analyse a car drive system.

Q2 Figure 17.33 shows a gear system. The smaller gear is connected to a motor running at 3240 rpm. Calculate the output speed of the system.

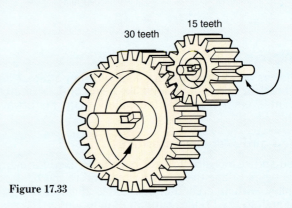

30 teeth   15 teeth

Figure 17.33

QUESTIONS

Q3 The chain and sprocket drive system of a bicycle is similar to a pulley drive system. What advantage does the chain and sprocket have over a pulley system?

Q4 Describe the difference between shell and frame structures. Give one example of each structural system.

Q5 Look back at Fig. 17.26, beam B. If the 500 N force was acting 1 m from X and 5 m from Y what then would be the X and Y reactions?

REMEMBER! Cover the answers if you want to.

ANSWERS

A1
a)
  i)   woodwork vice
  ii)   ratchet screwdriver
  iii)   car windscreen wipers

b)
  1   The reciprocating motion of the pistons is changed into rotary motion by the crank shaft.
  2   The rotary motion of the drive shaft, through the gear box, turns the wheels.
  3   The rotary motion of the wheels is changed into linear motion of the car through contact with the road.

A2 The gear ratio is 2 : 1.

The output speed will therefore be
$\frac{3240}{2} = 1620$ rpm

A3 The chain cannot slip over the sprockets whereas a pulley drive belt can slip.

A4 A shell structure is a continuous form like a dome shape or a drinks can. A frame structure is made up of different members that work together like the Eiffel Tower.

A5 The reaction at X would be 416.6 N and the

TUTORIALS

T1 *Questions sometimes assume that you have some knowledge of common technological systems, such as a car or a bicycle. You should always try to develop an understanding of those types of things with which you may come into contact on a regular basis.*

T2 *A very simple calculation like this can gain you easy marks. Always remember the units, in this case rpm (revolutions per minute).*

T3 *Another question that expects you to be able to apply your technological knowledge to answer a straightforward question.*

T4 *A good answer with suitable examples.*

T5 *By looking at this problem and applying a little logic you can see that as the force moves towards a reaction so one reaction increases and the other decreases. There is a process and formula for more complex examples of these problems called 'taking moments'. This is beyond the range of the current examination syllabuses.*

KEY WORDS

These are the key words. Tick them if you think you know what they mean. Otherwise check on them.

mechanism	gear ratio
mechanical advantage	bevel gears
rotary	worm and wormwheel
linear	rack and pinion
oscillating	energy
reciprocating	efficiency
lever	monocoque structure
pivot	frame structure
fulcrum	dynamic force
effort	compression
load	tension
velocity ratio	bending
lever classification	shear
linkages	torsion
cam	centrifugal
crank	beam
follower	strength-to-weight ratio
pulley	stability
gears	triangulation
gear train	cantilever

EXAMINATION CHECKLIST FOR THIS SECTION

After studying systems and control you should be able to:

- develop and control systems and sub-systems;
- demonstrate an understanding of the concepts associated with an 'input-process-output' model and appreciate the need for feedback within such a system to ensure stability;
- recognise and use mechanical, electronic, structural and process systems;
- identify the common components used in mechanical and structural systems.

EXAM PRACTICE

Sample Student's Answers & Examiner's Comments

1 The table below contains a list of everyday products.

Tick the boxes to show which type of system is used in the operation of each product.

The first one has been done for you.

PRODUCT	MECHANICAL SYSTEM	ELECTRICAL OR ELECTRONIC SYSTEM	
Food mixer	✓	✓	
G-clamp	✓		(1 mark)
Digital alarm clock		✓	(1 mark)
Clothes peg	✓		(1 mark)
Microwave oven	✓	✓	(1 mark)
CD Walkman	✓	✓	(1 mark)

These are correct responses to this question. Quick questions of this type are common at the beginning of the examination. You will notice that the example that is done for you has two ticks: this is to indicate to you that two ticks is an acceptable response.

2 A hedge trimmer uses an electric motor to make one blade move backwards and forwards over the top of another similar blade. A simple sketch of the blades and motor is shown below.

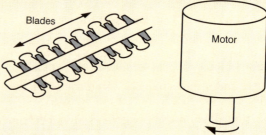

Blades

Motor

(a) Using sketches and notes, show a suitable mechanism that will make one of the blades move, as shown in the diagram above, when the motor turns.

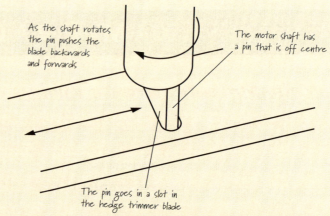

As the shaft rotates the pin pushes the blade backwards and forwards

The motor shaft has a pin that is off centre

The pin goes in a slot in the hedge trimmer blade

(b) To reduce the output speed of a motor, a worm and wheel is often used. Why might a worm and wheel be preferred to a gear train?

A worm and wormwheel takes up less space with fewer components than the gear train that would be needed to get the same kind of reduction.

AQA NEAB, 1998

Question to Answer

The answer to Question 3 can be found in Chapter 21.

3 Shown below is part of an internal view of a hand lawn mower. The intended speed ratio between the steel roller and the blades is 5 : 1.

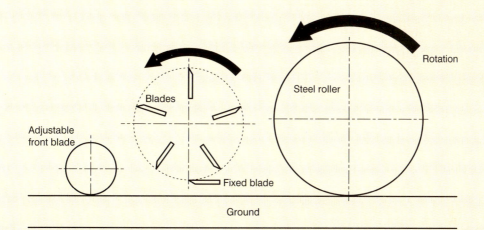

(i) Add appropriate detail to a copy of the sketch and explain fully how:
  • a mechanism would make the blades rotate in the same direction as the roller (3 marks)
  • a speed ratio of 5 : 1 would be produced (2 marks)
  • the fixed blade would remain a fixed distance above the ground (3 marks)

(ii) Show how the speed ratio has been calculated. (2 marks)

(iii) Name the mechanism you have used. (1 mark)

(iv) Name one other mechanism which would achieve the same ratio. (1 mark)

(v) Which of the two mechanisms do you consider the more suitable?
Give the reasons for your choice. (2 marks)

AQA NEAB, 1998

DESIGN AND MARKETING

Manufacturers of products need to make profits and to do this they must capture and keep their share of the market. The continually increasing rate of change as a result of consumer demand and improvements in manufacturing technologies means that it is impossible to stand still.

Keeping a hold on the market can be done in a number of ways:

- **Introducing a new product** is a costly process and can involve large research and design departments (R & D) in many months of work. Industrial design is a disciplined activity and must be carried out with a clear understanding of the manufacturing capability and potential of the company.

- **Improving an existing product** is about selecting an existing product, analysing its performance specification and setting about making it perform better or more economically.

- **Re-styling** is essentially a cosmetic exercise to make an existing product look 'better' or more modern. This has the effect of making competitor's products look old or out of date. Consumers tend to buy on the basis of appearance and fashion rather than performance.

- **Reducing the manufacturing costs** by taking advantage of new materials and new technologies means the cost of manufacture can be reduced or productivity increased. Thus the profit is increased or the retail price reduced so that a greater share of the market is taken. Another method of reducing manufacturing costs is to move production to other areas of the world where labour costs are lower.

- **Marketing** sells products. The price must be right, the product must be right, the promotion must be right, and, for consumer goods, the point of sale must be right. These are the 4 'P's of marketing and they all work together for successful manufacturing companies.

Figure 18.1 *A wide range of flat-pack furniture using standard parts.*

Many manufacturers carry out some or all of the above all of the time. It is important to remember therefore that the cost implication of a continual process of design and development must be built into the selling price of products produced and sold. Designing takes time and so it costs money, new equipment and processes also require an investment, and advertising and promotion can be very expensive.

Companies may have their own R & D (research and development) departments or they may use design consultants to investigate the market and to develop designs. Often a combination of in-house and external consultants is used.

Development costs can be considerably reduced by using standard component parts and sub-assemblies across a range of products. Look at flat-pack furniture - you will find the same hinges and fixings on all furniture whether it is for the kitchen, bedroom, lounge or office. Using standard components enables manufacturers to reduce storage, administrative and assembly costs.

Figure 18.2 *The Sony Walkman when first introduced was a totally new entertainment product that became an immediate success despite the fact that market research suggested that this would not be the case.*

Manufacturers have to consider carefully all investment and predict the time-scale from when they start work on a project to when their investment is covered and they begin to move back into profit. This is called the break-even point.

THE TECHNOLOGY PUSH

When working to develop new or existing products, designers and manufacturers often make demands upon existing technologies that result in new materials, processes and ways of working. Meeting the demand of the marketplace is a common driving force for manufacturing industry. Often, however, a new technology is developed for one application that then sets in motion a 'technology push' that can then be applied to other new and innovative products. Leading-edge industries such as the computer and space industries have started many technology pushes that are now very common within communications and the home. A good example of this is Teflon, a material developed to provide a very low coefficient of friction coating for space flight, which now also provides a non-stick surface for cooking utensils.

Figure 18.3 *The Teflon used to coat these pans was originally developed for use in space!*

MODERN INDUSTRY

There is a great danger in thinking that the industrial processes used for manufacturing are simply larger versions of those that you are familiar with in school. This is certainly not the case. Industrial manufacturing in the developed world has, over the last thirty years, become a computer dependent and highly sophisticated enterprise that relies upon a technologically expert work-force.

Manufacturing development in the UK and the developed world has resulted from:

- competition from the developing world where labour costs are low;
- the adoption of new management and working practices developed principally in Japan;
- flexible working arrangements that use better qualified and multi-skilled personnel;
- large reduction in the size of the work-force;
- computer-based technologies (see also Chapter 19).

In most manufacturing, raw materials tend to be cheap. The expensive items are investment in new technology, time and people. Money has to be spent on new technologies to be competitive and enable time to be saved and the work-force reduced. If these are reduced by even a small margin then large savings can be made. Figure 18.4 shows machine tool manufacture in 1954. You can see several people and many familiar tools and machines.

Figure 18.4 *Yardley's machine tool manufacturers, Liverpool, 1954.*

In Fig. 18.5 you can see an automated manufacturing cell used to machine gear box casings for tractors. There are a very few people associated with this manufacturing cell. The gear boxes are the parts painted red and they are mounted on special vehicles on a U-shaped track system. As each casing arrives at the machining centre, it is identified by the system and all of the necessary machining processes are carried out. The process is fast, efficient and flexible.

Figure 18.5 *An automated U-shaped manufacturing cell carrying out a variety of machining processes on tractor transmission systems.*

As they are scaled up, many manufacturing processes become very sophisticated in order to achieve maximum efficiency and cost effectiveness.

Over the last 30 years manufacturing output per worker in the UK has increased in some areas by 100 times. This way a much larger demand is supplied by a much reduced work-force. This does, of course, have social implications but it is a trend that cannot possibly be reversed; in fact, it is one that is likely to increase.

Figure 18.6 *Blow moulded bottles for household cleaner.*

Figure 18.7 *Hot forged car components emerging from a fully automated forging process.*

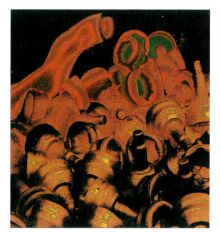

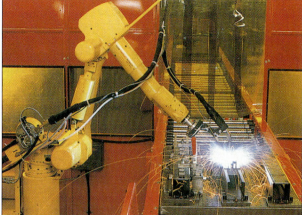

Figure 18.8 *A robot MIG welding.*

Figure 18.9 *Press-formed car body panels.*

Figure 18.10 *The Nissan car factory in Sunderland is amongst the world's best in terms of output per worker ratio.*

SCALE OF PRODUCTION

Types of manufacturing production are categorised according to their scale as follows:

- **Process production**, also known as **continuous production** Some processes such as steel manufacture are only economic if they are always kept running. Process production refers to the type of manufacture that is normally associated with primary processes such as refining, chemical manufacture and oil production. Process production requires a high investment in capital equipment.

- **Mass production** This is high volume production of products including personal computers, cars and televisions, and standardised sub-assemblies of these products like transformers and cathode ray tubes. As with process production, mass production requires specialised equipment but in this case often a large unskilled work-force particularly in assembly areas. Mass production processes are often broken down into small simple and easy-to-learn operations in order to provide the flexibility to move around an unskilled work-force.

- **Batch production** A batch can be any specified quantity of a product from a few to a few thousand. Batches or production runs

Figure 18.11

can be repeated any number of times as required. It is important with batch production that the work-force, the machines and the tooling are flexible and can change quickly from the batch production of one product to that of another. The change-over time is known as **down time**. Down time is non-productive and therefore expensive so it must be kept to a minimum.

● **Jobbing production**, also known as **one-off production** This refers to the manufacture of a single item usually produced to a specific customer's specification. This type of production has the highest cost per unit and includes products such as space craft, ships, bridges and individually designed jewellery. Jobbing production requires skilled personnel.

In reality most manufacturing is a combination of some of these types of production processes. Batch production often enables there to be variation to mass-produced products. When mass production of cars by Ford in America first meant that cars could be sold to ordinary people, each production line could produce one type in only one colour. Now it is possible even within mass production to have flexibility; each car progressing through a production line will have its own specification. This is achieved by producing ranges of engine sizes, wheel trims, upholstery types, etc. in small batches that can be fed into the mass-production process as required. Control of such systems has only become possible by using advanced integrated computer systems; see Chapter 19.

MANUFACTURING SYSTEMS

GCSE syllabuses make reference to a number of manufacturing systems as the means by which manufacturing is organised. These systems are really ways of organising different aspects of manufacture and they overlap each other. It is important to understand that a manufacturer does not use just one system or another. The several systems used are often compatible with each other.

Cell production

Production cells usually consist of a number of work-stations grouped together to produce a single component or a number of similar components. The work-

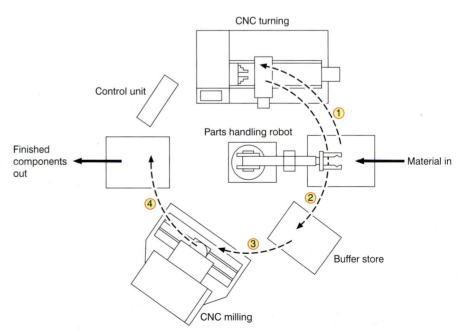

Figure 18.12 *Fully automated manufacturing cell with CNC turning and milling and robot parts handling.*

stations within a cell may be machining processes, hand processes, assembly or inspection. The cell may have a team of people with a team leader or it may be an automated cell. Production cells operate like mini-enterprises within a larger company. The production cell team is responsible for every aspect of production including quality control and scheduled maintenance.

In-line production and assembly

In-line systems are associated with mass production like the car assembly line in Fig. 18.11. Changes to lines are expensive to make, so in-line systems are less flexible than cell manufacture. There are advantages with this system as there are with all forms of mass production. Low cost, unskilled labour tends to be used with just a few semi-skilled people who are flexible and able to change tasks as required to ensure a smooth flow. Fig. 18.13 shows an in-line production process for wheel component manufacture. This particular system is semi-automated with the operator moving between work-stations to ensure continuous flow.

Figure 18.13 *In-line production.*

Flexible manufacturing systems (FMS)

The term flexible has been used many times within this book. It is currently regarded as the key to successful manufacturing. 'This is my job and that's your job' attitudes are not tolerated within modern forward-looking manufacturing industry. But it is not only people who must be flexible; the manufacturing system itself must be flexible. Flexible manufacturing is best suited to batch production where the ability to change quickly is critical. Flexible manufacturing has come about through development in computer control in the widest sense not just specific to one particular machine or function.

Computers within manufacturing is the theme of Chapter19.

Just-in-time (JIT)

The 'just-in-time' philosophy was developed in Japan in an effort to get rid of expensive stock. Stocks of resources, materials and components have to be transported, stored and controlled in addition to the cost of the stock itself. The JIT principle is to aim to carry no stock or finished products. Delivery is arranged so that materials and components arrive at the exact time that they are needed and products are dispatched immediately upon completion. Suppliers are responsible for supplying on time, not early or late, and manufacturers must keep their order books full and keep to their supply targets for their customers. The system is also fast and flexible, there is less paperwork and stock does not have to be used up before changes can be implemented.

Concurrent engineering

Traditionally in manufacturing, a design department completed a design and then handed it to the product engineering department who began trialling and developing a manufacturing specification, etc. and so gradually the process moved towards production. Concurrent engineering or simultaneous engineering aims to shorten the time it takes to get a product into production.

This happens by tackling designing, specifying, prototyping and piloting production in parallel with each other. Doing this gets all aspects of R & D involved and encourages better communication between departments and a much improved lead time between concept and manufacture.

Figure 18.14 *Model of concurrent engineering.*

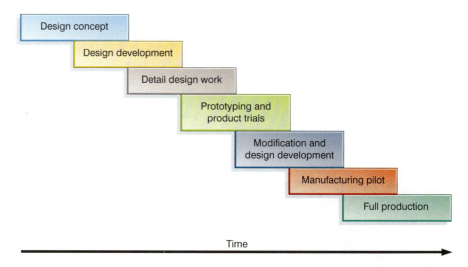

QUALITY ASSURANCE

Cost is not the only factor that influences consumer and manufacturer product choice. Quality of design, manufacture (build quality), performance and customer satisfaction are often the main reasons why one product is chosen in preference to another. Quality assurance involves all aspects of manufacturing performance from design to delivery. **ISO 9000** is the International Standard of Quality that is awarded to companies who demonstrate the highest quality standards throughout their organisations. It is part of the pursuit of **Total Quality Management (TQM)**, a concept that is about establishing attitudes of quality that permeate a whole company not just the manufacturing sectors. The responsibility for TQM is led by management teams who lead through example, encouraging the establishment of **quality circles** within production areas to meet and discuss any issues that will effect the quality of the product outcome.

QUALITY CONTROL

This is a part of the quality assurance function. Quality control is about meeting agreed quality standards and monitoring these standards at every stage from the raw material or supplier through to the finished product. Quality control involves inspection and testing. (See also 'Tolerance and gauge inspection'.)

Inspection

Inspection is the examination of the product and the materials from which it is made to determine if it meets the specified standard. This will include:

- dimensional accuracy;
- surface finish;
- appearance;
- material composition and structure.

Testing

Testing is concerned with the functional aspects of the product:

- Does it function as it should?
- Will it continue to function over its expected lifetime?
- Will it continue to function in a range of environments: hot, cold, corrosive, etc.?

Some tests push the product to the limits to determine when it will fail; for some products this can be an expensive exercise. Most testing is **non-destructive testing (NDT)**.

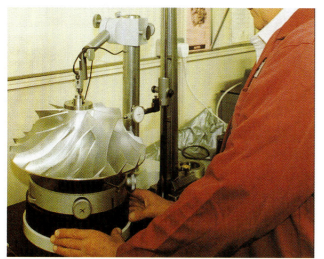

Figure 18.15 *A turbine motor being inspected using dial indicators to test for flatness and concentricity.*

Figure 18.16 *An NDT track using a light sensitive crack detection method.*

TOLERANCE

In practice all manufactured products and components are made to a level of acceptability or tolerance. To work towards absolute precision where there is no need would be a waste of time and resources that would greatly increase the eventual cost of the product. The term '**tolerance**' describes the acceptable degree that the size of a component may vary from the **nominal size**. Tolerance is an important concept.

For example:

Consider a simple wheel for a trolley or barrow that is designed to run freely on a fixed axle as shown in Fig. 18.18.

Clearly there must be some clearance between the wheel's bearing surface and the axle, otherwise it would be tight and not able to rotate. Look at Fig. 18.18.

- **Axle** The nominal size of the axle is given as 20 mm and it must not be larger than this, but it is acceptable to be smaller by up to 0.3 mm. Its size is said to be $20\,\text{mm}^{+0.00}_{-0.30}$
- **Bearing** The wheel bearing must always be larger than the axle by at least 0.2 mm so that there will always be clearance. Its size can be said to be $20\,\text{mm}^{+0.20}_{+0.50}$

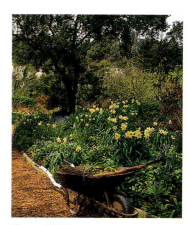

Figure 18.17

In Fig. 18.18 you can see these dimensions expressed in an alternative manner.

Figure 18.18 *Dimensioned wheel bearing and axle.*

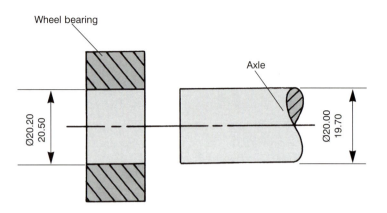

It is essential to know that when a product reaches the assembly stage that any components that are designed to fit together will do so without needing to be selected. In the above example any wheel made to these tolerances will have a clearance fit with any axle made to the tolerance.

GAUGE INSPECTION

In order to determine whether or not a component is within its tolerance limit gauge inspection can be used. This is much quicker and less prone to error than measuring. Gauges are precision-made instruments, sometimes pneumatic or electronic, but very often as simple as the gap gauge and plug gauge shown in Fig. 18.19. The key point to remember is that gauges do not indicate a size, they indicate acceptability by determining that the component is within tolerance.

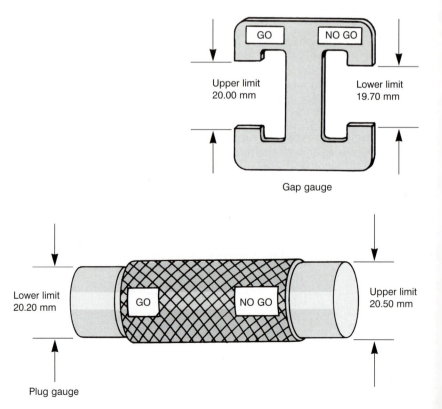

Figure 18.19 *Simple gauges.*

STATISTICAL QUALITY CONTROL

It is usually unnecessary to inspect or test every product manufactured by a mass production or batch production process. Inspection and testing is often only applied to a selected sample. The results of sample inspection and testing can then be recorded on quality control charts like the one in Fig. 18.20.

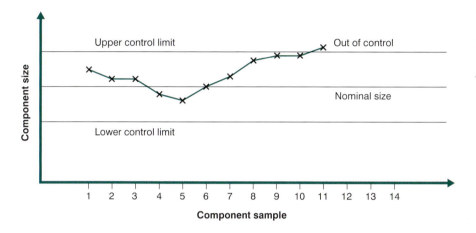

Figure 18.20 *Quality control chart for a turned component, showing the size variation of samples inspected by a computer-controlled gauging machine.*

The size and frequency of the sample taken for inspection and testing depends upon the nature of the product and the scale of production. Quantities and times will be determined by the application of mathematical formulae to ensure that representative samples are inspected and tested at intervals that are appropriate to the component and the process.

The aim of the exercise is to look for manufacturing variations and take action before the process goes out of control and produces components that are out of tolerance. Variations can result from:

- human errors;
- tool wear;
- machine failure;
- variations in the materials and components used;
- environmental conditions.

When a sample goes 'out of control', that is, outside of the defined acceptable tolerance, then action has to be taken to remedy the problem.

Often this process is performed by computer-controlled machines with the actual inspection carried out by sensors that are controlled by and communicate with the computer. Coordinate measuring machines like the one in Fig. 18.21 are used for sampling off-line. They employ a probe which has the ability to move in three-dimensional space providing a precise record of dimensional and geometrical features such as:

- hole locations and diameters;
- linear dimensions;
- sphere centre and diameter;
- flatness;
- angular measurement between two planes.

Figure 18.21 *A coordinate measuring machine in use.*

Check yourself

QUESTIONS

Q1 Explain two ways by which a manufacturer of electronic products could consider regaining a larger share of the consumer market.

Q2 Consider a job or manufacturing process that existed during the 18th century at the time of the industrial revolution. Describe how aspects of the job have changed over the last 200 years.

Q3 Cell production has become a favoured manufacturing arrangement particularly within large companies. What advantages does this offer a large company?

Q4 Describe the steps that a manufacturing company can take so that quality can be assured rather than just controlled.

REMEMBER! Cover the answers if you want to.

ANSWERS

A1 The manufacturer could re-style the products so that they appeal to a wider range of consumer. This could mean targeting a younger market for products such as television sets and CD players.

Another thing that the manufacturer could do is to improve the technical specification of the product by making it perform better for the same cost.

Whatever the manufacturer chooses to do, it is important to then promote and advertise.

A2 Refer to the tutorial section.

A3 Cell production has the effect of breaking a large company down into smaller manufacturing units where people take responsibility for their particular contribution to the whole product. This has advantages in terms of flexible working arrangements and quality control.

A4 Quality can be assured by paying attention to quality issues at all stages. It is about designing quality into a product and about establishing a feeling of responsibility for quality throughout all of the stages of manufacture. The company should ensure that quality in management sets an example.

TUTORIALS

T1 *This answer has picked up on two good points and has added the comment on marketing for good measure. Other alternatives would have been the introduction of a new product, although this is the most expensive option, and looking at ways of reducing the manufacturing costs in order to pass this saving on to the consumer.*

T2 *The answer here will depend upon the job chosen by you but this is a very valuable exercise to carry out. Use other books and an encyclopaedia, and talk to older people. You could look at welding. This was once part of the blacksmith's job and has now developed into a computer-controlled robot operation, but there are a number of stages along the way. There were no plastics and no electricity in the 18th century; what influences have these developments had upon manufacturing industry?*

T3 *This is not a particularly full answer. Flexibility is gained within the cell because people share the responsibility and work together towards a common goal. It is about using teams and belonging to a team increases work-force morale. We all like to feel part of something and contribute to its success. Production line workers can often feel quite the opposite and so the quality of their work declines and absentee rates increase.*

T4 *This is a good answer. Quality assurance is about the whole approach to all aspects of quality within a company and not just about the control of quality within the production processes.*

KEY WORDS

These are the key words. Tick them if you think you know what they mean. Otherwise check on them.

manufacturing
production
profit
re-styling
marketing
R & D (research and development)
standard components
technology push
manufacturing output
scale of production
process production
mass production
batch production
jobbing production
down time
cell production/manufacturing cells

in-line production
assembly line
flexible manufacturing systems (FMS)
just-in-time (JIT)
concurrent engineering
quality assurance
total quality management (TQM)
ISO 9000
quality control
inspection
testing
tolerance
nominal size
gauge inspection
statistical quality control

CHAPTER 19

COMPUTERS WITHIN MANUFACTURING INDUSTRY

The inclusion of computer technology within all aspects of manufacturing industry and within GCSE examinations is growing. Most examination papers will contain some reference to ICT (information and communication technology), often more directly to computer control of processes and the application of computers within industry and commerce. The GCSE syllabuses vary in terms of their specific reference to the application of computers although all expect an awareness of how computers are used and how they have assisted in the development of the new approaches to manufacturing mentioned in the previous chapter.

Note!

This chapter deals with computers within manufacturing industry. The underpinning use of computers within designing and making are covered in early chapters of this book. You should use these references for that essential information. Refer to:

- Chapter 10: **CAD** computer-aided design
  CADD computer-aided design and drafting
- Chapter 13: **CNC** computer numerical control
  CAM computer-aided manufacture
  CAD/CAD computer-aided design and manufacture

Without computer technology, manufacturing industry in the developed world would not able to compete. Computers have made the single greatest contribution to increasing manufacturing productivity. Productivity is the relationship between the quantity of products produced and the cost of producing them: the lower the cost the higher the productivity.

COMPUTER-INTEGRATED MANUFACTURING (CIM)

Early references to computers dealt with their use for specific design and manufacturing functions: CAD, CAM, etc. Computer-integrated manufacturing is the joining together of all of these functions with other computer assisted functions.

Figure 19.1 *Computer integration within the manufacturing cycle.*

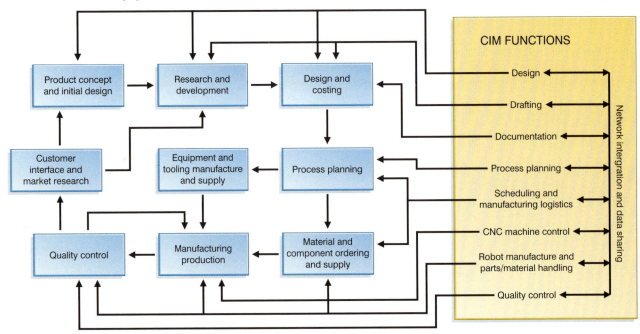

Figure 19.2 *A CNC turning centre.*

Figure 19.3 *Detail of tool turrets and drive spindles.*

Industrial manufacturing is a very complex network of operations. Figure 19.1 shows an overview of a typical manufacturing system with all of the computer functions that can be integrated by a central mainframe or server system. The degree of communication within the system allows design changes, resource requirements and unforeseen delays to be instantly transferred to all aspects of manufacture, and suitable action taken. The JIT concept mentioned in the previous chapter could not function without this degree of integration.

The industrial scale of manufacture has led to the evolution of multi-functional machine tools that tend to be variations of tools familiar to most school workshops. Figures 19.2 and 19.3 show a CNC turning centre that combines all of the operations of a traditional lathe in a single machine. The tools are mounted on a turret and the computer program instructs the machine to select the appropriate tool, sets the feeds and speeds, turns on the coolant, positions and holds the components, performs all the machining operations and then ejects the component upon completion. The machine in the photographs has two spindles and two 12-station tool turrets. Following one operation the part-finished component can be fed to the other turret so that work can commence on the other end. Both turning operations can be carried out at the same time.

The same CNC principles are applied to material removal from sheet stock, such as pressing, punching, cropping , bending and cutting, as well as other process operations such as welding, forging, assembling, inspection and packaging. The results are greater accuracy, more consistent quality and greatly reduced waste. These and other processes may form part of a flexible manufacturing system.

Figure 19.4 *An FMS system.*

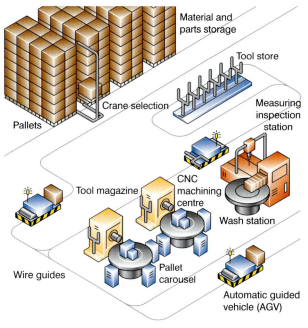

Figure 19.5 *Robot assembly and welding production cell, components enter and leave via a conveyer system.*

FLEXIBLE MANUFACTURING SYSTEMS (FMS)

FMS and cell production was introduced in Chapter 18. With CIM, production cells can be linked within a flexible manufacturing arrangement. A flexible manufacturing system may consist of a group of cells or work-stations, usually Computer Numerical Control (CNC) machines, joined together by an automated materials handling system all controlled by an integrated computer system.

Within this type of flexible manufacturing system there will be a team of technical operators whose job it is to set up the machines and the tools, maintain the equipment and make repairs as necessary. They are responsible for monitoring the process, the computer systems and carrying out quality control functions.

AUTOMATICALLY GUIDED VEHICLES (AGVS)

In many manufacturing organisations the movement of materials, components and tools between manufacturing centres and FMS cells requires a more flexible means of transportation than conveyors and overhead cranes. AGVs can be programmed to travel along pre-determined paths to specified locations. They are usually guided by inductive wires running on top of or below the factory floor and so are free to go wherever the wiring has been laid. Route programming can be achieved by an on-board microprocessor which is able to respond to sensors incorporated in the vehicle. These enable it to communicate information regarding location and loading back to the main system.

ROBOTS

Materials and parts handling is a major consideration within all manufacturing processes and has an even higher priority within a system like FMS that represents a large investment of capital and may be operating a JIT system. Components and parts need to be transported to and between processes and onto and off machines.

Robots have many benefits within manufacturing industry:

- They increase machine use.
- They eliminate the need for people to undertake boring, repetitive tasks.
- They can operate in hazardous and unfriendly conditions.
- They are more accurate, stronger and have a greater reach than humans.
- Modern computer technology enables robots to be quickly reprogrammed making them flexible, adaptable and able to perform many varied tasks.

The main feature of most industrial robots is the mechanical arm designed to reproduce human-like motions. Some robots, however, are of a much simpler design for 'pick and place' operations. These are particularly popular for inserting components in electronic circuit boards.

Figure 19.6 *Robot MIG welding.*

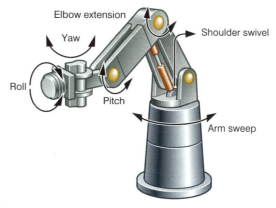

Figure 19.7 *Robot anatomy.*

Industrial robots comprise four basic systems:

- **The mechanical structure** as an articulated arm or a simpler configuration;

- **The drive system** which may be electrical (d.c. servo motors or stepper motors), pneumatic, hydraulic or a combination of each;

- **The tooling (end effector)** which will depend upon the task the robot is expected to perform. The most common means for materials handling is the mechanical gripper in which the component is held between one or more sets of mechanical fingers usually shaped to match the form of the component.

- **The controller** which is most often a closed loop control system that provides positional feedback signals from the joints and end effectors to ensure that there is continuous accuracy and repeatability of movement. Advanced robot controllers can interact with other machines to avoid clashes, make decisions when things go wrong, provide data and respond to sensory inputs such as machine vision.

Robot programming

There are three ways of programming or teaching robots a sequence of movements:

- **Walk through (Nose led)** An operator manually moves the arm of the robot through the required sequence. The robot then retains the positional data to use again.

Figure 19.8 *End effector.*

- **Lead through** This is a similar method to walk through but the movements are initiated from a joystick or a control box.

- **Off-line (Remote computer link)** An important aspect of CIM is the ability to program robotic involvement from remote computer work-stations in the same way that CNC machines can receive instructions. Robot actions can be planned and simulated using animated graphic software at design, development and production planning stages.

KEY WORDS

These are the key words. Tick them if you think you know what they mean. Otherwise check on them.

CAD	**productivity**	**robots**
CADD	**computer-integrated manufacturing (CIM)**	**material and parts handling**
CNC	**machining centres**	**pick and place**
CAM	**FMS**	**end effector**
CAD/CAM	**automatically guided vehicles (AGV)**	**off-line programming**

Check yourself

QUESTIONS

Q1 How does computer integration support flexibility within a manufacturing system?

Q2 Look back at Fig. 19.4 'An FMS system'. What is the function of the wash station within this system?

Q3
a) Identify two methods by which a robot is programmed.

b) Outline some advantages and disadvantages of robots within manufacturing industry.

....
REMEMBER! Cover the answers if you want to.
....

ANSWERS

A1 The manufacturing and quality control within the system is provided with data by the computer system. When changes need to be made and the system is called upon to be flexible, it is very easy with an integrated system to update all aspects without delay.

A2 Wash stations within automated manufacturing systems are necessary to ensure that components are not transferred from one process to the next with swarf and debris that would upset the location for the next operation.

A3
a) A robot can be programmed by leading it through the movements that it will be required to repeat or by programming it off-line.

b) Robots can work in hostile environments such as paint and chemical spraying where people risk injury, and they do boring repetitive jobs. They can also work long hours and do not need a break.

The disadvantage with robots is that they take jobs from people even if they are boring jobs.

TUTORIALS

T1 *The key point about computer integration is communication; what this answer misses is the recognition that integration supports the flexibility required by the whole manufacturing system. Flexibility cannot be achieved in one or two areas alone. Integration means that all contributory parts are informed and updated: material and component suppliers, planning, materials and parts handling, administration and product despatch as well as manufacturing and quality control.*

T2 *A question of this nature is not asking you to recall knowledge that you may have; it is expecting you to apply reason and understanding of manufacturing processes. It is asking you 'Why do you think that a wash station is needed?' rather than 'Do you know why a wash station is needed?'.*

T3
a) *This is a good concise response. Lead through is the type of programming used with paint spraying where the actual movements that a human takes are very complex. Off-line programming is also an important concept.*

b) *This is a very interesting response. The advantages are clear and these along with others are identified in the chapter. The disadvantages identified in terms of employment is a response that is not to be encouraged. The fact is that for industry to succeed it must be efficient and competitive. If a company fails to be productive because of high employment costs then it will not be able to continue to function at all and all the jobs will be lost.*

CONFLICT OF INTERESTS

Within design and technology it is important to develop responsible values towards technological advances. It is too easy sometimes to be impressed by the 'wow' factor and lose sight of the consequences. Conflicts of interests often arise when the far-reaching effects of technological advances are not considered and when the needs of individuals are placed above the needs of society. In a free society we do not consider it unreasonable for individuals to own and use a car; a significant problem arises however if the rest of the world wants one as well.

The traditional view of manufacturing industry has been of grimey chimneys belching out sulphurous, choking smoke. The Control of Pollution Act, the Environmental Protection Act and the Environment Act places legal requirements upon industry to ensure protection for the environment. Legislation of this type, however, must always have a price and results in increased manufacturing costs that are passed on through the industry eventually to the consumer.

Figure 20.1 *The manufacturing industry's effect on the environment is a cause for concern.*

Manufacturing continues to contribute to:

- the drain upon the world's non-renewable resources;
- the 'greenhouse effect';
- waste created by a multitude of industrial activities;
- changes in society and social living patterns.

Consumers have a considerable responsibility. The current tendency is to:

- buy cheap rather than durable products;
- generate waste as a result of fashion considerations;
- demand an excessive level of packaging;
- fail to recycle;
- encourage manufacturing to respond to their demands;
- waste energy through over-heating and lighting of inefficient and under-used buildings;
- waste energy on inefficient transport systems.

Figure 20.2 *Traditional skills, like those of blacksmiths, may be lost forever.*

Here are some interesting figures:

- Oil consumption in the period 1960–1970 in the developed economies alone was equal to the total oil produced before 1960.
- Coal consumption since 1940 has exceeded all the coal used in the previous nine hundred years.
- The richest 25% of the worlds population consumes:
  - 80% of the world's energy;
  - 85% of the world's chemical production;
  - 90% of the world's automobile production.

Computer technology should have a positive role to play but it brings with it other problems that directly affect the communities that have traditionally hosted manufacturing industries. We have seen that the ever-increasing demand for higher productivity in manufacturing industry has resulted in the growth of computerised, automated production systems and how productivity gains are offset by the reduction in human resources. The effect upon individuals and local communities can be considerable. Securing work for some has resulted in widespread, long-term unemployment for others. As a result, social patterns and living conditions are forced to change as a wealth of traditional manufacturing skills and knowledge that is incompatible with computer technology, has been lost to industry.

WASTE

The period since 1945 has seen a dramatic increase in the production of consumer products and therefore of waste. For many years the increase in waste proceeded unchecked.

- Products that do not need to be frequently replaced are often not considered good for business.
- Durability depresses purchasing, replacement and repairs.
- Fashion and marketing encourage the 'throw-away society'.

Much of the solid waste generated is disposed of either through landfill or incineration.

Figure 20.3 *Industrial effluent.*

LANDFILL

Landfill is usually accompanied by the emission of landfill gases which, on entering the atmosphere, act as greenhouse agents. Liquid waste can also end up in landfill sites and great care has to be taken to avoid such substances leaching into surrounding land and water courses. Other liquid wastes can be disposed of into rivers at predetermined levels, although ensuring these levels are adhered to is a very difficult task. Almost all manufacturing industries use, and have to dispose of, chemicals at some point in the production process.

INCINERATION

Incineration can result in residual ash and the emission of combustion gases that may contain toxic dioxins. Furans are produced from the burning of chlorine-containing compounds such as plastics and bleached paper. The control of such emissions is monitored by government agencies and plants have to reach the highest standards for the filtration of such pollutants. New technology has resulted in the recovery of heat and electrical energy from

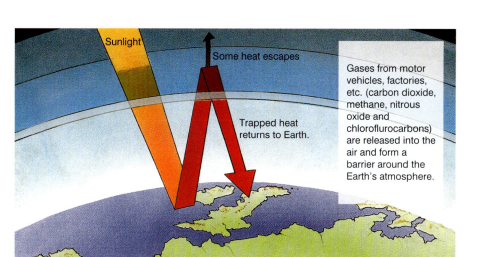

Figure 20.4 *The greenhouse effect.*

incineration plants although Britain still lags behind our major industrial competitors in the amount of energy recovered from waste.

In an attempt to reduce the effect of industrial waste, work is being done to find ways of turning waste from one process into the raw materials for others.

LIFE CYCLE ANALYSIS (LCA)

Life cycle analysis aims to reduce waste from manufactured products and the processes used to make them. LCA involves making detailed measurements of the lifetime of a product, from the extraction of the raw materials, through its manufacture, use, possible recycling and eventual disposal. Manufacturers are able to quantify how much energy and raw materials are used, and how much solid, liquid and gaseous waste is generated at each stage of the product life cycle. The resulting data is an indication to the manufacturer of the impact the product will have upon the environment. Such information can then be used to develop products that are more environmentally friendly and less demanding upon resources and energy. In an environmentally conscious world manufacturers are beginning to recognise that products designed on the basis of LCA will have a competitive edge.

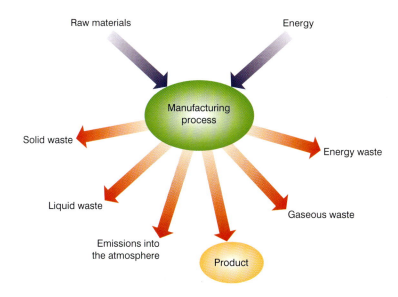

Figure 20.5 *Life cycle analysis.*

Raw material + 20 units of energy = 1 can

Recycled material + 1 unit of energy = 1 can

Figure 20.6 *Recycling.*

RECYCLING

Recycling of waste materials and waste energy wherever possible is vital for the long-term prosperity of all the Earth's inhabitants. Recycling can be extremely energy efficient if the waste is readily available. It is often the collection, transportation and sorting of recyclable waste that makes the whole process expensive and non-viable.

Look at Fig. 20.6. It is 20 times as efficient, in terms of energy usage, to recycle aluminium rather than produce it from raw bauxite ore.

Recycling waste:

- conserves non-renewable resources and the sites from which they are taken;
- reduces energy consumption and greenhouse gas emissions;
- controls the pollution involved in the manufacturing, treatment and disposal processes;
- reduces the dependence on raw materials.

Increasingly, industries within the developed industrial nations have a responsible attitude and do prefer to recycle waste. Many products, particularly those made from wood pulp, such as paper and card, are promoted on the fact that they are made from recycled raw materials. Recycling is being proven to be good for business. The term 'recyclable', however, is used on many products but this can be a means of leaving the responsibility to somebody else.

Governments also help by offering incentives through tax and legislation to encourage recycling. Industry in poorer countries, however, is less likely to be able to look further than the gains that enable them to be competitive with their richer neighbours. To make the situation worse, many countries within the developing world have ready access to minerals, timber and fossil fuels that can be consumed in response to the increasing demand for manufactured consumer goods.

Targets for recycling:

- **Waste minimisation and prevention** This is best dealt with in manufacturing production processes where it is estimated 90% of pollution originates. The message is 'Don't create the waste in the first place'.

- **Pre-consumer recycling and re-using of production waste** It is easier and more economical for industry to recycle than to recycle materials that have been in the hands of the consumer.

- **Product re-use** Reclamation and/or repair prolongs a product's usefulness e.g. returnable drinks containers, re-treading of car tyres, etc.

- **Primary recovery** Recycling waste to produce new raw materials is appropriate for paper, card, fabrics, metals and many types of plastics.

- **Secondary recovery** Reclaiming energy from waste includes electrical energy from incineration plants and the recovery of landfill gas as a fuel source,

Figure 20.7 *The green parts of this car are recyclable whilst the blue parts are already made from recycled material.*

REDUCTION	RE-USE	RECOVERY	DISPOSAL
Reduce the production of waste in the first place	Put objects such as bottles back into use	Recycle, compost or burn to recover energy	The least attractive option where no benefit can be obtained

Figure 20.8 *A waste/recycling strategy.*

Check yourself

QUESTIONS

Q1 Explain the following terms:
i)   non-renewable resources;
ii) the greenhouse effect;
iii) pre-consumer recycling.

Q2 Explain how life cycle analysis contributes towards a more responsible approach towards environmental issues.

Q3 What action can governments take to reduce pollution and waste?

REMEMBER! Cover the answers if you want to.

ANSWERS

A1
i)   Non-renewable resources are those such as coal and oil that once used can never be used again.
ii) The greenhouse effect concerns the build-up of gasses around the Earth's atmosphere that create global warming.
iii) Pre-consumer recycling is the recycling of waste before it leaves the manufacturer.

A2 Life cycle analysis is about the energy and raw materials that make up a product and how this information can be used to help to design more environmentally friendly products.

A3 Governments can pass laws like the Environment Act and they can then fine manufacturers who make pollution and waste.

TUTORIALS

T1 *These are good answers, some additional points to consider are:*
i)   *Other non-renewable resources include metal ores.*
ii) *It is called a greenhouse effect because it lets the sunlight through and then traps the heat like a greenhouse does.*
iii) *Pre-consumer recycling is much cheaper than collecting waste after the product has been sold. It is less likely to need transporting or sorting.*

T2 *This is only part of the answer. LCA is also about waste produced and the potential recyclability of the waste and the product. It is about developing a total understanding of the product in order to provide information for future designs.*

T3 *Again this is just part of the answer. Governments can also provide tax incentives and grants to enable manufacturers to clean up. They can also set examples through their own activities in areas such as government administration and the armed forces.*

KEY WORDS

These are the key words. Tick them if you think you know what they mean. Otherwise check on them.

conflict	**life cycle analysis (LCA)**	**recover**
responsibility	**recycle**	**landfill**
greenhouse effect	**reduce**	**incinerate**
waste	**reuse**	

EXAMINATION CHECKLIST FOR THIS SECTION

After studying industrial manufacturing you should understand the scale and differences between industrial manufacturing and practices in school in relation to:

- designing and marketing within industry;
- the scale of industrial practice;
- the organisation of manufacturing;
- manufacturing systems;
- quality assurance and control;
- the application of computer-based systems for organisation and manufacture.

You should be aware of the environmental issues and concerns that exist in respect of industrial manufacturing and the environment.

EXAM PRACTICE

Sample Student's Answers & Examiner's Comments

EXAMINER'S COMMENTS

(a) *This is a good range of well-reasoned responses. The student should, however have made reference to batch production for chair A and mass production for chair B. The reasons are in the answer provided but the terminology is not used.*

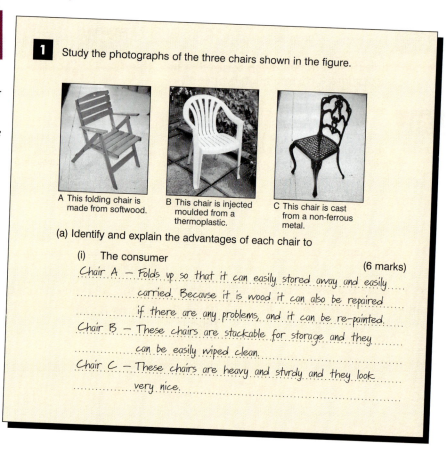

1 Study the photographs of the three chairs shown in the figure.

A This folding chair is made from softwood.

B This chair is injected moulded from a thermoplastic.

C This chair is cast from a non-ferrous metal.

(a) Identify and explain the advantages of each chair to

(i) The consumer (6 marks)

Chair A – Folds up so that it can easily stored away and easily carried. Because it is wood it can also be repaired if there are any problems, and it can be re-painted.

Chair B – These chairs are stackable for storage and they can be easily wiped clean.

Chair C – These chairs are heavy and sturdy and they look very nice.

(ii)   The manufacturer   (6 marks)

Chair A — Can be made with very conventional tools and softwood is easily available.

Chair B — These chairs are made by injection moulding so they are expensive to set up for manufacture but they are then very cheap to make.

Chair C — These chairs are more expensive but they have very fancy designs and can fit in with a range of furniture such as tables.

In the advertising literature it is claimed that chair A is made from a renewable resource and chair C is made from a recycled material.

(b)   With reference to the chairs explain the difference between a renewable resource and recycled material.   (4 marks)

A renewable resource like that used for chair A is a material such as softwood that can be grown again as trees get cut down. The chair in C will be made from metal that has been reclaimed from scrap, this is an example of recycling.

Some products carry a symbol on them to show that they are made from a recycled material.

(c)   In the space provided sketch the symbol used.   (2 marks)

AQA, NEAB, 1998

(b)   *These answers are good and to the point. The term 'scrap' however is one that is misused in most instances. If a material can be recycled it is not scrap. The student failed to mention the metal used for the chair. This will be aluminium.*

(c)   *This question is relying upon your general knowledge in terms of manufacturing and recycling. It is a very common symbol that you must have seen before.*

EXAMINER'S COMMENTS

(a) *This is a good answer, the words inspection and testing could have been used in relation to quality control.*

(b) *Correct*

(c) *This is a correct answer as far as it goes but it does miss some of the key points. Gauge inspection is used to ensure that sizes are within tolerance - this is an important word. The student could also have added that gauge inspection removes the need to make measurements and is therefore quicker and there is less chance of errors.*

---

2 Quality control is a function of quality assurance.

(a) Explain the relationship between quality control and quality assurance.

(4 marks)

Quality control is a part of quality assurance. Quality assurance is about the total attitude of a company towards quality whereas quality control is used to check that the manufacture of the product is satisfactory.

In order to ensure quality control, products must be inspected.

(b) Name a type of gauge inspection.

(2 marks)

A plug gauge for checking holes

(c) Explain what is meant by 'gauge inspection'.

(4 marks)

Gauge inspection is when gauges such as plug and gap gauges are used to check that features of components are correct.

Question to Answer

The answer to Question 3 can be found in Chapter 21.

3 Many manufacturing companies are adopting concurrent engineering practices. Discuss this modern manufacturing philosophy with reference to:

(a) Reduced lead times

(b) Quality assurance

MEG, 1998

SECTION 2 MATERIALS AND COMPONENTS

Answer

2 For kitchen products such as kettles and saucepans designers need to consider the following factors:

The environment
A kitchen is a place where things get spilt and splashed around so the material must not be one that stains easily.

Durability
Kitchen products often get knocked when they are put into cupboards and taken out a large number of times. They will also be subjected to heating and rapid cooling so the material must be able to withstand these extremes.

Fashion
Kitchen products need to be fashionable and stylish and they must be available in a range of colours. The material used must look good and keep its colour. It should be self-coloured or be able to be finished in a colour.

Examiner's Comments

This is a good range of responses because they are all related to materials suitable for the kitchen and the needs of kitchen products. Often the responses by students to questions of this nature drift away from the point and deal with design in a very general way focusing on points such as size, cost, safety and issues that are very broad and could relate to any product. If the question is specific then make sure that your answer is specific.

SECTION 3 DESIGNING

Answer

2 a) i)

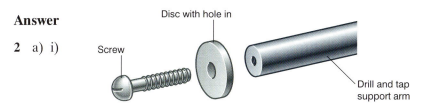

Screw   Disc with hole in   Drill and tap support arm

ii)

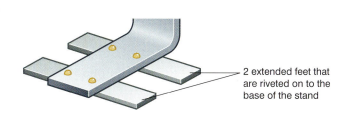

2 extended feet that are riveted on to the base of the stand

Examiner's Comments

There will always be a number of possible solutions to design questions of this type. The answers here both satisfy the criteria required by the question. Solutions to part (i) should stop the roll falling off and also enable it to be changed easily when empty, therefore any permanent fixing to the arm would not be acceptable. Marks would be lost in part (ii) if the method of fixing the 'feet' had not been made clear.

Answer

b) i)   So that there are no sharp corners that could scratch people or furniture.

ii)   So that the roll runs freely when the wire is being pulled off.

Examiner's Comments

These are the correct answers. Part (ii) could also include the ability to replace the roll easily and quickly.

SECTION 4 **MAKING**

Answer

2 a) i)

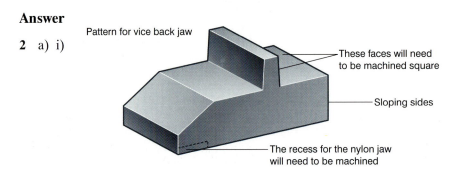

Pattern for vice back jaw

These faces will need to be machined square

Sloping sides

The recess for the nylon jaw will need to be machined

Examiner's Comments

This flat-faced pattern is a good solution, it will be easier to cast than one that includes the recess for the nylon jaw as this would need to be a split pattern. When asked about casting patterns always be sure to include the casting 'draft' that enables the pattern to be removed from the sand. It is not easy to show this on a sketch so the answer here indicates 'sloping sides'.

The question also asks you to indicate the faces that require finish machining. The important concept is to only spend time machining those faces that need to be flat or square. In this case the part that will locate on the edge of a bench or table, and the recess for the nylon jaw. The rest of the jaw can remain 'as cast'. Marks would be lost for machining the jaw any more than necessary.

Answer

ii)   1. Protective clothing such as gloves and leather apron
2. Full face mask
3. Fume extraction unit
4. Clear area without people too close

Examiner's Comments

These are all good points that will gain the marks available. It would not be acceptable however to simply list four items of protective clothing.

Answer

b) i)   Engineer's square
Vee block and clamp
G-clamp

Examiner's Comments

This is not an easy question unless you have experienced this within your own project work. To drill a hole through a bar requires accurate setting up and clamping. The engineer's square (not a try square) is used to align the hole position. The vee block is need to locate the round main screw with the vee block clamp holding it in the block. A G-clamp or some other form of clamping is then needed to hold it all down to the drilling machine table.

Answer

ii)

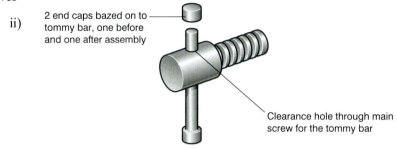

2 end caps bazed on to tommy bar, one before and one after assembly

Clearance hole through main screw for the tommy bar

Examiner's Comments

This is a clear sketch that shows how the tommy bar and main screw could be assembled and allow free movement. There is no mention however of the manufacture of the two end caps for the tommy bar. The addition of the word 'turned' would have been sufficient. (2 turned end caps...)

SECTION 5 SYSTEMS AND CONTROL

Answer

3 i) A belt or chain would make the blades turn in the same direction as the roller.
The ratio would be achieved by a toothed belt with five times the teeth on the large pulley than the small pulley.
The fixed blade can be set a distance above the ground by making the front roller height adjustable.

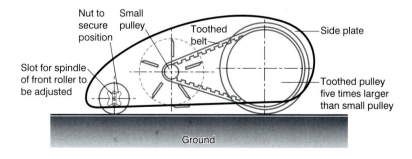

Nut to secure position

Small pulley

Toothed belt

Side plate

Slot for spindle of front roller to be adjusted

Toothed pulley five times larger than small pulley

Ground

Examiner's Comments

This is a good response. Alternatives could show a chain drive system or even a gear system with an intermediate gear to keep the roller and blades rotating in the same direction.

171

Answer

ii) Speed ratio = $\dfrac{\text{driver}}{\text{driven}} = \dfrac{35 \text{ teeth}}{7 \text{ teeth}} = 5:1$

Examiner's Comments

These are the candidate's own figures but it does show a ratio that works. The ratio with a toothed belt is calculated the same way as with a gear ratio.

Answer

iii) Toothed belt drive

Examiner's Comments

An easy one mark that is used to focus the candidate on the next part of the question.

Answer

iv) Chain drive

Examiner's Comments

Yes, any workable alternative would be acceptable here.

Answer

v) Toothed belt drive
This is the better system because it will be quieter in use and it is easier to replace a belt than a chain.

Examiner's Comments

This is a good answer. Other advantages could have included 'will not rust' or 'cheaper to replace'.

SECTION 6 **INDUSTRIAL MANUFACTURING**

Answer

3   a) The reduction in lead times is the main aim of concurrent engineering. It means that products can get from design to customer quicker. This is made possible by overlapping the various functions such as designing and modelling and encouraging better communication between departments.

b) The increased communication that comes about with concurrent engineering encourages greater responsibility and this leads to better attitudes towards all aspects of quality.

Examiner's Comments

This is a difficult question that is targeted at the A* candidate. These are good answers that only miss the finer points of the psychology. By involving people more in the process of manufacturing from concept to marketing you encourage a feeling of 'ownership' in the company and the product being made, this is the most positive step in quality assurance.

This final chapter contains five more examination questions taken from recent years' papers. Five questions would typically make up a complete examination.

Notice how each question is extended to cover a number of aspects of design and technology. This is typical of most examination questions.

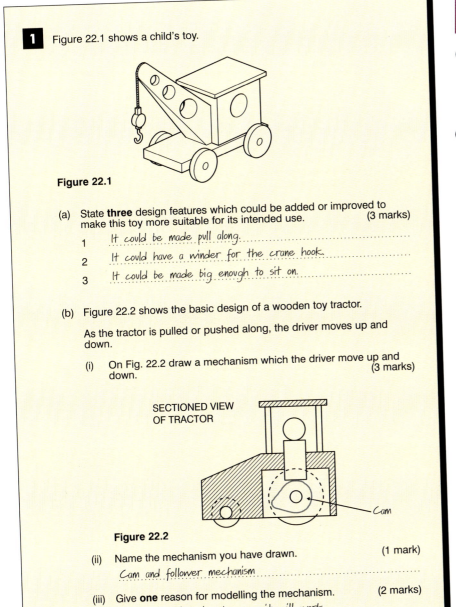

1 Figure 22.1 shows a child's toy.

Figure 22.1

(a) State **three** design features which could be added or improved to make this toy more suitable for its intended use. (3 marks)

1 _It could be made pull along._

2 _It could have a winder for the crane hook_

3 _It could be made big enough to sit on._

(b) Figure 22.2 shows the basic design of a wooden toy tractor.

As the tractor is pulled or pushed along, the driver moves up and down.

(i) On Fig. 22.2 draw a mechanism which the driver move up and down. (3 marks)

SECTIONED VIEW
OF TRACTOR

Cam

Figure 22.2

(ii) Name the mechanism you have drawn. (1 mark)

Cam and follower mechanism

(iii) Give **one** reason for modelling the mechanism. (2 marks)

To try it out and make sure it will work

(c) *(i) The simple jig for drilling will work effectively but could be improved by having some means of clamping it into place. The sketch does not show how the two side members are held onto the top plate. A note about brazing or welding would have been appropriate.*
(ii) The wheels must be secured to the axle to be able to drive the cam mechanism and PVA is the correct type of glue to use. You should remember the name.

(iv) Draw a mechanism which will make the driver rise slowly and fall rapidly when pulled along. (1 mark)

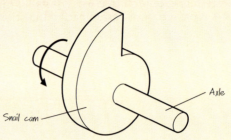

(v) Name the mechanism you have drawn. (1 mark)
This is a snail cam.

(vi) Explain **one** disadvantage of using this type of mechanism. (2 marks)
It will not work if the tractor is pushed backwards.

(c) Twenty tractors are to be manufactured.

The roof and body of the tractor are connected by means of dowels. The positions are shown in Figure 22.3.

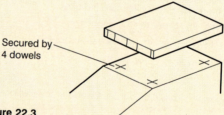

Secured by 4 dowels

Figure 22.3

(i) Design a jig so that the four holes in the roof and body of the tractor can be drilled quickly and accurately. (3 marks)

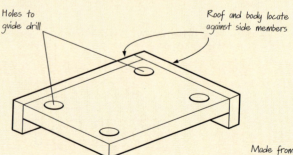

Holes to guide drill

Roof and body locate against side members

Made from mild steel

(ii) Describe how the wheels of the wooden toy could be attached to the rear axle. (2 marks)
The wheels are made of wood and could be attached to the wooden axle using PVA wood glue.

MEG, Specimen paper

2 Figure 22.4 shows some of the parts of a pulley block.

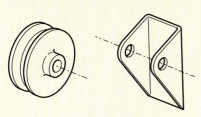
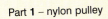
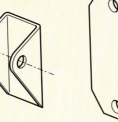

Part **1** – nylon pulley   Part **2** – mild steel bearing bracket   Part **3** – mild steel back plate

Figure 22.4

(a) The pulley block is assembled with the addition of a mild steel shaft, part No. 4, which is not shown.

(i) Complete the following parts list for the pulley block assembly.
(2 marks)

PART NO.	NAME	MATERIAL	QTY
1	pulley	nylon	1
2	bearing bracket	mild steel	1
3	back plate	mild steel	1
4	shaft	mild steel	1

(ii) The pulley in Fig. 22.4 has a raised central boss on each side. Explain the reason for this common design feature of pulleys.
(2 marks)

It has a small area of contact and therefore there is less friction.

EXAMINER'S COMMENTS

(a) *Part (i) is straightforward and is 2 easy marks; part (ii) however needs a little bit of reasoning. You may well have seen pulleys like this many times. It is important to look at simple mechanical things and question their design.*

(b) *These are correct responses. Notice that is not necessary to section features such as pulleys and shafts when drawing sectional views.*

(b) Figure 22.5 shows an incomplete sketch of a section through the assembled pulley block.

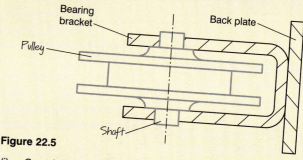

Figure 22.5

(i) Complete the sketch by adding the other components. (2 marks)

(ii) Give two methods for permanently joining the bearing bracket and the back plate.
(2 marks)

1 *Brazing*

2 *Riveting*

(iii) It is necessary for the pulley to be removable from the pulley block assembly.

Explain why it is an advantage to be able to take apart mechanical products.
(2 marks)

For maintenance, so that you can replace worn parts.

(iv) The pulley is 'free running' on the shaft.

Give two reasons why it is better for the pulley to run free on the shaft than for the shaft to run free in the bearing bracket.

Reason 1 *Nylon will run easily against steel.*
(2 marks)

Reason 2 *The steel shaft would rust to the steel bearing.*
(2 marks)

MEG, 1998

(a) *Other factors could have included: corrosion, cost of replacement, vandalism and fungal attack.*

(b) *Here there are also a number of answers with different woods and metal and also plastics. If the answer is that no treatment is needed then be sure to say why.*

3 Consideration needs to be given when selecting materials for products used outdoors.

(a) One factor may be to withstand wet conditions, give two others.
2 marks)

1 *Changes in temperature*

2 *Ultra violet light*

(b) Name two materials from the woods, metals and plastics you have studied which are suitable for outdoor products. State any special treatment they need. If none is required, state why not. Give a reason for your choice of each material.
(6 marks)

1 Name of material and reason
Softwood, cheap and easy to work

Special treatment (if needed)
Preservatives or painting

2 Name of material and reason
Aluminium, light and cheap

Special treatment (if needed)
No treatment is needed, not corrosive

Many years ago seed trays were made from wood, as shown below. Today, trays are vacuum formed from plastics.

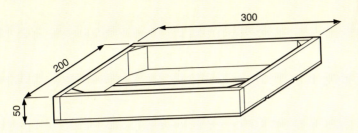

Figure 22.6

(c) Give **two** reasons for the change from wood to plastic. (2 marks)

1 Plastic is cheaper than wood.

2 Plastic trays can be mass produced cheaper.

(d) Name a suitable plastic for making vacuum formed trays. (1 mark)

Polystyrene

(e) (i) Using sketches and notes, produce a suitable design for a vacuum formed seed tray based on the dimensions given on the wooden seed tray. Consideration should be given to the following specification.
- the tray must be strong when held at one side while full of soil or compost (4 marks)
(1 mark)
- the tray must drain excess water
- provision must be made for transporting large quantities of empty trays (2 marks)

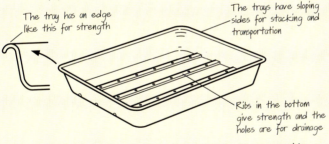

The tray has an edge like this for strength

The trays have sloping sides for stacking and transportation

Ribs in the bottom give strength and the holes are for drainage

(ii) Draw and label a cross-sectional view of the former used to produce the seed tray. (4 marks)

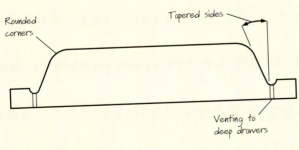

Rounded corners

Tapered sides

Venting to deep drawers

EXAMINER'S COMMENTS

(f) *With a question like this you should break your response down, like this one has been, into a list of points. Do not be tempted to provide an essay type of answer.*

(g) *Yes.*

(f) Injection moulding is an alternative method of producing larger trays.

(i) Figure 22.7 shows a section through a plastics moulding machine.

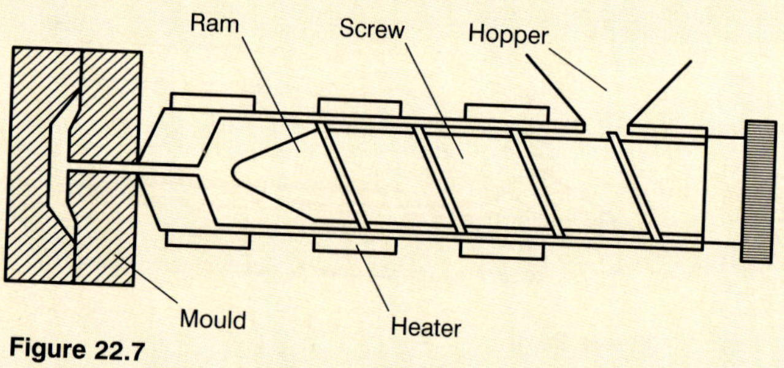

Figure 22.7

Describe the main points of the injection moulding process.

(6 marks)

1 Granules of plastic come down the hopper.
2 The screw turns and the granules move forwards and are plasticised by the heaters.
3 The screw is used as a ram to force the plastic into the mould.
4 When the plastic is solid the mould is opened and the product is taken out.

(ii) When in continuous use, the mould gets hot. This slows down the solidifying process of the component being made. Describe how the mould can be prevented from getting hot.

(2 marks)

By being cooled with water running through it.

(g) Name the manufacturing process that would be used to produce 3 metre lengths of the PVC channel, as shown in the cross-section.

(1 mark)

Cross-section of channel

Figure 22.8

Extrusion

AQA, NEAB, 1998

4 Figure 22.9 shows the basic design for a small adjustable mirror. The side view shows details of a mirror tile and its backing material.

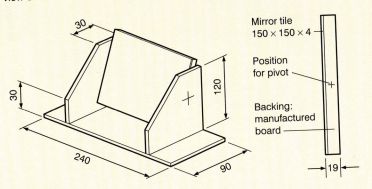

Mirror tile
150 × 150 × 4

Position
for pivot

Backing:
manufactured
board

Figure 22.9

(a) The base and uprights are to be made from a single length of hardwood as shown in Figure 22.10.

Complete Fig. 22.10 to show how the base and uprights should be marked out to avoid wasting hardwood.   (3 marks)

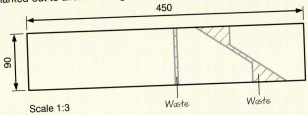

Scale 1:3

Waste   Waste

Figure 22.10

(b) Name a suitable construction for joining the base to the uprights.
                                                                        (1 mark)

Housing joint

Figure 22.11 shows a side view of the adjustable mirror with the right-hand upright removed. The mirror is pivoted between the uprights and is to be held at any angle between 0° and 45°.

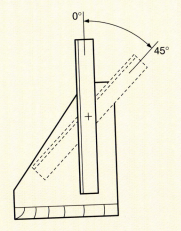

Figure 22.11

(a) *This part of the question draws upon your experience of working with materials and avoiding waste. It is also expected that you will be able to translate the 1 : 3 scale. This is a good answer that gains from including a small waste allowance for cleaning up between the base and the uprights.*

(b) *There are a number of suitable joints including simply butt jointing.*

(c) *This is an excellent response as far as it goes but it does not satisfy the whole of the question. This fitting will allow the mirror to tilt and to lock in any position but there is nothing to limit the movement to between 0° and 45°. Simple dowel pegs could be used to satisfy this requirement. You must make certain that you study the question carefully and do not respond too quickly and miss bits out.*

(a) *This is the most relevant reason for using aluminium in this application.*

(b) *Safety questions often appear on examination question papers. With respect to the number of teeth; soft materials have a coarse pitch and hard materials have a fine pitch but you should always use a fine pitch with tubes and thin sections in order to keep more teeth in contact.*

(c) *Yes, a push fit should require no more than a light tap to assemble and it should not drop out.*

(c) In the space below, use sketches and notes to show a suitable pivot and a locking method by which the mirror can be held at any angle, (0°–45°), between the uprights. Name the materials and any fittings used.

(8 marks)

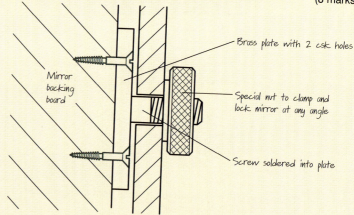

Mirror backing board

Brass plate with 2 csk holes

Special nut to clamp and lock mirror at any angle

Screw soldered into plate

MEG, Specimen

5 Figure 22.12 shows a foot assembly for a display system. The legs are made from tubular aluminium I/D 25 mm, O/D 30 mm. The feet are a 'push fit' into the legs and are height adjustable.

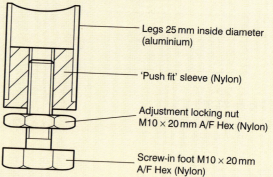

Legs 25 mm inside diameter (aluminium)

'Push fit' sleeve (Nylon)

Adjustment locking nut M10 × 20 mm A/F Hex (Nylon)

Screw-in foot M10 × 20 mm A/F Hex (Nylon)

Figure 22.12

(a) Give one reason why tubular aluminium is a good choice of material for a display system.

(1 mark)

Tubular aluminium is light.

(b) The aluminium tube for the legs is to be cut to length using a hand hacksaw.

List three checks to be made to the blade of the hacksaw to ensure its safe and accurate use for this task.

(3 marks)

1   Check the blade is not cracked.

2   Check that the tension is correct.

3   Check that it is the right blade i.e. the correct number of teeth.

(c) Explain what is meant by 'push fit'.

(1 mark)

Fits tightly when assembled without having to be forced together.

(d) Figure 22.13 shows the first stage in making the 'screw-in' foot. In the space below describe step by step how a centre lathe would be used to make the 'screw-in' foot, to this stage, on the end of a stock length of 20 mm A/F hexagonal Nylon rod. (8 marks)

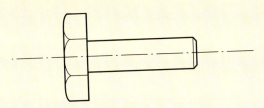

Figure 22.13

1 Roughing out
2 Finish turn to size
3 Chamfer end
4 Part off
5 Chamfer the other end

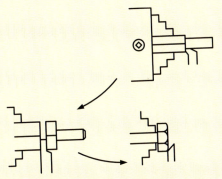

(e) The company developing the display system have identified a potential market that will require 8000 Nylon screw-in feet per month.

(i) Name a process suitable for producing this volume of feet. (1 mark)

Injection moulding

(ii) Give **two** reasons for the company using the process you have named in part (i) instead of machining each foot from the 20 mm A/F Hex Nylon rod. (2 marks)

1 The unit costs are very low.
2 The quality will be good enough for the job they have to do.

MEG, Specimen

(d) *This answer is correct but the description of the operations is rather brief: for example, there is no reference to calipers or a micrometer to check the size of the component. If you know the information then include it in your answer. You can never be certain how much detail the examiner is looking for.*

(e) *(i) Yes*
(ii) Clearly there would be a high investment cost in tooling but the unit costs are then very low. The quality of injection moulded products can be very high dependant upon the quality of the mould and the speed of the process.

ACKNOWLEDGEMENTS

Published by Collins Educational
An imprint of HarperCollins*Publishers* Ltd
77–85 Fulham Palace Road
London W6 8JB

The HarperCollins website address is www.**fire**and**water**.com

First published 1999

Reprinted 2000

ISBN 0 00 323523 8

Colin Chapman asserts the moral right to be identified as the author of this work.

British Library Cataloguing in Publication Data
A catalogue record for this publication is available from the British Library

Edited by Margaret Shepherd
Production by Anna Pauletti
Picture Research by Tamsin Miller
Cover design by BCG Communications
Book design by Rupert Purcell and produced by Gecko Limited
Index compiled by Marie Lorimer
Printed and bound in Hong Kong

Acknowledgements
The Author and Publishers are grateful to the following for permission to reproduce copyright material:
British Standards Institution (p. 59, Fig. 9.5). Extracts from BS 5940: Part 1: 1980 are reproduced with the permission of BSI under licence no. PD\1998 1847. Complete editions of the standards can be obtained by post from BSI Customer Services, 389 Chiswick High Road, London W4 4AL.

London Examinations, a division of Edexcel Foundation (pp. 6 [Fig. 1.4], 121–123)
Edexcel Foundation , London Examinations accepts no responsibility whatsoever for the accuracy or method of working in the answers given.
Northern Examinations and Assessment Board (pp. 5 [Fig. 1.3], 83–84, 142–143, 166–167, 176–178)
The author is responsible for the possible answers/solutions and the commentaries on the past questions from the Northern Examinations and Assessment Board. They may not constitute the only possible solutions.
Oxford Cambridge and RSA Examinations (p. 3, [Fig.1.2]). Reproduced by permission of the University of Cambridge Local Examinations Syndicate/Midland Examining Group (pp. 55, 85, 124, 168, 173–176, 179–181)
The University of Cambridge Local Examinations Syndicate/Midland Examining Group bears no responsibility for the example answers to questions taken from its past question papers which are contained in this publication.
Southern Examining Group (p. 2, [Fig. 1.1])

Rebecca Capper, Spalding Girls' High School (pp.20–1, Fig. 3.15)
Hannah Loy, Lincoln Christ's Hospital School (pp. 16–17, Figs. 3.7–3.11)
Xerxes Sethna, William Farr Comprehensive School (pp.18–19, Figs.3.12–3.14)
Jason Gunn, Past Design and Technology Student Teacher of the University of Greenwich (pp.21–4, Figs. 3.16–3.19). These design sheets have been taken from a set of 'Display Materials' produced by the Centre for Design and Technology at the University of Greenwich. If you would like further details of these and other materials please phone 0181 331 8040, fax 0181 331 8034 or e-mail HYPERLINK mailto:j.w.golden@gre.ac.uk

Photographs
Black & Decker (12.16); BMW (20.7); Boxford Ltd (13.17, 13.19, 19.3); British Steel (18.16); BT Archives (7.1, 7.2); Colin Chapman (3.6); Draper Tools (12,8, 12.13, 12.14, 12.15, 13.9, 13.31); Dupont (18.3); EMA model supplies (10.9, 10.10); Mike Finney (1.1a, 2.1); Great Universal (18.1); Sally & Richard Greenhill (9.3,6.9); Halfords (16.1); Hulton Getty (18.4); Julia Kendall (10.15); Liberty (3.3); Massey Ferguson (18.5, 18.12, 18.13); Moore & Wright (3.24); Tom Morgan, De Aston School, Market Rasen (3.4, 3.5, 10.16); NEAB (20.9a, 20.9b, 20.9c); Nissan (18.10); Mel Peace (6.8, 3.103); Peugeot Partnership Centre (18.21); Fredk.Pollard & Co Ltd (19.2); Record Tools (7.5, 12.17, 13.2, 13.14, 13.15); RPC containers (7.3, 18.6); John H Rundle Ltd (14.25); Science Photo Library (4.2, 5.1, 5.2, 16.7, 17.21, 17.22, 18.7, 20.1, 20.2, 20.3); Sony (18.2); Stäubli Unimation (18.8, 19.5); Telegraph Colour Library (18.9); Tony Stone Images (9.4).

Illustrations
Karen Donnelly, Mike Badrocke, Tim Cooke, Sam Denley, Gecko Ltd, Simon Girling Associates (Graham Bingham, Alex Pang, Stephen Sweet, Chris Etheridge, Mike Taylor), Dalton Jacobs, Graham-Cameron Illustration (Jeremy Bays, Tony Dover), David Lock, Linda Rogers Associates (Ann Baum), Malcolm Ryan, Ken Vail Graphic Design.

Every effort has been made to contact the holders of copyright material, but if any have been inadvertently overlooked, the Publishers will be pleased to make the necessary arrangements at the first opportunity.

INDEX